THEORY OF INTEREST
AND LIFE CONTINGENCIES
WITH PENSION APPLICATIONS

A Problem-Solving Approach

Third Edition

Michael M. Parmenter
ASA, Ph.D.

ACTEX Publications
Winsted, Connecticut

To my Mother and the memory of my Father

Manufactured in the United States of America

10 9 8 7 6 5 4 3

Cover design by MUF

Library of Congress Cataloging-in-Publication Data

Parmenter, Michael M.
    Theory of interest and life contingencies, with pension
applications: a problem-solving approach / Michael M. Parmenter.
    p.   cm.
      Includes index.
      ISBN 1-56698-333-9
      1. Insurance, Life--Mathematics--Problems, exercises, etc.
2.   Interest--Problems, exercises, ets.   3.   Annuities--Problems,
exercises, etc.   I. Title
HG8781. P29   1999
368.2'2'011076--dc 19   88-38947

ISBN: 1-56698-333-9

TABLE OF CONTENTS

PREFACE

It is impossible to escape the practical implications of compound interest in our modern society. The consumer is faced with a bewildering choice of bank accounts offering various rates of interest, and wishes to choose the one which will give the best return on her savings. A home-buyer is offered various mortgage plans by different companies, and wishes to choose the one most advantageous to him. An investor seeks to purchase a bond which pays coupons on a regular basis and is redeemable at some future date; again, there are a wide variety of choices available.

Comparing possibilities becomes even more difficult when the payments involved are dependent on the individual's survival. For example, an employee is offered a variety of different pension plans and must decide which one to choose. Also, most people purchase life insurance at some point in their lives, and a bewildering number of different plans are offered.

The informed consumer must be able to make an intelligent choice in situations like those described above. In addition, it is important that, whenever possible, she be able to make the appropriate calculations herself in such cases. For example, she should understand why a given series of mortgage payments will, in fact, pay off a certain loan over a certain period of time. She should also be able to decide which portion of a given payment is paying off the balance of the loan, and which portion is simply paying interest on the outstanding loan balance.

The first goal of this text is to give the reader enough information so that he can make an intelligent choice between options in a financial situation, and can verify that bank balances, loan payments, bond coupons, etc. are correct. Too few people in today's society understand how these calculations are carried out.

In addition, however, we are concerned that the student, besides being able to carry out these calculations, understands why they work. It is not enough to memorize a formula and learn how to apply it; you should understand why the formula is correct. We also wish to present the material in a proper mathematical setting, so the student will see how the theory of interest is interrelated with other branches of mathematics.

Let me explain why the phrase "Problem-Solving Approach" appears in the title of this text. We will prove a very small number of formulae and then concentrate our attention on showing how these formulae can be applied to a wide variety of problems. Skill will be needed to take the data presented in a particular problem and see how to rearrange it so the formulae can be used. This approach differs from many texts, where a large number of formulae are presented, and the student tries to memorize which problems can be solved by direct application of a particular formula. We wish to emphasize understanding, not rote memorization.

A working knowledge of elementary calculus is essential for a thorough understanding of all the material. However, a large portion of this book can be read by those without such a background by omitting the sections dependent on calculus. Other required background material such as geometric sequences, probability and expectation, is reviewed when it is required.

Each chapter in this text includes a large number of examples and exercises. It should be obvious that the most efficient way for a student to learn the material is for her to work all the exercises.

Finally, let us stress that it is assumed that every student has a calculator (with a y^x button) and knows how to use it. It is because of our ability to use a calculator that many formulae mentioned in older texts on the subject are now unnecessary.

This book is naturally divided into two parts. Chapters 1-5 are concerned solely with the Theory of Interest, and Life Contingencies is introduced in Chapters 6-11.

In Chapter 1 we present the basic theory concerning the study of interest. Our goal here is to give a mathematical background for this area, and to develop the basic formulae which will be needed in the rest of the book. Students with a weak calculus background may wish to omit Section 1.6 on the force of interest, as it is of more theoretical than practical importance. In Chapter 2 we show how the theory in Chapter 1 can be applied to practical problems. The important concept of equation of value is introduced, and many worked examples of numerical problems are presented. Chapter 3 discusses the extremely important concept of annuities. After developing a few basic formulae, our main emphasis in this chapter is on practical problems, seeing how data for such problems can be substituted in the basic formulae. It is in this section especially that we have left out many of the formulae presented in other texts, preferring to concentrate on problem-solving techniques rather than rote memorization. Chapters 4 and 5 deal with further applications of the material in Chapters 1 through 3, namely amortization, sinking funds and bonds.

Chapter 6 begins with a review of the important concepts of probability and expectation, and then illustrates how probability can be combined with the theory of interest. In Chapter 7 we introduce life tables, discussing how they are constructed and how they can be applied. Chapter 8 is concerned with life annuities, that is annuities whose payment are conditional on survival, and Chapter 9 discusses life insurance. These ideas are generalized to multi-life situations in Chapter 10.

Finally, Chapter 11 demonstrates how many of these concepts are applied in the extremely important area of pension plans.

Chapters 1 through 6 have been used for several years as the text material for a one semester undergraduate course in the Theory of Interest, and I would like to thank those students who pointed out errors in earlier drafts. In addition, I am deeply indebted to Brenda Crewe and Wanda Heath for an excellent job of typing the manuscript, and to my colleague, Dr. P. P. Narayanaswami, for his invaluable technical assistance.

Chuck Vinsonhaler, University of Connecticut, was strongly supportive of this project, and introduced me to the people at ACTEX Publications, for which I owe him a great deal. Dick London did the technical content editing, Marilyn Baleshiski provided the electronic typesetting, and Marlene Lundbeck designed the text's cover. I would like to thank them for taking such care in turning a very rough manuscript into what I hope is a reasonably comprehensive yet friendly and readable text book for actuarial students.

St. John's, Newfoundland   Michael M. Parmenter
December, 1988

PREFACE TO THE
REVISED EDITION

In the fifteen months since the original edition of this text was published, a number of comments have been received from teachers and students regarding that edition.

We are pleased to note that most of the comments have been quite complimentary to the text, and we are making no substantial modifications at this time.

A significant, and thoroughly justified, criticism of the original edition is that time diagrams were not used to illustrate the examples given in the second half of the text, and that deficiency has been rectified by the inclusion of thirty-five additional figures in the Revised Edition.

Thus it is fair to say that there are no *new topics* contained in the Revised Edition, but rather that the pedagogy has been strengthened. For this reason we prefer to call the new printing a Revised Edition, rather than a Second Edition.

In addition we have corrected the errata in the original edition. We would like to thank all those who took the time to bring the various errata to our attention.

February, 1990   M.M.P.

PREFACE TO THE
THIRD EDITION

It is now more than ten years since the original publication of this textbook. In that time, several very significant developments have occurred to suggest that a new edition of the text is now needed, and those developments are reflected in the modifications and additions made in this Third Edition.

First, improvements in calculator technology give us better approaches to reach numerical results. In particular, many calculators now include iteration algorithms to permit direct calculation of unknown annuity interest rates and bond yield rates. Accordingly, the older approximate methods using interpolation have been deleted from the text.

Second, with the discontinued publication of the classic textbook *Life Contingencies* by C.W. Jordan, our text has become the only one published in North America which provides the traditional presentation of contingency theory. To serve the needs of those who still prefer this traditional approach, including the use of commutation functions and a deterministic life table model, we have chosen to include various topics contained in Jordan's text but not contained in our earlier editions. These include insurances payable at the moment of death (Section 9.3), life contingent accumulation functions (Section 8.2), the table of uniform seniority concept for use with Makeham and Gompertz annuity values (Section 11.1), simple contingent insurance functions (Section 11.1), and an expansion of the material regarding multiple-decrement theory (Section 7.6).

Third, actuaries today are interested in various concepts of finance beyond those included in traditional interest theory. To that end we have introduced the ideas of real rates of return, investment duration, modified duration, and so on, in this Third Edition.

Fourth, the new edition provides a gentle introduction to the more modern stochastic view of contingency theory, in the completely new Chapter 10, to supplement the traditional presentation.

In connection with the expansion of topics, the new edition contains over forty additional exercises and examples. As well, the numerical answers to the exercises have been made more precise and the errata in the previous edition have been corrected. We would like to thank everyone who brought such errata to our attention.

With the considerable modifications made in the new edition, we believe this text is now appropriate for two major audiences: pension actuaries, who wish to understand the use of commutation functions and deterministic contingency theory in pension mathematics, and university students, who seek to understand basic contingency theory at an introductory level before undertaking a study of the more mathematically sophisticated stochastic contingency theory.

As with the original edition of this text, the staff at ACTEX Publications has been invaluable in the development of this new edition. Specifically I would like to thank Denise Rosengrant for her text composition and typesetting work, and Dick London, FSA, for his technical content editing.

February, 1999   M.M.P

CHAPTER ONE
INTEREST: THE BASIC THEORY

1.1 ACCUMULATION FUNCTION

The simplest of all financial transactions is one in which an amount of money is invested for a period of time. The amount of money initially invested is called the *principal* and the amount it has grown to after the time period is called the *accumulated value* at that time.

This is a situation which can easily be described by functional notation. If t is the length of time for which the principal has been invested, then the amount of money at that time will be denoted by $A(t)$. This is called the *amount function*. For the moment we will only consider values $t \geq 0$, and we will assume that t is measured in years. We remark that the initial value $A(0)$ is just the principal itself.

In order to compare various possible amount functions, it is convenient mathematically to define the *accumulation function* from the amount function as $a(t) = \dfrac{A(t)}{A(0)}$. We note that $a(0) = 1$ and that $A(t)$ is just a constant multiple of $a(t)$, namely $A(t) = k \cdot a(t)$ where $k = A(0)$ is the principal.

What functions are possible accumulation functions? In theory, any function $a(t)$ with $a(0) = 1$ could represent the way in which money accumulates with the passage of time. Certainly, however, we would hope that $a(t)$ is increasing. Should $a(t)$ be continuous? That depends on the situation; if $a(t)$ represents the amount owing on a loan t years after it has been taken out, then $a(t)$ may be continuous if interest continues to accumulate for non-integer values of t. However, if $a(t)$ represents the amount of money in your bank account t years after the initial deposit (assuming no deposits or withdrawals in the meantime), then $a(t)$ will stay constant for periods of time, but will take a jump whenever interest is paid into the account. The graph of such an $a(t)$ will be a step function. We will normally assume in this text that $a(t)$ is continuous; it is easy to make allowances for other situations when they turn up.

In Figure 1.1 we have drawn graphs of three different types of accumulation functions which occur in practice:

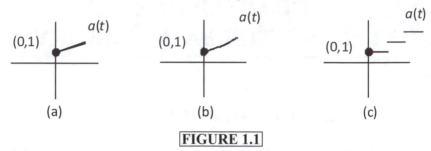

FIGURE 1.1

Graph (a) represents the case where the *amount* of interest earned is constant over each year. On the other hand, in cases like (b), the amount of interest earned is increasing as the years go on. This makes more sense in most situations, since we would hope that as the principal gets larger, the interest earned also increases; in other words, we would like to be in a situation where "interest earns interest". There are many different accumulation functions which look roughly like the graph in (b), but the exponential curve is the one which will be of greatest interest to us.

We remarked earlier that a situation like (c) can arise whenever interest is paid out at fixed periods of time, but no interest is paid if money is withdrawn between these time periods. If the amount of interest paid is constant per time period, then the "steps" will all be of the same height. However, if the amount of interest increases as the accumulated value increases, then we would expect the steps to get larger and larger as time goes on.

We have used the term interest several times now, so perhaps it is time to define it!

$$Interest = Accumulated\ Value - Principal$$

This definition is not very helpful in practical situations, since we are generally interested in comparing different financial situations to determine which is most profitable. What we require is a standardized measure for interest, and we do this by defining the *effective rate of interest i* (per year) to be the interest earned on a principal of amount 1 over a period of one year. That is,

$$i = a(1) - 1. \tag{1.1}$$

We can easily calculate i using the amount function $A(t)$ instead of $a(t)$, if we recall that $A(t) = k \cdot a(t)$. Thus

$$i = a(1) - 1 = \frac{a(1) - a(0)}{a(0)} = \frac{A(1) - A(0)}{A(0)}. \tag{1.2}$$

Verbally, the effective rate of interest per year is the amount of interest earned in one year divided by the principal at the beginning of the year. There is nothing sacred about the term "year" in this definition. We can calculate an effective rate of interest over any time period by simply taking the numerator of the above fraction as being the interest earned over that period.

More generally, we define the effective rate of interest in the nth year by

$$i_n = \frac{A(n) - A(n-1)}{A(n-1)} = \frac{a(n) - a(n-1)}{a(n-1)}. \tag{1.3}$$

Note that i_1, calculated by (1.3), is the same as i defined by either (1.1) or (1.2).

| Example 1.1 |

Consider the function $a(t) = t^2 + t + 1$.
(a)   Verify that $a(0) = 1$.
(b)   Show that $a(t)$ is increasing for all $t \geq 0$.
(c)   Is $a(t)$ continuous?
(d)   Find the effective rate of interest i for $a(t)$.
(e)   Find i_n.

| Solution |

(a) $a(0) = (0)^2 + (0) + 1 = 1$.
(b)   Note that $a'(t) = 2t + 1 > 0$ for all $t \geq 0$, so $a(t)$ is increasing.
(c)   The easiest way to solve this is to observe that the graph of $a(t)$ is a parabola, and hence $a(t)$ is continuous (or recall from calculus that all polynomial functions are continuous).
(d) $i = a(1) - 1 = 3 - 1 = 2$.
(e) $i_n = \dfrac{a(n) - a(n-1)}{a(n-1)} = \dfrac{n^2 + n + 1 - [(n-1)^2 + (n-1) + 1]}{(n-1)^2 + (n-1) + 1}$

$\qquad = \dfrac{2n}{n^2 - n + 1}.$ $\qquad\qquad\qquad\square$

1.2 SIMPLE INTEREST

There are two special cases of the accumulation function $a(t)$ that we will examine closely. The first of these, *simple interest*, is used occasionally, primarily between integer interest periods, but will be discussed mainly for historical purposes and because it is easy to describe. The second of these, *compound interest*, is by far the most important accumulation function and will be discussed in the next section. Keep in mind that in both of these cases $a(t)$ is continuous, and also that there are some practical settings where modifications must be made.

Simple interest is the case where the graph of $a(t)$ is a straight line. Since $a(0) = 1$, the equation must therefore be of the general form $a(t) = 1 + bt$ for some b. However, the effective rate of interest i is given by $i = a(1) - 1 = b$, so the formula is

$$a(t) = 1 + it, \quad t \geq 0. \tag{1.4}$$

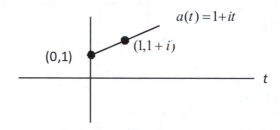

$$\boxed{\text{FIGURE 1.2}}$$

Remarks

1. This is case (a) graphed in Figure 1.1. In this situation, the amount of interest earned each year is constant. In other words, only the original principal earns interest from year to year, and interest accumulated in any given year does not earn interest in future years.

2. The formula $a(t) = 1 + it$ applies to the case where the principal is $A(0) = a(0) = 1$. More generally, if the principal at time 0 is equal to k, the amount at time t will be $A(t) = k(1 + it)$.

3. We noted above that the "i" in $a(t) = 1 + it$ is also the effective rate of interest for this function. Note however that

$$i_n = \frac{1 + in - [1 + i(n-1)]}{1 + i(n-1)}$$

$$= \frac{i}{1 + i(n-1)}. \tag{1.5}$$

Observe that i_n is not constant. In fact, i_n decreases as n gets larger, a fact which should not surprise us. If the amount of interest stays constant as the accumulated value increases, then clearly the effective rate of interest is going down.

4. Clearly $a(t) = 1 + it$ is a formula which works equally well for all values of t, integral or otherwise. However, problems can develop in practice, as illustrated by the following example.

Example 1.2

Assume Jack borrows 1000 from the bank on January 1, 1996 at a rate of 15% simple interest per year. How much does he owe on January 17, 1996?

Solution

The general formula for the amount owing at time t in general is $A(t) = 1000(1 + .15t)$, but the problem is to decide what value of t should be substituted into this formula. An obvious approach is to take the number of days which have passed since the loan was taken out and divide by the number of days in the year, but should we count the number of days as 16 or 17? Getting really picky, should we worry about the time of day when the loan was taken out, or the time of day when we wish to find the value of the loan? Obviously, any value of t is only a convenient approximation; the important thing is to have a consistent rule to be used in practice. Two techniques are common:

(a) The first method is called *exact simple interest*, and with it we use

$$t = \frac{number\ of\ days}{365}. \tag{1.6}$$

When counting the number of days it is usual to count the last day, but not the first. In our case this would lead to $t = \frac{16}{365}$ so Jack owes $1000\left[1 + (.15)\left(\frac{16}{365}\right)\right] = 1006.58$.

(b)   The second method is called *ordinary simple interest* (or the *Banker's Rule*), and with it we use

$$t = \frac{number\ of\ days}{360}.$$ (1.7)

The same procedure as above is used for calculating the number of days. In our case, we would have $t = \frac{16}{360}$ so the debt is

$$1000\left[1 + (.15)\left(\frac{16}{360}\right)\right] = 1006.67.$$

The common practice in Canada is to use exact simple interest, whereas ordinary simple interest is used in the United States and in international markets.   □

1.3 COMPOUND INTEREST

The most important special case of the accumulation function $a(t)$ is the case of compound interest. Intuitively speaking, this is the situation where money earns interest at a fixed effective rate; in this setting, the interest earned in one year earns interest itself in future years.

If i is the effective rate of interest, we know that $a(1) = 1 + i$, so 1 becomes $1 + i$ after the first year. What happens in the second year? Consider the $1 + i$ as consisting of two parts, the initial principal 1 and the interest i earned in the first year. The principal 1 will earn interest in the second year and will accumulate to $1 + i$. The interest i will also earn interest in the second year and will grow to $i(1 + i)$. Hence the total amount after two years is $1 + i + i(1+i) = (1 + i)^2$. By continuing this reasoning, we see that the formula for $a(t)$ is

$$a(t) = (1 + i)^t, \quad t \geq 0.$$ (1.8)

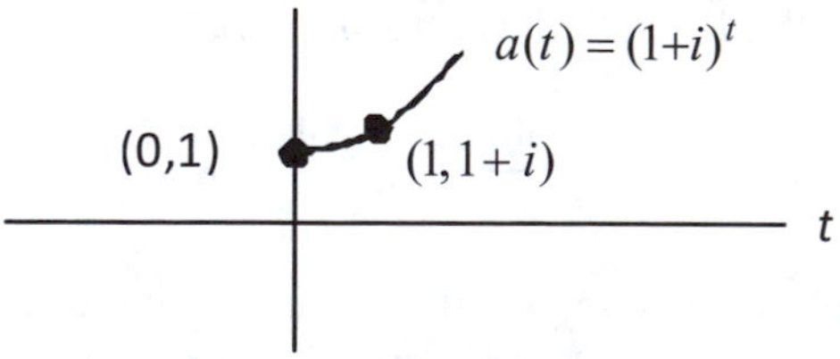

FIGURE 1.3

Remarks

1.   This is an example of the type of function shown in part (b) of the graph in Figure 1.1.

2.   The formula $a(t) = (1 + i)^t$ applies to the case where the principal is $A(0) = a(0) = 1$. More generally, if the principal at time 0 is equal to k, the amount at time t will be $A(t) = k(1 + i)^t$.

3.   Observe that the "i" in $(1 + i)^t$ is the effective rate of interest. More generally,

$$i_n = \frac{(1 + i)^n - (1 + i)^{n-1}}{(1 + i)^{n-1}} = 1 + i - 1 = i. \qquad (1.9)$$

Hence, in this case i_n is the same for all positive integers n. We shouldn't be surprised, since this fits with our idea that, in compound interest, the effective rate of interest is constant.

4.   Mathematically, any value of t, whether integral or not, can be substituted into $a(t) = (1 + i)^t$. This is an easier task for us today than it was fifty years ago; we just have to press the appropriate buttons on our calculators! Again, there are problems determining what value of t should be used, but we can deal with them as we did in the last section.

   In practical situations, however, a very different solution is sometimes used in the case of compound interest. To find the amount of a loan (for example) when t is a fraction, first find the amounts for the integral values of t immediately before and immediately after the fractional value in question. Then use linear interpolation between the two computed amounts to calculate the required answer.

   This is equivalent to saying that compound interest is used for integral values of t, and simple interest is used between integral values. In Figure 1.4, the solid line represents $a(t) = (1 + i)^t$, whereas the dotted lines indicate the graph of $a(t)$ if linear interpolation is used.

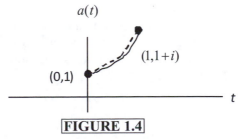

FIGURE 1.4

As we will see later, this common procedure benefits the lender in a financial transaction, and (consequently) is detrimental to the borrower if she has to repay the loan at a duration between integral values.

| Example 1.3 |

Jack borrows 1000 at 15% compound interest.
(a)   How much does he owe after 2 years?
(b)   How much does he owe after 57 days, assuming compound interest between integral durations?
(c)   How much does he owe after 1 year and 57 days, under the same assumption as in part (b)?
(d)   How much does he owe after 1 year and 57 days, assuming linear interpolation between integral durations?
(e)   In how many years will his principal have accumulated to 2000?

| Solution |

(a) $1000(1.15)^2 = 1322.50$.

(b)   The most suitable value for t is $\frac{57}{365}$, and the accumulated value is
$1000(1.15)^{\frac{57}{365}} = 1022.07$.

(c) $1000(1.15)^{1\frac{57}{365}} = 1175.38$

(d)   We must interpolate between $A(1) = (1000)(1.15) = 1150.00$ and $A(2) = 1000(1.15)^2 = 1322.50$.   The difference between these values is $A(2) - A(1) = 172.50$.   The portion of this difference which will accumulate in 57 days, assuming simple interest, is $\left(\frac{57}{365}\right)(172.50) = 26.94$. Thus the accumulated value after 1 year and 57 days is $1150.00 + 26.94 = 1176.94$.   Observe that the borrower owes more money in this case than he does in part (c).

(e)   We seek t such that $1000(1.15)^t = 2000$, or that $(1.15)^t = 2$. Using logs we obtain

$$t = \frac{\log 2}{\log 1.15} = 4.9595 \text{ years.} \qquad \square$$

To close this section, we will compare simple interest and compound interest to see which gives the better return. In Figure 1.5, graphs for both simple interest and compound interest are drawn on the same set of axes.

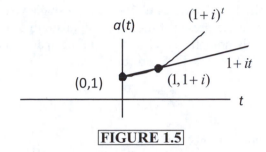

FIGURE 1.5

We know that the exponential function $(1 + i)^t$ is always concave up (because the second derivative is $(1 + i)^t [ln\,(1 + i)]^2$, which is greater than zero), whereas $1 + it$ is a straight line. These facts tell us that the only points of intersection of these graphs are the obvious ones, namely $(0,1)$ and $(1, 1 + i)$. They also give us the two important relationships

$$(1 + i)^t < 1 + it, \quad \text{for} \quad 0 < t < 1 \tag{1.10}$$

and

$$(1 + i)^t > 1 + it, \quad \text{for} \quad t > 1. \tag{1.11}$$

Hence we conclude that compound interest yields a higher return than simple interest if $t > 1$, whereas simple interest yields more if $0 < t < 1$. The first of these statements does not surprise us, since for $t > 1$, we have interest as well as principal earning interest in the $(1 + i)^t$ case. The second statement reminds us that, for periods of less than a year, simple interest is more beneficial to the lender than compound interest, a fact which was illustrated in Example 1.3.

1.4 PRESENT VALUE AND DISCOUNT

In Section 1.1 we defined accumulated value at time t as the amount that the principal accumulates to over t years. We now define the *present value t years in the past* as the amount of money that will accumulate to the principal over t years. In other words, this is the reverse procedure of that which we have been discussing up to now.

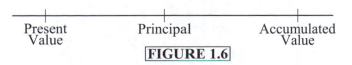

FIGURE 1.6

For example, 1 accumulates to $1 + i$ over a single year. How much money is needed, at the present time, to accumulate to 1 over one year? We will denote this amount by v, and, recalling that v accumulates to $v(1 + i)$, we have $v(1 + i) = 1$. Therefore

$$v = \frac{1}{1 + i}. \tag{1.12}$$

These two accumulations are shown in Figure 1.7.

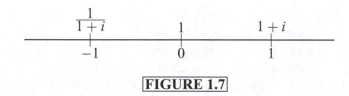

FIGURE 1.7

From now on, unless explicitly stated otherwise, we will assume that we are in a compound interest situation, where $a(t) = (1 + i)^t$. In this case, the present value of 1, t years in the past, will be $v^t = \frac{1}{(1 + i)^t}$. We summarize this on the time diagram shown in Figure 1.8.

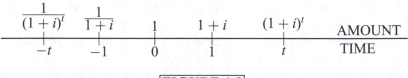

FIGURE 1.8

Observe that, since $v^t = (1 + i)^{-t}$, the function $a(t) = (1 + i)^t$ expresses all these values, for both positive and negative values of t. Hence $(1 + i)^t$ gives the value of one unit (at time 0) at any time t, past or future. The graph is shown in Figure 1.9.

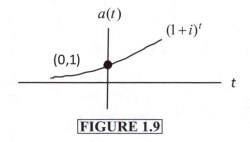

FIGURE 1.9

| Example 1.4 |

The Kelly family buys a new house for 93,500 on May 1, 1996. How much was this house worth on May 1, 1992 if real estate prices have risen at a compound rate of 8% per year during that period?

| Solution |

We seek the present value, at time $t = -4$, of 93,500 at time 0. This is

$93{,}500 \left(\frac{1}{1.08} \right)^4 = 68{,}725.29.$ □

What happens to the calculation of present values if simple interest is assumed instead of compound interest? The accumulation function is now $a(t) = 1 + it$. Hence, the present value of one unit t years in the past is given by x, where $x(1 + it) = 1$. Thus the present value is

$$x = \frac{1}{1 + it}. \qquad (1.13)$$

The time diagram for this case is shown in Figure 1.10.

| FIGURE 1.10 |

In Exercise 15, you are asked to sketch the graph of this situation. Unlike the compound interest case, this graph changes dramatically as it passes through the point $(0, 1)$.

We now turn our attention to the concept of discount. For the moment we will not assume compound interest, since any accumulation function will be satisfactory.

Imagine that 100 is invested, and that one year later it has accumulated to 112. We have been viewing the 100 as the "starting figure," and have imagined that interest of 12 is added to it at the end of the year. However, we could also view 112 as the basic figure, and imagine that 12 is deducted from that value at the start of the year. From the latter point of view, the 12 is considered an amount of *discount*.

Students sometimes get confused about the difference between interest and discount, but the important thing to remember is that the only difference is in the point of view, not in the underlying financial transaction. In both situations we have 100 accumulating to 112, and nothing can change that.

Since discount focuses on the total at the end of the year, it is natural to define the effective rate of discount, d, as

$$d = \frac{a(1) - 1}{a(1)}. \tag{1.14}$$

In other words, standardization is achieved by dividing by $a(1)$ instead of $a(0)$, as was done in (1.2) to define the effective rate of interest i.

More generally, the effective rate of discount in the nth year is given by

$$d_n = \frac{a(n) - a(n-1)}{a(n)}. \tag{1.15}$$

(Compare this with the definition of i_n, given by (1.3).)

Now we will derive some basic identities relating d to i. One identity follows immediately from the definition of d, namely,

$$d = \frac{a(1) - 1}{a(1)} = \frac{(1+i) - 1}{1+i} = \frac{i}{1+i}. \tag{1.16}$$

Since $1 + i > 1$, this tells us that $d < i$.

Immediately from the above we obtain

$$1 - d = 1 - \frac{i}{1+i} = \frac{1}{1+i} = v. \tag{1.17}$$

Actually, this identity is exactly what we would expect from the definition of d. The fact that $1 - d$ accumulates to 1 over one year is the exact analogy of 1 accumulating to $1 + i$ over the same period.

Solving either of the above identities for i, we obtain

$$i = \frac{d}{1-d}. \tag{1.18}$$

The reader will be asked to derive other identities in the exercises and to give verbal arguments in support of them. We note that all identities derived so far hold for any accumulation function. For the rest of this section, it will be assumed that $a(t) = (1 + i)^t$.

In Section 1.3 we learned that to find the accumulated value t years in the future we multiply by $(1 + i)^t$, whereas to find the present value t years in the past we multiply by $\frac{1}{(1 + i)^t}$. However, identity (1.17) tells us that $1 - d = \frac{1}{1 + i}$. Hence, if d is involved, the rules for present and accumulated value are reversed: present value is obtained by multiplying by $(1 - d)^t$, and accumulated value by multiplying by $\frac{1}{(1 - d)^t}$.

| Example 1.5 |

1000 is to be accumulated by January 1, 1995, at a compound rate of discount of 9% per year.
(a)   Find the present value on January 1, 1992.
(b)   Find the value of i corresponding to d.
| Solution |
(a) $1000(1 - .09)^3 = 753.57.$
(b) $i = \frac{d}{1 - d} = \frac{.09}{.91} = .0989.$ □

| Example 1.6 |

Jane deposits 1000 in a bank account on August 1, 1996. If the rate of compound interest is 7% per year, find the value of this deposit on August 1, 1994.
| Solution |
Some students think that the answer to this question should be 0, because the money hasn't been deposited yet! However, in a mathematical sense, we know that money has value at all times, past or future, so the correct answer is $1000\left(\frac{1}{1.07}\right)^2 = 873.44.$ □

1.5   NOMINAL RATE OF INTEREST

We will assume $a(t) = (1 + i)^t$ throughout this section and, unless stated otherwise, in all remaining sections of the book.

| Example 1.7 |

A man borrows 1000 at an effective rate of interest of 2% per month. How much does he owe after 3 years?

Solution
What we want is the amount of the debt after three years. Since the
effective interest rate is given per month, three years is 36 interest
periods. Thus the answer is $1000(1.02)^{36} = 2039.89$.   □

The point of the above example is to illustrate that effective rates
of interest need not be given per year, but can be defined with respect to
any period of time. To apply the formulae developed to this point, we
must be sure that t is the number of *effective interest periods* in any
particular problem.

In many real-life situations, the effective interest period is not a
year, but rather some shorter period. Perhaps the lender tries to keep this
fact hidden, as it might be to his benefit to do so! For example, suppose
you want to take out a mortgage on a house and you discover a rate of
12% per year. When you dig a little, however, what you find out is that
this rate is "convertible semiannually", which means that it is really 6%
effective per half-year. Is that the same thing? Not at all. Consider what
happens to an investment of 1. After half a year it has accumulated to
1.06. After one year (two interest periods) it has become
$(1.06)^2 = 1.1236$. So, over a one-year period, the amount of interest
gained is .1236, which means the effective rate of interest per year is
actually 12.36%. Although it may not be clear from the advertising,
many mortgage loans are convertible semiannually, so the effective rate
of interest is higher than the rate quoted.

As another example, consider a well-known credit card which
charges 18% per year convertible monthly. This means that the actual
rate of interest is $\frac{.18}{12} = .015$ effective per month. Over the course of a
year, 1 will accumulate to $(1.015)^{12} = 1.1956$, so the effective rate of
interest per year is actually 19.56%.

The 18% in the last example is called a *nominal* rate of interest,
which means that it is convertible over a period other than one year. In
general, we use the notation $i^{(m)}$ to denote a nominal rate of interest
convertible m times per year, which implies an effective rate of interest
of $\frac{i^{(m)}}{m}$ per m^{th} of a year. If i is the effective rate of interest per year, it
follows that

$$1 + i = \left[1 + \frac{i^{(m)}}{m}\right]^m. \tag{1.19}$$

Example 1.8

Find the accumulated value of 1000 after three years at a rate of interest of 24% per year convertible monthly.

Solution

This is really 2% effective per month, so the answer is the same as Example 1.7, namely $1000(1.02)^{36} = 2039.89$. □

Remark

An alternative method of solving Example 1.8 is to find i, the effective rate of interest per year, and then proceed as in Section 1.3. We would have $i = \left(1 + \frac{i^{(m)}}{m}\right)^m - 1 = (1+.02)^{12} - 1 = .26824$, and the answer would be $1000 (1.26824)^3 = 2039.88$.

Notice the difference of .01 in the two answers. This is because not enough decimal places were kept in the value of i, and some error crept in. Of course, if you use the memory in your calculator it is unlikely that this type of error will occur. Nevertheless, the first solution is still preferable; time spent on unnecessary calculations can be significant in examination situations.

It will be extremely important in later sections of the text to be able to convert from one nominal rate of interest to another whose convertible frequency is different. Here is an example of this.

Example 1.9

If $i^{(6)} = .15$, find the equivalent nominal rate of interest convertible semiannually.

Solution

We have $\left(1 + \frac{i^{(2)}}{2}\right)^2 = \left(1 + \frac{.15}{6}\right)^6$, so $i^{(2)} = 2[(1.025)^3 - 1] = .15378$.
□

In the same way that we defined a nominal rate of interest, we could also define a nominal rate of discount, $d^{(m)}$, as meaning an effective rate of discount of $\frac{d^{(m)}}{m}$ per m^{th} of a year. Analogous to identity (1.19), it is easy to see that

$$1 - d = \left[1 - \frac{d^{(m)}}{m}\right]^m. \tag{1.20}$$

Since $1 - d = \frac{1}{1+i}$, we conclude that

$$\left[1 + \frac{i^{(m)}}{m}\right]^m = 1 + i = (1-d)^{-1} = \left[1 - \frac{d^{(n)}}{n}\right]^{-n}, \quad (1.21)$$

for all positive integers m and n.

Example 1.10

Find the nominal rate of discount convertible semiannually which is equivalent to a nominal rate of interest of 12% per year convertible monthly.

Solution

$$\left[1 - \frac{d^{(2)}}{2}\right]^{-2} = \left[1 + \frac{i^{(12)}}{12}\right]^{12}, \text{ so } 1 - \frac{d^{(2)}}{2} = (1.01)^{-6} = .942045, \text{ from}$$

which we find $d^{(2)} = 2(1 - .942045) = .11591.$ $\square$

1.6 FORCE OF INTEREST

We note before starting this section that it is somewhat theoretical, and is independent of the rest of the text. Anyone wishing to proceed directly to more practical problems can safely omit this material. In particular, more background knowledge is required for a full understanding here than is required for any other section; students with only a sketchy knowledge of calculus might omit this on first reading.

Assume that the effective annual rate of interest is $i = .12$, and that we want to find nominal rates $i^{(m)}$ equivalent to i. The formula $i^{(m)} = m\left[(1+i)^{1/m} - 1\right]$, which comes from identity (1.19), is used to calculate these values which are shown in Table 1.1.

TABLE 1.1

m	1	2	5	10	50
$i^{(m)}$	.12	.1166	.1146	.1140	.1135

We observe that $i^{(m)}$ decreases as m gets larger, a fact which we will be able to prove later in this section. We also observe that the values of $i^{(m)}$ are decreasing very slowly as we go further and further along; in the language of calculus, $i^{(m)}$ seems to be approaching a limit. This is, in fact, what is happening, and we can use L'Hopital's rule to see what the limit is. There is no need to assume $i = .12$ in our derivation, so we proceed with arbitrary i.

$$\lim_{m \to \infty} i^{(m)} = \lim_{m \to \infty} m\left[(1+i)^{1/m} - 1\right] = \lim_{m \to \infty} \frac{(1+i)^{1/m} - 1}{\frac{1}{m}} \quad (1.22)$$

Since (1.22) is of the form $\frac{0}{0}$, we take derivatives top and bottom, cancel, and obtain

$$\lim_{m \to \infty} i^{(m)} = \lim_{m \to \infty} \left[(1+i)^{1/m} \cdot ln(1+i)\right] = ln(1+i), \quad (1.23)$$

since $\lim_{m \to \infty} (1+i)^{1/m} = 1$.

This limit is called the *force of interest* and is denoted by δ, so we have

$$\delta = ln(1+i). \quad (1.24)$$

In our example, $\delta = ln(1.12) = .11333$. The reader should compare this with the entries in Table 1.1.

Intuitively, δ represents a nominal rate of interest which is convertible *continuously*, a notion of more theoretical than practical importance. However, δ can be a very good approximation for $i^{(m)}$ when m is large (for example, a nominal rate convertible daily), and has the advantage of being very easy to calculate.

We note that identity (1.24) can be rewritten as

$$e^\delta = 1 + i. \quad (1.25)$$

The usefulness of this form is shown in the next example. Again we stress the importance of being able to convert a rate of interest with a given conversion frequency to an equivalent rate with a different conversion frequency.

| Example 1.11 |

A loan of 3000 is taken out on June 23, 1997. If the force of interest is 14%, find each of the following:
(a)   The value of the loan on June 23, 2002.
(b)   The value of i.
(c)   The value of $i^{(12)}$.

| Solution |

(a)   The value 5 years later is $3000(1+i)^5$. Using $e^\delta = 1+i$, we obtain $3000(e^{.14})^5 = 3000\,e^{.7} = 6041.26$.

(b) $i = e^{.14} - 1 = .15027$.

(c) $\left(1 + \dfrac{i^{(12)}}{12}\right)^{12} = 1 + i = e^{.14}$, so we have the result

$$i^{(12)} = 12(e^{.14/12} - 1) = .14082. \qquad \square$$

Remark

Note that if we tried to solve part (a) by first obtaining $i = .15027$ (as in part (b)), and then calculating $3000(1.15027)^5$, we would get 6041.16, an answer differing from our first answer by .10. There is nothing wrong with this second method, except that not enough decimal places were carried in the value of i to guarantee an accurate answer. Let us repeat an earlier admonition: it is always wise to do as few calculations as necessary.

Observe that $D[(1+i)^t] = (1+i)^t \cdot ln(1+i)$, where D stands for the derivative with respect to t.   Hence we see that

$$\delta = ln(1+i) = \frac{D[(1+i)^t]}{(1+i)^t} = \frac{D[a(t)]}{a(t)}. \qquad (1.26)$$

Let us see why this fact happens to be true. Recall from the definition of the derivative that $D[a(t)] = \lim\limits_{h \to 0} \dfrac{a(t+h) - a(t)}{h}$, so

$$\frac{D[a(t)]}{a(t)} = \lim_{h \to 0} \frac{a(t+h) - a(t)}{h \cdot a(t)} = \lim_{h \to 0} \frac{\frac{a(t+h) - a(t)}{a(t)}}{h}. \qquad (1.27)$$

The term $\dfrac{a(t+h)-a(t)}{a(t)}$ in (1.27) is just the effective rate of interest over a very small time period h, so $\dfrac{\frac{a(t+h)-a(t)}{a(t)}}{h}$ is the nominal annual rate corresponding to that effective rate, which agrees with our earlier definition of δ.

The above analysis does more than that, however. It also indicates how the force of interest should be defined for arbitrary accumulation functions.

First, let us observe that $\delta = ln\,(1+i)$ is independent of t. However, this is a special property of compound interest, corresponding to a constant i_n. For arbitrary accumulation functions, we define the force of interest at time t, δ_t, by

$$\delta_t = \frac{D[a(t)]}{a(t)}, \tag{1.28}$$

since we would normally expect δ_t to depend on t.

For certain functions, it is more convenient to use the equivalent definition

$$\delta_t = D[ln\,(a(t))]. \tag{1.29}$$

We also remark that, since $A(t) = k \cdot a(t)$, it follows that

$$\delta_t = \frac{D[A(t)]}{A(t)} = D[ln\,(A(t))]. \tag{1.30}$$

| Example 1.12 |

Find δ_t in the case of simple interest.

| Solution |

$$\delta_t = \frac{D(1+it)}{1+it} = \frac{i}{1+it}. \qquad \square$$

We now have a method for finding the force of interest, δ_t, given any accumulation function $a(t)$. What if we are given δ_t instead, and wish to derive $a(t)$ from it?

To start with, let us write our definition of δ_t from (1.29) using a different variable, namely $\delta_r = D[ln\,(a(r))]$, where D now means the derivative with respect to r. Integrating both sides of this equation from 0 to t, we obtain

$$\int_0^t \delta_r \, dr = \int_0^t D[\ln(a(r))] \, dr = \ln(a(r)) \Big|_0^t$$

$$= \ln(a(t)) - \ln(a(0))$$

$$= \ln(a(t)), \qquad (1.31)$$

since $a(0) = 1$ and $\ln 1 = 0$. Then taking the antilog we have

$$a(t) = e^{\int_0^t \delta_r \, dr}. \qquad (1.32)$$

Example 1.13

Prove that if δ is a constant (i.e., independent of r), then $a(t) = (1 + i)^t$ for some i.

Solution

If $\delta_r = c$, the right hand side of (1.32) is $e^{\int_0^t c \, dr} = e^{ct} = (e^c)^t$. Hence the result is proved with $i = e^c - 1$. □

Example 1.14

Prove that $\displaystyle\int_0^n A(t) \delta_t \, dt = A(n) - A(0)$ for any amount function $A(t)$.

Solution

The left hand side is

$$\int_0^n A(t) \delta_t \, dt = \int_0^n A(t) \left[\frac{D[A(t)]}{A(t)} \right] dt = \int_0^n D[A(t)] \, dt$$

$$= A(t) \Big|_0^n = A(n) - A(0) \text{ as required.}$$

□

The identity in the above example has an interesting verbal interpretation. The term $\delta_t \, dt$ represents the effective rate of interest at time t for the infinitesimal "period of time" dt. Hence $A(t) \delta_t \, dt$ represents the amount of interest earned in this period, and $\int_0^n A(t) \delta_t \, dt$ represents the total amount of interest earned over the entire period, a number which is clearly equal to $A(n) - A(0)$.

We now return to the compound interest case where we have $a(t) = (1 + i)^t$. It is interesting to write some of the formulae already developed as power series expansions. For example $\delta = \ln(1 + i)$ becomes

$$\delta = i - \frac{i^2}{2} + \frac{i^3}{3} - \frac{i^4}{4} + \cdots. \qquad (1.33)$$

Convergence is a concern here, but as long as $|i| < 1$, which is usually the case, the above series does converge.

Another important formula was $i = e^\delta - 1$, which becomes

$$i = \delta + \frac{\delta^2}{2!} + \frac{\delta^3}{3!} + \cdots. \tag{1.34}$$

Since all terms on the right hand side are positive, this allows us to conclude immediately that $i > \delta$. We note in passing that this series converges for all δ.

Next let us expand the expression $i = \frac{d}{1-d} = d(1-d)^{-1}$, which becomes

$$i = d(1 + d + d^2 + d^3 + \cdots) = d + d^2 + d^3 + \cdots. \tag{1.35}$$

Again this shows us very clearly that $i > d$. We also note that we must have $|d| < 1$ for this series to converge. In fact, trying to put $d = 2$ yields an amusing result: the left hand side is $i = \frac{2}{1-2} = -2$, whereas the right hand side becomes $2 + 2^2 + 2^3 + \cdots$, all of which are positive terms. Thus we have "proven" that -2 is a positive number!

Next let us expand $i^{(m)}$ as a function of i. From (1.19) we have $i^{(m)} = m[(1+i)^{1/m} - 1]$, so

$$\begin{aligned}
i^{(m)} &= m\left[1 + \frac{1}{m}i + \frac{\frac{1}{m}(\frac{1}{m}-1)}{2!}i^2 + \frac{(\frac{1}{m})(\frac{1}{m}-1)(\frac{1}{m}-2)}{3!}i^3 + \cdots - 1\right] \\
&= i + \left[\frac{\frac{1}{m}-1}{2!}\right]i^2 + \frac{(\frac{1}{m}-1)(\frac{1}{m}-2)}{3!}i^3 + \cdots. \tag{1.36}
\end{aligned}$$

Again, this converges for $|i| < 1$.

Why are we interested in power series expansions? Well, we have already seen that they sometimes allow us to easily conclude facts like $i > \delta$ (although they certainly aren't needed for that). They also give us a quick means of calculating some of these functions, since often only the first few terms of the series are necessary for a high degree of accuracy. If you ask your calculator to do this work for you instead, it will oblige, but the program used for the calculation will often be a variation of one of those described above.

As a final example, let us expand $d^{(m)}$ in terms of δ. We have

$$\left[1 - \frac{d^{(m)}}{m}\right]^m = (1+i)^{-1} = e^{-\delta},\qquad(1.37)$$

so

$$
\begin{aligned}
d^{(m)} &= m[1 - e^{-\delta/m}] \\
&= m\left[1 - \left(1 + \left(-\frac{\delta}{m}\right) + \frac{(-\frac{\delta}{m})^2}{2!} + \frac{(-\frac{\delta}{m})^3}{3!} + \cdots\right)\right] \\
&= m\left[\frac{\delta}{m} - \frac{\delta^2}{2!m^2} + \frac{\delta^3}{3!m^3} - \cdots\right] \\
&= \delta - \frac{\delta^2}{2!m} + \frac{\delta^3}{3!m^2} - \cdots .\qquad(1.38)
\end{aligned}
$$

From this we easily see that $\lim\limits_{m\to\infty} d^{(m)} = \delta$. In other words, there is no need to define a force of discount, because it will turn out to be the same as the force of interest already defined.

EXERCISES

1.1 Accumulation Function;   1.2 Simple Interest;
1.3 Compound Interest

1-1. Alphonse has 14,000 in an account on January 1, 1995.
    (a) Assuming simple interest at 8% per year, find the accumulated value on January 1, 2001.
    (b) Assuming compound interest at 8% per year, find the accumulated value on January 1, 2001.
    (c) Assuming exact simple interest at 8% per year, find the accumulated value on March 8, 1995.
    (d) Assuming compound interest at 8% per year, but linear interpolation between integral durations, find the accumulated value on February 17, 1997.

1-2. Mary has 14,000 in an account on January 1, 1995.
   (a)   Assuming compound interest at 11% per year, find the accumulated value on January 1, 2000.
   (b)   Assuming ordinary simple interest at 11% per year, find the accumulated value on April 7, 2000.
   (c)   Assuming compound interest at 11% per year, but linear interpolation between integral durations, find the accumulated value on April 7, 2000.

1-3. For the $a(t)$ function given in Example 1.1, prove that $i_{n+1} < i_n$ for all positive integers n.

1-4. Consider the function $a(t) = \sqrt{1 + (i^2 + 2i)t^2}$, $i > 0$, $t \geq 0$.
   (a)   Show that $a(0) = 1$ and $a(1) = 1 + i$.
   (b)   Show that $a(t)$ is increasing and continuous for $t \geq 0$.
   (c)   Show that $a(t) < 1 + it$ for $0 < t < 1$, but $a(t) > 1 + it$ for $t > 1$.
   (d)   Show that $a(t) < (1 + i)^t$ if t is sufficiently large.

1-5. Let $a(t)$ be a function such that $a(0) = 1$ and i_n is constant for all n.
   (a)   Prove that $a(t) = (1 + i)^t$ for all integers $t \geq 0$.
   (b)   Can you conclude that $a(t) = (1 + i)^t$ for all $t \geq 0$?

1-6. Let $A(t)$ be an amount function. For every positive integer n, define $I_n = A(n) - A(n-1)$.
   (a)   Explain verbally what I_n represents
   (b)   Prove that $A(n) - A(0) = I_1 + I_2 + \cdots + I_n$.
   (c)   Explain verbally the result in part (b).
   (d)   Is it true that $a(n) - a(0) = i_1 + i_2 + \cdots + i_n$? Explain.

1-7. (a)   In how many years will 1000 accumulate to 1400 at 12% simple interest?
   (b)   At what rate of simple interest will 1000 accumulate to 1500 in 6 years?
   (c)   Repeat parts (a) and (b) assuming compound interest instead of simple interest.

1-8.   At a certain rate of simple interest, 1000 will accumulate to 1300
       after a certain period of time. Find the accumulated value of 500 at
       a rate of simple interest $\frac{2}{3}$ as great over twice as long a period of
       time.

1-9.   Find the accumulated value of 6000 invested for ten years, if the
       compound interest rate is 7% per year for the first four years and
       11% per year for the last six.

1-10. Annual compound interest rates are 13% in 1994, 11% in 1995 and
       15% in 1996. Find the effective rate of compound interest per year
       which yields an equivalent return over the three-year period.

1-11. At a certain rate of compound interest, it is found that 1 grows to 2
       in x years, 2 grows to 3 in y years, and 1 grows to 5 in z years.
       Prove that 6 grows to 10 in $z - x - y$ years.

1-12. If 1 grows to K in x periods at compound rate i per period and 1
       grows to K in y periods at compound rate $2i$ per period, which one
       of the following is always true? Prove your answer.
       (a) $x < 2y$
       (b) $x = 2y$
       (c) $x > 2y$
       (d) $y = \sqrt{x}$
       (e) $y > 2x$

1.4   Present Value and Discount

1-13. Henry has an investment of 1000 on January 1, 1998 at a
       compound annual rate of discount $d = .12$.
       (a)   Find the value of his investment on January 1, 1995.
       (b)   Find the value of i corresponding to d.
       (c)   Using your answer to part (b), rework part (a) using i instead
              of d. Do you get the same answer?

1-14. Mary has 14,000 in an account on January 1, 1995.
       (a)   Assuming compound interest at 12% per year, find the
              present value on January 1, 1989.
       (b)   Assuming compound discount at 12% per year, find the
              present value on January 1, 1989.
       (c)   Explain the relative magnitude of your answers to parts (a)
              and (b).

1-15. (a) Sketch a graph of $a(t)$ with its extension to present value in the case of simple interest.

(b) Explain, both mathematically and verbally, why $1 - it$ is not the correct present value t years in the past, when simple interest is assumed.

1-16. Prove that d_n is constant in the case of compound interest.

1-17. Prove each of the following identities mathematically. For parts (a), (b) and (c), give a verbal explanation of how you can see that they are correct.

(a) $d = iv$

(b) $d = 1 - v$

(c) $i - d = id$

(d) $\frac{1}{d} - \frac{1}{i} = 1$

(e) $d\left(1 + \frac{i}{2}\right) = i\left(1 - \frac{d}{2}\right)$

(f) $i\sqrt{1 - d} = d\sqrt{1 + i}$

1-18. Four of the following five expressions have the same value (for $i > 0$). Which one is the exception?

(a) $\dfrac{d^3}{(1 - d)^2}$ (b) $\dfrac{(i - d)^2}{1 - v}$ (c) $(i - d)d$ (d) $i^3 - i^3 d$ (e) $i^2 d$

1-19. The interest on L for one year is 216. The equivalent discount on L for one year is 200. What is L?

1.5 Nominal Rate of Interest

1-20. Acme Trust offers three different savings accounts to an investor.

Account A: compound interest at 12% per year convertible quarterly.

Account B: compound interest at 11.97% per year convertible 5 times per year.

Account C: compound discount at 11.8% per year convertible 10 times per year.

Which account is most advantageous to the investor? Which account is most advantageous to Acme Trust?

1-21. Phyllis takes out a loan of 3000 at a rate of 16% per year convertible 4 times a year. How much does she owe after 21 months?

1-22. The Bank of Newfoundland offers a 12% mortgage convertible semiannually. Find each of the following:
(a) i (b) $d^{(4)}$ (c) $i^{(12)}$
(d) The equivalent effective rate of interest per month.

1-23. 100 grows to 107 in 6 months. Find each of the following:
(a) The effective rate of interest per half-year.
(b) $i^{(2)}$ (c) i (d) $d^{(3)}$

1-24. Find n such that $1 + \dfrac{i^{(n)}}{n} = \dfrac{1 + \frac{i^{(6)}}{6}}{1 + \frac{i^{(8)}}{8}}$.

1-25. Express $d^{(7)}$ as a function of $i^{(5)}$.

1-26. Show that $v\left(1 + \dfrac{i^{(3)}}{3}\right) = \left(1 + \dfrac{i^{(30)}}{30}\right)\left(1 - \dfrac{d^{(5)}}{5}\right)\sqrt{1 - d}$.

1-27. Prove that $i^{(4)}d^{(8)} \geq i^{(8)}d^{(4)}$.

1-28. (a)   Prove that $i^{(m)} - d^{(m)} = \dfrac{i^{(m)}d^{(m)}}{m}$.

     (b)   Prove that $\dfrac{1}{d^{(m)}} - \dfrac{1}{i^{(m)}} = \dfrac{1}{m}$.

1.6   Force of Interest

1-29. Find the equivalent value of δ in each of the following cases.
(a) $i = .13$
(b) $d = .13$
(c) $i^{(4)} = .13$
(d) $d^{(5)} = .13$

1-30. In Section 1.3, it was shown that for $0 < t < 1$, $(1+i)^t < 1 + it$. Show that $1 + it - (1+i)^t$ is maximized at $t = \frac{1}{\delta}[\ln i - \ln \delta]$.

1-31. Assume that the force of interest is doubled.
    (a)   Show that the effective annual interest rate is more than doubled.
    (b)   Show that the effective annual discount rate is less than doubled.

1-32. Show that $\lim\limits_{i \to 0} \dfrac{i - \delta}{\delta^2} = .50$.

1-33. Find $a(t)$ if $\delta_t = .04(1 + t)^{-1}$.

1-34. Obtain an expression for δ_t if $A(t) = ka^{t+1} b^{t^3} c^{d^t}$.

1-35. Using mathematical induction, prove that for all positive integers n, $\dfrac{d^m}{dv^n}(v^{n-1}\delta) = -(1 + i)(n - 1)!$, where $\dfrac{d}{dv}$ denotes derivative with respect to v.

1-36. Express v as a power series expansion in terms of δ.

1-37. Express d as a power series expansion in terms of i.

1-38. Prove that $i^{(n)} < i^{(m)}$ if $n > m$.

1-39. Prove that $d < d^{(n)} < \delta < i^{(n)} < i$ for all $n > 1$.

1-40. Show that $D(\delta_t) = \dfrac{D^2 A(t)}{A(t)} - (\delta_t)^2$, where D is the derivative with respect to t.

1-41. Show that $\delta = \dfrac{d+i}{2} + \dfrac{d^2 - i^2}{4} + \dfrac{d^3 + i^3}{6} + \cdots$.

1-42. Which is larger, $i - \delta$ or $\delta - d$? Prove your answer.

1-43. (a)   Write a computer program which will take a given value of i
              and output values of $i^{(m)}$ for a succession of values of m.

       (b)   Extend the program in part (a) to also give you a value for δ,
              using $\delta = \lim\limits_{m \to \infty} i^{(m)}$.

1-44. Write a computer program which will take a given value of δ and
       output the equivalent value of i. (*Use the power series expansion.*)

CHAPTER TWO
INTEREST: BASIC APPLICATIONS

2.1 EQUATION OF VALUE

In its simplest terms, every interest problem involves only four quantities: the principal originally invested, the accumulated value at the end of the period of investment, the period of investment, and the rate of interest. Any one of these four quantities can be calculated if the others are known.

In this section we will present a number of examples illustrating the determination of principal, accumulated value, and period of investment; determining the rate of interest will be explored in Sections 2.2 and 2.3. More complicated situations involving several "principals" invested at different times will arise in practice, and we will examine some of these as well.

The most important tool in dealing with such problems is the time diagram, which we encountered in chapter one, and the first step in any solution should be to draw such a diagram. After that, all entries on the diagram should be "brought" to the same point in time, in order that they can be compared. Then an *equation of value* is set up at that point in time, and a solution is obtained by algebraic means. The student should carefully study the examples in this section to see how these steps are carried out in practice.

We remark that before calculators came into general use, the calculations involved in some of these problems were quite difficult, and it was necessary to develop a collection of techniques to deal with them. Interest tables and log tables were in frequent use, and values which did not appear in the interest tables were handled by interpolation or other approximate methods. For example, the power series expansions given in the previous chapter could be used for calculation, since the first few terms often give a good approximation to the correct answer. We, however, will use our calculators freely and will generally not need to employ the older techniques. That does not mean that every question can be solved by pushing the appropriate button, however; in particular we will see cases where some approximate method (e.g., linear interpolation) is required to obtain an answer. In addition it is often necessary to first analyze the data very carefully, and organize it in such a way such that the calculator can then be called upon to assist in solving the problem. After all, your calculator is only an aid to mechanical computation. The person with the problem still has to solve it!

| Example 2.1 |

Find the accumulated value of 500 after 173 months at a rate of interest of 14% convertible quarterly, assuming compound interest throughout.
| Solution |
The effective rate of interest is .035 per 3 month period, and there are a total of $57\frac{2}{3}$ periods. Hence the answer is $500(1.035)^{173/3} = 3635.22$. □

Remarks

1. It is quite common to assume compound interest over integral durations, but simple interest between integral durations. Under that assumption, the answer to this example would be $500(1.035)^{57}\left[1 + (.035)\left(\frac{2}{3}\right)\right] = 3635.69$. Observe that this answer is larger than the one in the example, agreeing with our earlier observation that simple interest gives a higher return when the period is less than a year.

2. In pre-calculator days the calculation of $500(1.035)^{173/3}$ would require some work. Log tables, if available, could give the answer quickly but if only interest tables were available, you might have to write the product as $500(1.035)^{50}(1.035)^{7}(1.035)^{2/3}$. The values of $(1.035)^{50}$ and $(1.035)^{7}$ could be found in the interest tables, in particular in the $n = 50$ and $n = 7$ rows of the $i = 3\frac{1}{2}\%$ table. There is no $n = 57$ row of most interest tables, which is why $(1.035)^{57}$ would have to be broken up into two parts. The term $(1.035)^{2/3}$ presents a special problem. Usually only integral values of n are given in the interest tables, along with common fractional values such as $\frac{1}{2}$, $\frac{1}{4}$ and $\frac{1}{12}$, but not $\frac{2}{3}$. One could work this out by observing that $(1.035)^{2/3} = [(1.035)^{1/12}]^{8}$, but otherwise log tables or a power series expansion would be required.

Example 2.2

Alice borrows 5000 from The Friendly Finance Company at a rate of interest of 18% per year convertible semiannually. Two years later she pays the company 3000. Three years after that she pays the company 2000. How much does she owe seven years after the loan is taken out?

Solution

We will use a time diagram to aid in our solution:

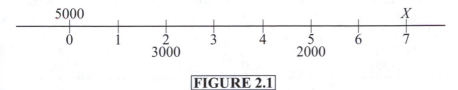

FIGURE 2.1

Let X be the amount still owing. In this type of problem, our goal is to obtain an equation of value which will yield the solution. To do that, all entries on the time diagram should be brought to the same point in time so an equation can be found. Any point in time can be chosen, but the most convenient one in this example is $t = 7$. The amount owing will equal the accumulated value at time 7 of the loan, minus the accumulated value at time 7 of the payments already made. Since the actual rate of interest is .09 effective per half-year, we have $X = 5000(1.09)^{14} - 3000(1.09)^{10} - 2000(1.09)^4 = 6783.38$. ☐

Example 2.3

Eric deposits 8000 in an account on January 1, 1995. On January 1, 1997, he deposits an additional 6000 in the account. On January 1, 2001, he withdraws 12,000 from the account. Assuming no further deposits or withdrawals are made, find the amount in Eric's account on January 1, 2004, if $i = .05$.

Solution

In this example, we see that withdrawals can be viewed as "negative deposits" in an equation of value.

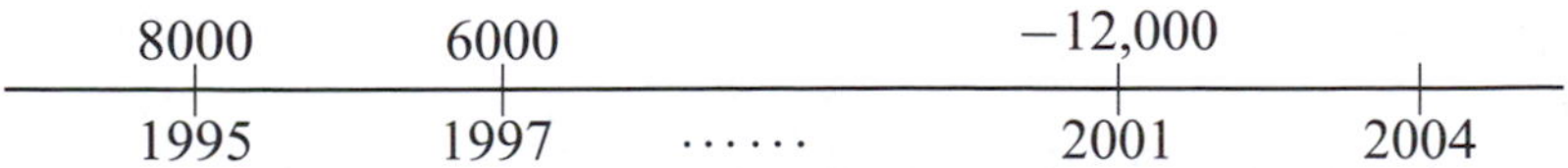

8000	6000		−12,000	
1995	1997	......	2001	2004

FIGURE 2.2

The resulting balance is

$$X = 8000(1.05)^9 + 6000(1.05)^7 - 12,000(1.05)^3 = 6961.73. \qquad \square$$

Example 2.4

John borrows 3000 from The Friendly Finance Company. Two years later he borrows another 4000. Two years after that he borrows an additional 5000. At what point in time would a single loan of 12,000 be equivalent if $i = .18$?

Solution

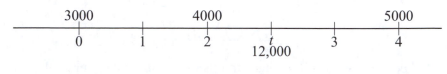

FIGURE 2.3

We let t be the number of years after the 3000 loan at which a single loan of 12,000 would be equivalent, and form the equation of value at time 0 as $12,000v^t = 3000 + 4000v^2 + 5000v^4$, where $v = \frac{1}{1.18}$. Then $v^t = \frac{3 + 4v^2 + 5v^4}{12}$. Taking logs of both sides of this equation we find $t = \frac{ln(3+4v^2+5v^4) - ln\,12}{ln\,v} = 2.11789$. $\qquad \square$

   We remark that there is an approximate method of solving problems like Example 2.4, called the *method of equated time*, but we will not need to examine it here since there are no difficulties in obtaining an exact solution.

   To conclude this section, we give a very simple example where the rate of interest is the unknown.

Example 2.5

Find the rate of interest such that an amount of money will triple itself over 15 years.

Solution

Let i be the required effective rate of interest. We have $(1 + i)^{15} = 3$, so that $i = 3^{1/15} - 1 = .07599$. $\qquad \square$

2.2 UNKNOWN RATE OF INTEREST

When the rate of interest is the unknown in an equation of value, complications often arise. To illustrate this, consider the following example.

Example 2.6

Joan deposits 2000 in her bank account on January 1, 1995, and then deposits 3000 on January 1, 1998. If there are no other deposits or withdrawals and the amount of money in the account on January 1, 2000 is 7100, find the effective rate of interest she earns.

Solution

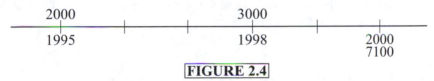

FIGURE 2.4

$2000(1+i)^5 + 3000(1+i)^2 = 7100$ is the equation of value on January 1, 2000. Now we have a problem. This equation is a fifth degree polynomial in i, and there is no exact formula for finding its solution. Most students will have a subroutine available on their calculators which will enable them to approximate the answer with a high degree of accuracy, and we encourage this approach. To show how these approximations are actually obtained, we will work out this example numerically.

Let $f(i) = 2000(1+i)^5 + 3000(1+i)^2 - 7100$. We wish to find two values for i, i_1 and i_2, such that $f(i_1) < 0$ and $f(i_2) > 0$, where i_1 and i_2 are close together. Then linear interpolation will be used to approximate a value i_0 such that $f(i_0) = 0$. To find i_1 and i_2, we use trial and error, aided by the fact that $f(i)$ is an increasing function. We eventually obtain $f(.11) = -33.58$ and $f(.12) = 187.88$.

Linear interpolation assumes that the function is a straight line between .11 and .12. The total change in the value of the function between $i = .11$ and $i = .12$ is $187.88 - (-33.58) = 221.46$. The amount of this change that occurs between .11 and a value i_0 such that $f(i_0) = 0$ is $0 - (-33.58) = 33.58$. Hence the fraction of the change occurring between .11 and i_0 is $\frac{33.58}{221.46} = .15163$, and i_0 must be that fraction of the distance between .11 and .12. This reasoning leads us to the conclusion that $i_0 = .11 + (.15163)(.01) = .1115163$, or $i_0 = .11152$ to five decimal places.   □

Example 2.7

Obtain a more exact answer to Example 2.6.

Solution

To improve on the answer, we will start with values i_1 and i_2 such that $f(i_1) < 0$ and $f(i_2) > 0$, where i_1 and i_2 are closer together than they were in the solution to Example 2.6. For instance, using $i_1 = .111$ and $i_2 = .112$, we find $f(.111) = -11.71$ and $f(.112) = 10.22$. Using these values, we obtain

$$i_0 = .111 + \left[\frac{11.71}{10.22 - (-11.71)} \right] (.001) = .11153. \qquad \square$$

We remark that standard calculator techniques give $i_0 = .11153$ as the correct answer (to five decimal places).

2.3   TIME-WEIGHTED RATE OF RETURN

The rate of interest calculated in Section 2.2 is often called the *dollar-weighted* rate of investment return. A very different procedure is used to calculate the *time-weighted* rate of investment return, and that is what we will consider here. We remark before starting that in this section the compound interest assumption is no longer being made.

To calculate the time-weighted rate of return, it is necessary to know the accumulated value of an investment fund just before each deposit or withdrawal occurs. Let B_0 be the initial balance in a fund, B_n the final balance, $B_1, \ldots, B_{n-1}$ the intermediate values just preceding deposits or withdrawals, and $W_1, \ldots, W_{n-1}$ the amount of each deposit or withdrawal, where $W_i > 0$ for deposits and $W_i < 0$ for withdrawals. Let $W_0 = 0$. Then

$$i_t = \frac{B_t}{B_{t-1} + W_{t-1}} - 1 \qquad (2.1)$$

represents the rate of interest earned in the time period between balances B_{t-1} and B_t. The time-weighted rate of return is then defined by

$$i = (1 + i_1)(1 + i_2) \cdots (1 + i_n) - 1. \qquad (2.2)$$

Example 2.8

On January 1, 1999, Graham's stock portfolio is worth 500,000. On April 30, 1999, the value has increased to 525,000. At that point, Graham adds 50,000 worth of stock to his portfolio. Six months later, the value has dropped to 560,000, and Graham sells 100,000 worth of stock. On December 31, 1999, the portfolio is again worth 500,000. Find the time-weighted rate of return for Graham's portfolio during 1999.

Solution

The accumulation rate from January 1 to April 30 is given by the factor $1 + i_1 = \frac{525,000}{500,000} = 1.05.$ Immediately after the April 30 stock purchase, the portfolio is worth 575,000. Hence the accumulation rate from May 1 to October 31 is $\frac{560,000}{575,000} = .97391.$ Finally, the accumulation rate in the last two months of the year is $\frac{500,000}{460,000} = 1.08696.$ The time-weighted rate of return for the year is found from the interval accumulation factors as $(1.05)(.97391)(1.08696) - 1 = .11153.$ □

Note in Example 2.8 that the value of the portfolio decreased during the period from May 1 to October 31, so we see that compound interest is clearly not operating here. Nevertheless, it is still possible to calculate a dollar-weighted rate of return by considering only deposits and withdrawals, and ignoring intermediate balances. Setting up the equation of value by accumulating all quantities to December 31, 1999, we obtain

$$500,000(1+i) + 50,000(1+i)^{2/3} - 100,000(1+i)^{1/6} = 500,000.$$

This could be solved by linear interpolation, as in Section 2.2, but an alternative approach to this type of problem is to assume simple interest for periods less than a year. We would then obtain

$$500,000(1+i) + 50,000(1+\tfrac{2}{3}i) - 100,000(1+\tfrac{1}{6}i) = 500,000.$$

Since this equation is linear in i, the result $i = \frac{300,000}{3,100,000} = .09677$ is easily obtained.

In Chapter 12 we will see how the theories of dollar-weighted and time-weighted rates of investment return are applied to pension funds.

EXERCISES

2.1   Equation of Value

2-1.   Brenda deposits 7000 in a bank account. Three years later, she withdraws 5000. Two years after that, she withdraws an additional 3000.   One year after that, she deposits an additional 4000. Assuming $i = .06$, and that no other deposits or withdrawals are made, how much is in Brenda's account ten years after the initial deposit is made?

2-2.   Eileen borrows 2000 on January 1, 1997. On January 1, 1998, she borrows an additional 3000. On January 1, 2001, she repays 4000. Assuming $i = .13$, how much does she owe on January 1, 2005?

2-3.   Boswell wishes to borrow a sum of money. In return, he is prepared to pay as follows: 200 after 1 year, 500 after 2 years, 500 after 3 years and 700 after 4 years. If $i = .12$, how much can he borrow?

2-4.   Payments of 800, 500 and 700 are made at the ends of years 2, 3 and 6 respectively. Assuming $i = .13$, find the point at which a single payment of 2100 would be equivalent.

2-5.   A vendor has two offers for a house: (i) 40,000 now and 40,000 two years hence, or (ii)   28,750 now, 23,750 in one year, and 27,500 two years hence. He makes the remark that one offer is "just as good" as the other. Find the two possible rates of interest which would make his remark correct.

2-6.   (a)   The present value of 2 payments of 1000 each, to be made at the end of n years and $n + 4$ years, is 1250. If $i = .08$, find n.
        (b)   Repeat part (a) if the payments are made at the end of n years and $4n$ years.

2-7.   In return for payments of 400 at the end of 3 years and 700 at the end of 8 years, a woman agrees to pay X at the end of 4 years and $2X$ at the end of 6 years. Find X if $i = .14$.

2-8. How long should 1000 be left to accumulate at $i = .12$ in order that it may amount to twice the accumulated value of another 1000 deposited at the same time at 8% effective?

2-9. Fund A accumulates at 9% effective and Fund B at 8% effective. At the end of 10 years, the total of the two funds is 52,000. At the end of 8 years, the amount in Fund B is three times that in Fund A. How much is in Fund A after 15 years?

2-10. John pays Henry 500 every March 15 from 1996 to 2000 inclusive. He also pays Henry 300 every June 15 from 1998 to 2001 inclusive. Assuming $i^{(4)} = .17$, find the value of these payments on (a) March 15, 2005; (b) March 15, 1999; (c) March 15, 1995.

2.2 Unknown Rate of Interest

2-11. A consumer purchasing a refrigerator is offered two payment plans:
Plan A: 150 down, 200 after 1 year, 250 after 2 years
Plan B: 87 down, 425 after 1 year, 50 after 2 years
Determine the range of interest rates for which Plan A is better for the consumer.

2-12. Find the effective rate of interest if payments of 300 at the present, 200 at the end of one year, and 100 at the end of two years accumulate to 800 at the end of three years.

2-13. Bernie borrows 5000 on January 1, 1995, and another 5000 on January 1, 1998. He repays 3000 on January 1, 1997, and then finishes repaying his loans by paying 10,000 on January 1, 2000. What effective annual rate of interest is Bernie being charged?

2-14. John buys a TV for 600 from Jean. John agrees to pay for the TV by making a cash down payment of 50, then paying 100 every four months for one year (i.e. three payments of 100), and finally making a single payment 16 months after the purchase (i.e. four months after the last payment of 100).
(a) Find the amount of the final payment if John is charged interest at an effective rate of 12% per year.
(b) Find the effective annual interest rate if John's final payment is 350.

2-15. A trust company pays 7% effective on deposits at the end of each year. At the end of every four years, a 5% bonus is paid on the balance at that time. Find the effective rate of interest earned by an investor if he leaves his money on deposit for (a) 3 years; (b) 4 years; (c) 5 years.

2-16. The present value of a series of payments of 1 at the end of every 3 years forever is equal to $\frac{125}{91}$. Find the effective rate of interest per year.

2.3 Time-Weighted Rate of Return

2-17. Emily's trust fund has a value of 100,000 on January 1, 1997. On April 1, 1997, 10,000 is withdrawn from the fund, and immediately after this withdrawal the fund has a value of 95,000. On January 1, 1998, the fund's value is 115,000.
   (a)   Find the time-weighted rate of investment return for this fund during 1997.
   (b)   Find the dollar-weighted annual rate of investment return for Emily's fund, assuming simple interest.
   (c)   Find the rate of return for Emily's fund using simple interest, and assuming a uniform distribution throughout the year of all deposits and withdrawals.

2-18. Assume in Question 17 that, in addition to the information given, there is also a 5000 deposit to the fund on July 1, 1997.
   (a)   Find the dollar-weighted annual rate of investment return for the fund, assuming simple interest.
   (b)   Find the rate of return for Emily's fund using simple interest and assuming a uniform distribution throughout the year of all deposits and withdrawals.
   (c)   Is it possible to calculate the time-weighted rate of return? If not, why not?

2-19. Let A be the balance in a fund on January 1, 1999, B the balance on June 30, 1999, and C the balance on December 31, 1999.

    (a)   If there are no deposits or withdrawals, show that the dollar-weighted and time-weighted rates of return for 1999 are both equal to $\dfrac{C-A}{A}$.

    (b)   If there was a single deposit of W immediately *after* the June 30 balance was calculated, find expressions for the dollar-weighted and time-weighted rates of return for 1999. (Assume simple interest for periods of less than a year.)

    (c)   If there was a single deposit of W immediately *before* the June 30 balance was calculated, find expressions for the dollar-weighted and time-weighted rates of return for 1999. (Assume simple interest for periods of less than a year.)

    (d)   Give a verbal explanation for the fact that the dollar-weighted rates of return in parts (b) and (c) are equal.

    (e)   Show that the time-weighted rate of return in part (b) is larger than the time-weighted rate of return in part (c).

CHAPTER THREE

ANNUITIES

3.1 ARITHMETIC AND GEOMETRIC SEQUENCES

Before beginning the study of annuities, we will briefly review some basic facts about arithmetic and geometric sequences. The formulae we develop for geometric sequences will be used a number of times later in the chapter.

Recall that an arithmetic sequence is a sequence of numbers $X_1, X_2, \ldots$ where the difference between consecutive terms is constant. For example, the sequence 4, 7, 10, 13, ... is an arithmetic sequence with constant difference 3 (assuming the apparent pattern continues). The sequence 5, 1, -3, -7, ... is also arithmetic, having common difference -4.

Any arithmetic sequence is determined by its first term and its common difference; if the first term is a and the common difference d, the sequence is

$$a, \ a+d, \ a+2d, \ a+3d, \ \cdots. \tag{3.1}$$

There are two important formulae about arithmetic sequences which we would like to develop.

$\boxed{\text{Theorem 3.1}}$

Consider an arithmetic sequence with first term a and common difference d.

(a)   The nth term of this sequence is

$$a + (n-1)d.$$

(b)   The sum of the first n terms of this sequence is given by the formula

$$\tfrac{n}{2}[2a + (n-1)d].$$

Proof

(a)   Informally, we see from the pattern $a, a + d, a + 2d, a + 3d, \cdots$ that the nth term will be $a + (n-1)d$. A formal proof can be given using mathematical induction. We will leave this as an exercise for the reader.

(b)   Let S_n denote the sum of the first n terms. Using the result of part (a), we have

$$S_n = a + (a + d) + (a + 2d) + \cdots + [a + (n-1)d]. \qquad (3.2a)$$

Writing the terms on the right hand side of (3.2a) in the reverse order, we have

$$S_n = [a + (n-1)d] + [a + (n-2)d] + \cdots + (a+d) + a. \quad (3.2b)$$

Adding together (3.2a) and (3.2b) by combining first terms together, then second terms together, and so on, we obtain

$$2S_n = [a + a + (n-1)d] + [(a+d) + a + (n-2)d]$$
$$+ \cdots + [a + (n-1)d + a]. \quad (3.2c)$$

There are n equal terms on the right side of (3.2c), so we have $2S_n = n[2a + (n-1)d]$, or

$$S_n = \tfrac{n}{2}[2a + (n-1)d], \qquad (3.2d)$$

as required. As an exercise, the reader should give an alternate derivation of (3.2d) using mathematical induction. ∇

Example 3.1

Find the 32nd term and the sum of the first 18 terms of the arithmetic sequence $5, 9, 13, 17, \ldots$.

Solution

We have $a = 5$ and $d = 4$. Hence, the 32nd term is $5 + (31)(4) = 129$. Using (3.2d) the sum of 18 terms is $\tfrac{18}{2}[10 + (17)4] = 702$. $\square$

Now we will consider geometric sequences. Recall that a geometric sequence is a sequence of numbers $X_1, X_2, \ldots$ where each consecutive term is obtained from the previous term by multiplying by a fixed number. For example, the sequence 2, 6, 18, 54, ... is geometric with common ratio 3, and the sequence $5, -\frac{5}{2}, \frac{5}{4}, -\frac{5}{8}, \ldots$ is geometric with common ratio $-\frac{1}{2}$. The general geometric sequence with first term a and common ratio r will be

$$a, \ ar, \ ar^2, \ ar^3, \ldots . \tag{3.3}$$

Theorem 3.2

Consider a geometric sequence with first term a and common ratio r.

(a) The nth term of the sequence is ar^{n-1}

(b) The sum of the first n terms of the sequence is $\frac{a(1 - r^n)}{1 - r}$.

Proof

(a) As before, the pattern $a, ar, ar^2, \ldots$ leads us to believe that ar^{n-1} is the correct term, but a formal proof requires mathematical induction. We will leave this proof as an exercise for the reader.

(b) Let S_n be the sum of the first n terms. Using the result of part (a), we have

$$S_n = a + ar + \cdots + ar^{n-1}. \tag{3.4a}$$

Multiplying both sides by r, we obtain

$$rS_n = ar + ar^2 + \cdots + ar^n. \tag{3.4b}$$

Subtracting the second line from the first, we observe that many terms cancel, and we obtain

$$S_n - rS_n = a + ar - ar + ar^2 - ar^2 + \cdots$$
$$+ ar^{n-1} - ar^{n-1} - ar^n = a - ar^n. \tag{3.4c}$$

Thus we have $S_n(1 - r) = a(1 - r^n)$, or

$$S_n = \frac{a(1 - r^n)}{1 - r}, \tag{3.4d}$$

as required. ∇

Example 3.2

Find the 13th term and the sum of the first 9 terms of the geometric sequence $48, -24, 12, -6, 3, -\frac{3}{2}, \ldots$.

Solution

We have $a = 48$ and $r = -\frac{1}{2}$. Using part (a) of Theorem 3.2, we find that the 13th term is $48(-\frac{1}{2})^{12} = \frac{3}{256}$. Using (3.4d), the sum of the first 9 terms is $48 \left[\dfrac{1 - (-\frac{1}{2})^9}{1 - (-\frac{1}{2})} \right] = 48 \left[\dfrac{1 + \frac{1}{512}}{\frac{3}{2}} \right] = \frac{513}{16}.$ $\square$

3.2 BASIC RESULTS

John borrows 1500 from a finance company and wishes to pay it back with equal annual payments at the end of each of the next ten years. If $i = .17$, what should his annual payment be?

Jacinta buys a house and takes out a 50,000 mortgage. If the mortgage rate is 13% convertible semiannually, what should her monthly payment be to pay off the mortgage in 20 years?

Eileen deposits 2000 in a bank account every year for 11 years. If $i = .06$, how much has she accumulated at the time of the last deposit?

All of these questions have one thing in common: they involve a series of payments made at regular intervals. Such a series of payments is called an *annuity*. In the three cases above, the payments are of equal amount, and that will be the case with all annuities studied in this section. Later, however, we will study more general annuities.

Annuities turn up in many different types of financial transactions. From the point of view of practical applications, a complete understanding of annuities is an absolute must!

We shall start by considering an annuity under which payments of 1 are made at the end of each period for n periods. Sometimes a period will be one year, as with John's loan above, but other periods are certainly possible. It will be assumed throughout that, as with John's loan, the interest period and the payment period are equal. When this is not the case, as with Jacinta's mortgage, for example, we will first find the equivalent rate of interest per payment period and then proceed with our solution.

Level payments of an amount other than 1 can be handled by multiplying by the amount of the payment, as we shall see in the examples.

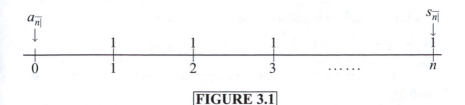

FIGURE 3.1

A time diagram showing n payments of 1 is given in Figure 3.1. The present value of this annuity at time 0 is denoted by $a_{\overline{n}|}$. The accumulated value of this annuity at time n is denoted by $s_{\overline{n}|}$.

We shall now derive a formula for $a_{\overline{n}|}$. Taking the value at time 0 of each of the payments in turn, we obtain

$$a_{\overline{n}|} = v + v^2 + v^3 + \cdots + v^n. \qquad (3.5)$$

This is the sum of n terms of a geometric sequence with $a = v$ and $r = v$. Using Formula (3.4d) developed in Section 3.1, we obtain

$$
\begin{aligned}
a_{\overline{n}|} &= \frac{v(1 - v^n)}{1 - v} \\
&= \frac{1 - v^n}{\frac{1}{v} - 1} \\
&= \frac{1 - v^n}{1 + i - 1} \\
&= \frac{1 - v^n}{i}. \qquad (3.6)
\end{aligned}
$$

Formula (3.6) is crucial, and will be used frequently throughout the rest of the text.

It is easy now to get a formula for $s_{\overline{n}|}$. Since $s_{\overline{n}|}$ is the value of the same annuity n years after $a_{\overline{n}|}$ has been calculated, it follows that

$$
\begin{aligned}
s_{\overline{n}|} &= a_{\overline{n}|}(1 + i)^n \\
&= \left[\frac{1 - v^n}{i}\right](1 + i)^n \\
&= \frac{(1 + i)^n - v^n(1 + i)^n}{i} \\
&= \frac{(1 + i)^n - 1}{i}. \qquad (3.7)
\end{aligned}
$$

Let us immediately proceed to some practical examples.

| Example 3.3 |

Find John's payment in the problem stated in the first paragraph of this section.

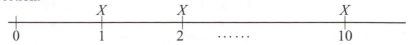

FIGURE 3.2

| Solution |

Let the payment be X. Since the present value of 10 payments of 1 is $a_{\overline{10}|}$, the present value of 10 payments of X will be $X \cdot a_{\overline{10}|}$. Thus we have

$$1500 = X \cdot a_{\overline{10}|}. \text{ Then } X = \frac{1500}{a_{\overline{10}|}} = \frac{1500}{\frac{1 - v^{10}}{i}} = \frac{1500(.17)}{1 - (\frac{1}{1.17})^{10}} = 321.98.$$

$\square$

| Example 3.4 |

Find the accumulated value in Eileen's bank account in the problem stated in the third paragraph of this section.

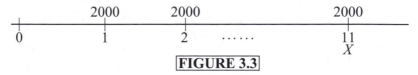

FIGURE 3.3

| Solution |

Since each deposit is 2000, the accumulated value will be given directly by $X = 2000 s_{\overline{11}|} = 2000\left[\frac{(1.06)^{11} - 1}{.06}\right] = 29{,}943.29.$ $\square$

| Example 3.5 |

Find Jacinta's mortgage payment in the problem stated in the second paragraph of this section.

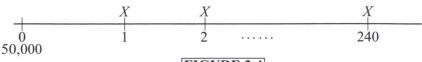

FIGURE 3.4

Solution
As mentioned earlier, we first have to find the effective monthly rate of interest equivalent to 13% convertible semiannually. This is because our formulae for $a_{\overline{n}|}$ and $s_{\overline{n}|}$ are based on the assumption that the interest period and payment period are the same. Letting this monthly rate be j, we have $1 + j = \left[1 + \frac{.13}{2}\right]^{1/6}$. Now we let the mortgage payment be X. Note that there are 240 monthly payments in the 20-year term of the mortgage, so we have $X \cdot a_{\overline{240}|} = 50{,}000$ and $X = \dfrac{50{,}000j}{1 - v^{240}} = 573.77$. $\square$

Example 3.6
Elroy takes out a loan of $5000 to buy a car. No payments are due for the first 8 months, but beginning with the end of the 9th month, he must make 60 equal monthly payments. If $i = .18$, find (a) the amount of each payment; (b) the amount of each payment if there is no payment-free period, (i.e., if the first payment is due in one month and the remaining 59 are made on a monthly basis thereafter).
Solution
(a) We first note that a monthly rate of interest j is required. Since $(1 + j)^{12} = 1.18$, we obtain $j = (1.18)^{1/12} - 1$. Let the amount of each payment be X.

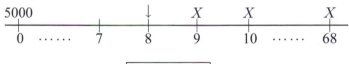

FIGURE 3.5

We now observe that this does not fit into the standard annuity pattern, since $X \cdot a_{\overline{60}|}$ will give us the value of the payments at month 8, one month before the first payment. The value of the loan at time 8 is $5{,}000(1+j)^8$, since it will accrue interest for eight months, even though no payments are required. Thus we have the equation of value $X \cdot a_{\overline{60}|} = 5000(1+j)^8$, so that $X = \dfrac{5000(1+j)^8}{a_{\overline{60}|}}$.

Evaluating $a_{\overline{60}|}$, $X = \dfrac{5000(1+j)^8 \cdot j}{1 - v^{60}} = 137.76$.

(b)   In this case, we just have $X \cdot a_{\overline{60}|} = 5000$, which we solve for
      $$X = \frac{5000j}{1 - (1+j)^{-60}} = 123.37.$$ This shows that, over the next 5
      years, the total amount of extra money paid for postponing the first
      payment for 8 months will be 863.40!   □

      The previous example beautifully demonstrates the power of our
calculators.   In pre-calculator days the evaluation of   the term
$a_{\overline{60}|} = \dfrac{1 - (1+j)^{-60}}{j}$ would have caused serious difficulties.   Even
interest tables would not have helped, because the interest rate j is not
one for which tables were constructed. All we do now, however, is press
a few buttons (in the right order) and the answer appears!

| Example 3.7 |

(a)   Prove the identity $1 = ia_{\overline{n}|} + v^n$.
(b)   Give a verbal interpretation of this identity.

| Solution |

(a) $a_{\overline{n}|} = \dfrac{1 - v^n}{i}$, so $ia_{\overline{n}|} = 1 - v^n$, and $1 = ia_{\overline{n}|} + v^n$, as required.
(b)   The term $ia_{\overline{n}|}$ can be thought of as the present value of an annuity
      with level payment i at the end of each year for n years (see Figure
      3.6). The term v^n is the present value of 1 at year n.

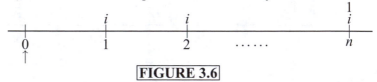

| FIGURE 3.6 |

      Imagine investing 1 at time 0. At the end of the first year, the
      interest is separated off from the original investment, and the
      amount of the investment is back to 1. This procedure continues
      for n years, leaving 1 at the end of n years and the annuity of i
      which was removed each year. The present value of these terms is
      v^n and $ia_{\overline{n}|}$, respectively.   □

      There are two other symbols in common usage with annuities,
namely $\ddot{a}_{\overline{n}|}$ and $\ddot{s}_{\overline{n}|}$.

$\ddot{a}_{\overline{n}|}$ is the present value of the annuity described earlier at the time of the first payment, and $\ddot{s}_{\overline{n}|}$ is the accumulated value one year after the last payment has been made. Our four functions, $a_{\overline{n}|}$, $\ddot{a}_{\overline{n}|}$, $s_{\overline{n}|}$ and $\ddot{s}_{\overline{n}|}$ are illustrated in Figure 3.7.

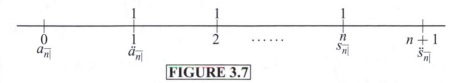

FIGURE 3.7

Mathematically, there is nothing very exciting going on here. We can see immediately from Figure 3.7 that $\ddot{a}_{\overline{n}|} = a_{\overline{n}|}(1 + i)$, and that $\ddot{s}_{\overline{n}|} = s_{\overline{n}|}(1 + i)$. These relationships lead to formulae for $\ddot{a}_{\overline{n}|}$ and $\ddot{s}_{\overline{n}|}$ that are analogous to Formulae (3.6) and (3.7) for $a_{\overline{n}|}$ and $s_{\overline{n}|}$, respectively. We have

$$
\begin{aligned}
\ddot{a}_{\overline{n}|} &= a_{\overline{n}|}(1 + i) \\[2mm]
&= \frac{1 - v^n}{i}(1 + i) \\[2mm]
&= \frac{1 - v^n}{\frac{i}{1+i}} \\[2mm]
&= \frac{1 - v^n}{d}, \tag{3.8}
\end{aligned}
$$

where d is the effective rate of discount defined in Chapter 1. Similarly, the reader should show that

$$
\ddot{s}_{\overline{n}|} = \frac{(1 + i)^n - 1}{d}. \tag{3.9}
$$

Observe that $\ddot{a}_{\overline{n}|}$ can also be described as the present value of payments of 1 made at the beginning of each period for n periods, and $\ddot{s}_{\overline{n}|}$ can be described as the accumulated value of the same payments at the end of the last period. Since the payments are at the beginnings of the periods, it follows that $\ddot{s}_{\overline{n}|}$ is their accumulated value a full period after the last payment.

There are many identities relating the four quantities we have introduced. In addition to the ones mentioned earlier, we note that

$$\ddot{s}_{\overline{n|}} = \ddot{a}_{\overline{n|}}(1+i)^n \qquad\qquad (3.10)$$

and

$$1 = d\ddot{a}_{\overline{n|}} + v^n, \qquad\qquad (3.11)$$

both of which have nice verbal interpretations. Other relationships will be presented as exercises.

Let us do an example. Imagine that Henry takes out a loan of 1000 and repays it with 10 equal yearly payments, the first one due at the time of the loan. In this case, if X is the amount of each payment, an appropriate equation of value would be

$$X \cdot \ddot{a}_{\overline{10|}} = 1000. \qquad\qquad (3.12a)$$

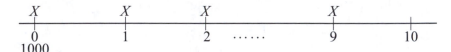

FIGURE 3.8

We use $\ddot{a}_{\overline{10|}}$ here because the annuity symbol $a_{\overline{10|}}$ assumes we are taking the present value *one year before* the first payment, and that is not the case with Henry's loan. An equally good equation of value would be

$$X \cdot a_{\overline{10|}} = 1000v, \qquad\qquad (3.12b)$$

because $1000v$ would be the value of the loan one year earlier, which allows us to use our first annuity symbol. Once the rate of interest i is known, we can find the amount of Henry's loan payment.

Let us observe as well that a third acceptable equation of value for Henry's problem would be

$$X(1 + a_{\overline{9|}}) = 1000. \qquad\qquad (3.12c)$$

> **Example 3.8**

Using all three equations of value, find Henry's loan payment if $i = .16$.

> **Solution**

(a)   First we consider Equation (3.12a), which is $X \cdot \ddot{a}_{\overline{10|}} = 1000$. Then $X = \dfrac{1000}{\ddot{a}_{\overline{10|}}} = \dfrac{1000d}{1 - v^{10}}$. To use this approach we need to find $d = \dfrac{i}{1+i} = \dfrac{.16}{1.16}$. This leads to the answer $X = 178.36$.

(b)   Equation (3.12b) states that $X \cdot a_{\overline{10|}} = 1000v$. Then we have

$$X = \frac{1000\left(\frac{1}{1.16}\right)(.16)}{1 - \left(\frac{1}{1.16}\right)^{10}} = 178.36.$$

(c)   Finally, consider Equation (3.12c), which gives us the equation

$$X = \frac{1000}{1 + a_{\overline{9|}}} = \frac{1000}{1 + \frac{1 - v^9}{i}} = 178.36. \qquad \square$$

The moral of Example 3.8 is that there is more than one way to work out this kind of problem. However, we reiterate the importance of keeping as many decimal places as possible during your calculations.

In many textbooks, the term *annuity-immediate* is used for the case where payments are made at the end of the period, and *annuity-due* is used when payments are made at the beginning of the period. As we have just illustrated, however, the same techniques can be used in both cases.

The following example illustrates that there are many possible ways of analyzing annuities.

> **Example 3.9**

Consider an annuity which pays 1 at the beginning of each year for $m + n$ years. Explain verbally why each of the following expressions gives the *current value* of this annuity at the end of year m. (See Figure 3.9 on the following page.)

(a) $a_{\overline{m+n|}}(1 + i)^{m+1}$

(b) $\ddot{a}_{\overline{m+n|}}(1 + i)^m$

(c) $s_{\overline{m+n|}} v^{n-1}$

(d) $\ddot{s}_{\overline{m+n|}} v^n$

(e) $s_{\overline{m+1|}} + a_{\overline{n-1|}}$

(f) $\ddot{s}_{\overline{m|}} + \ddot{a}_{\overline{n|}}$

(g) $1 + \ddot{s}_{\overline{m|}} + a_{\overline{n-1|}}$

FIGURE 3.9

Solution

In the time diagram for this annuity in Figure 3.9, we have denoted by ↑ the point at which we want the value of the annuity.

(a) $a_{\overline{m+n}|}$ is the value at year -1. To get to ↑, we must move $m + 1$ years into the future, so we have $a_{\overline{m+n}|}(1 + i)^{m+1}$.

(b) $\ddot{a}_{\overline{m+n}|}$ is the value at year 0. So $\ddot{a}_{\overline{m+n}|}(1 + i)^m$ moves us m years into the future.

(c) $s_{\overline{m+n}|}$ is the value at year $m + n - 1$. Hence we move back $n - 1$ years.

(d) $\ddot{s}_{\overline{m+n}|}$ is the value at year $m + n$, so we move back n years.

(e) $s_{\overline{m+1}|}$ is the value of the first $m + 1$ payments at time m, and $a_{\overline{n-1}|}$ is the value of the last $n - 1$ payments at time m.

(f) $\ddot{s}_{\overline{m}|}$ is the value of the first m payments at time m, and $\ddot{a}_{\overline{n}|}$ is the value of the last n payments at the same time.

(g) Here the single payment of 1 at time m is separated off from the $\ddot{a}_{\overline{n}|}$ in part (f), leaving $a_{\overline{n-1}|}$.   ☐

The above example should illustrate how careful we must be when working with these functions, but also that we have considerable flexibility in using them to express an annuity value at some point of time.

3.3 PERPETUITIES

A *perpetuity* is an annuity whose payments continue forever.   The time diagram is shown in Figure 3.10 below.

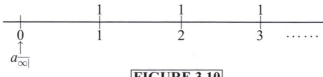

FIGURE 3.10

The value of this annuity one year before the first payment is $a_{\overline{\infty}|}$. We have

$$a_{\overline{\infty}|} = \lim_{n\to\infty} a_{\overline{n}|}$$

$$= \lim_{n\to\infty} \frac{1-v^n}{i}$$

$$= \frac{1}{i}, \tag{3.13}$$

since $\lim_{n\to\infty} v^n = 0$, as long as $i > 0$.

We can see verbally why Formula (3.13) should be true: if a principal of $\frac{1}{i}$ is invested at rate i, then the interest $\left(\frac{1}{i}\right) i = 1$ can be removed at the end of each year, leaving the original principal intact forever.

As in Section 3.2, the symbol $\ddot{a}_{\overline{\infty}|}$ represents the value of a perpetuity at the time of the first payment. The following identities are left as exercises for the reader:

$$\ddot{a}_{\overline{\infty}|} = a_{\overline{\infty}|}(1 + i), \tag{3.14}$$

$$\ddot{a}_{\overline{\infty}|} = 1 + a_{\overline{\infty}|}, \tag{3.15}$$

and

$$\ddot{a}_{\overline{\infty}|} = \frac{1}{d}. \tag{3.16}$$

3.4 UNKNOWN TIME AND UNKNOWN RATE OF INTEREST

We will consider here several examples involving annuities where the length of time or the rate of interest involved is the unknown.

| Example 3.10 |

A fund of 5000 is used to award scholarships of amount 500, one per year, at the end of each year for as long as possible. If $i = .09$, find the number of scholarships which can be awarded, and the amount left in the fund one year after the last scholarship has been awarded.

Solution

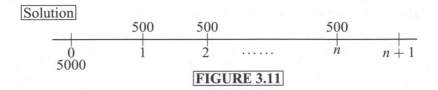

FIGURE 3.11

If n is the number of scholarships, then $500 \cdot a_{\overline{n}|} \leq 5000 < 500 \cdot a_{\overline{n+1}|}$, so that $a_{\overline{n}|} \leq 10 < a_{\overline{n+1}|}$. Putting $a_{\overline{n}|} = 10$, we obtain $\dfrac{1 - v^n}{i} = 10$. This reduces to $v^n = 1 - 10i$, so $n = \dfrac{\log(1 - 10i)}{\log v} = 26.7$. Hence, we conclude that 26 scholarships can be awarded. The amount in the fund one year after the last scholarship has been awarded will be $5000(1.09)^{27} - 500\ddot{s}_{\overline{26}|} = 363.84$.   □

Example 3.11

A trust fund is to be built by means of deposits of amount 5000 at the end of each year, with a terminal deposit, as small as possible, at the end of the final year. The purpose of this fund is to establish monthly payments of amount 300 into perpetuity, the first payment coming one month after the final deposit. If the rate of interest is 12% per year convertible quarterly, find the number of deposits required and the size of the final deposit.

Solution

We require effective yearly and monthly rates equivalent to $i^{(4)} = .12$. The yearly rate is $i = (1.03)^4 - 1$, whereas the monthly rate is $j = (1.03)^{1/3} - 1$. The value of the perpetuity one month before the first payment is $\dfrac{300}{j} = \dfrac{300}{(1.03)^{1/3} - 1} = 30{,}298.03$. We start with the inequality $5000\ddot{s}_{\overline{n}|} \leq 30{,}298.03 < 5000\ddot{s}_{\overline{n+1}|}$, so that $\ddot{s}_{\overline{n}|} \leq 6.06 < \ddot{s}_{\overline{n+1}|}$. Solving $\ddot{s}_{\overline{n}|} = 6.06$, we obtain $(1 + i)^n = 1.6758$, so $n = 4.4$. Hence four deposits of 5000 each are required.

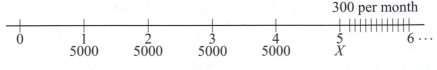

FIGURE 3.12

The size of the final deposit is given by X, and it is found from the equation $X = \frac{300}{j} - 5000\left[\frac{(1+i)^4 - 1}{i}\right](1+i) = 3184.30.$ □

Example 3.12

At what effective yearly rate of interest is the present value of 300 paid at the end of every month, for the next 5 years, equal to 15,000?

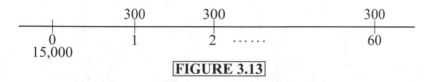

$$\begin{array}{ccccc} & 300 & 300 & & 300 \\ \hline \overset{\displaystyle 0}{15,000} & 1 & 2 & \cdots\cdots & 60 \end{array}$$

FIGURE 3.13

Let i be the monthly rate of interest; then we have $300 \cdot a_{\overline{60}|} = 15,000$ at rate i. Hence $a_{\overline{60}|} = 50$ and we must now solve for i. As in Chapter 2, we would expect students to solve this equation using standard calculator subroutines, since the equation $50 - a_{\overline{60}|} = 0$ is equivalent to $50i(1+i)^{60} - (1+i)^{60} + 1 = 0.$ However, we will also briefly outline two numerical methods for obtaining approximate solutions, partly for historical reasons and partly to show how the calculator subroutines actually work.

Solution One

Define $f(i) = 50 - a_{\overline{60}|}$. We will use linear interpolation to estimate the value of i for which $f(i) = 0$. Observe that $f(.006) = -.26213$, and $f(.007) = 1.14413$. Using linear interpolation between these values we obtain $i = .006 + \left[\frac{.26213}{1.40626}\right](.001) = .00619.$ The effective yearly rate is therefore $(1.00619)^{12} - 1 = .077.$

Solution Two

As an alternative to linear interpolation, we could use an interesting method called *successive approximation*. As before, we have $a_{\overline{60}|} = 50$, so $\frac{1 - v^{60}}{i} = 50$, or $i = \frac{1 - v^{60}}{50}$. The idea now is to substitute some trial value of i in the right hand side of the above equation. The value obtained is then used as the next trial value, and is substituted back into the right hand side. This procedure is continued until the required degree of accuracy is obtained.

For example, let us try $i_0 = .007$ as an initial estimate. We obtain
$i_1 = \dfrac{1 - v^{60}}{50} = \dfrac{1 - (1.007)^{-60}}{50} = .00684.$ Next   we   substitute
$i_1 = .00684$ in the right hand side, yielding $i_2 = \dfrac{1 - v^{60}}{50} = .00671.$
Continuing this procedure, we obtain the following values:

i_3	=	.00661	i_4 = .00653
i_5	=	.00647	i_6 = .00642
i_7	=	.00638	i_8 = .00634
i_9	=	.00631	i_{10} = .00629
i_{11}	=	.00627	i_{12} = .00625
i_{13}	=	.00624	i_{14} = .00623
i_{15}	=	.00622	i_{16} = .00621
i_{17}	=	.006205	i_{18} = .006201
i_{19}	=	.006198	i_{20} = .006195
i_{21}	=	.006193	i_{22} = .006191
i_{23}	=	.0061898	i_{24} = .0061887
i_{25}	=	.0061878	i_{26} = .0061870
i_{27}	=	.0061860	i_{28} = .0061858
i_{29}	=	.0061854	i_{30} = .0061850
i_{31}	=	.0061847	

In this solution we obtain $i = .006185$, to 6 decimal places. The yearly rate is therefore $(1.006185)^{12} - 1 = .0768.$ (Standard calculator subroutines show $i = .006183$ to 6 decimal places.)   □

We remark that successive approximation has the advantage of being iterative, and hence it is easy to write a computer program which will give you any degree of accuracy you require. However, care is needed since this procedure will not converge for all functions. In some cases convergence never occurs, whereas in others convergence will only occur if the starting value is close to the actual answer. Furthermore, convergence may depend on the form of the function used. For example when $s_{\overline{n}|}$ is involved, the expression $i = \dfrac{(1+i)^n - 1}{k}$, where k is a constant, diverges, whereas $i = (1+ik)^{1/n} - 1$ will converge.

A more detailed discussion of successive approximation will not be given here, but the interested reader should consult any standard text in numerical analysis.

3.5 CONTINUOUS ANNUITIES

A type of annuity which commonly arises in practice has monthly payments, but a quoted interest rate which is effective yearly or half-yearly. Mortgages are a good example of this type of annuity. In the last two sections we saw that this situation could easily be handled by converting the interest rate to a monthly rate. Older textbooks found that approach inconvenient, primarily because the new rate could not be found in interest tables. For this reason, symbols like $a_{\overline{n}|}^{(m)}$ and $s_{\overline{n}|}^{(m)}$ were developed, where $a_{\overline{n}|}^{(m)}$ represents the present value of an annuity with amount $\frac{1}{m}$ paid at the end of every m^{th} of an interest period for the next n periods. The basic idea is that the usual payment of 1 per period has now been divided into m parts of $\frac{1}{m}$ each.

The formulae developed for these new symbols are not required in our modern approach to annuities and will not be stated here. However, the limiting case is of interest. We define

$$\overline{a}_{\overline{n}|} = \lim_{m \to \infty} a_{\overline{n}|}^{(m)}. \tag{3.17}$$

$\overline{a}_{\overline{n}|}$ can be considered as an annuity lasting n periods, where the periodic payment of 1 is paid continuously throughout the period. To evaluate, sum becomes integral and we have

$$\overline{a}_{\overline{n}|} = \int_0^n v^t \, dt, \tag{3.18}$$

where the term $v^t \, dt$ in the integral can be thought of as the present value of an infinitesimally small amount dt payable at time t.

Such an annuity is called a *continuous annuity*. While it may not arise in practice, it serves as a good approximation to annuities where the payment period is very small (e.g., daily).

We easily obtain

$$\overline{a}_{\overline{n}|} = \int_0^n v^t \, dt$$

$$= \left[\frac{v^t}{\ln v}\right]_0^n$$

$$= \frac{v^n - 1}{\ln v}$$

$$= \frac{1 - v^n}{\ln(1 + i)}$$

$$= \frac{1 - v^n}{\delta}. \tag{3.19}$$

Formula (3.19) compares very nicely with Formulas (3.6) and (3.8) for $a_{\overline{n}|}$ and $\ddot{a}_{\overline{n}|}$, respectively, derived earlier in this chapter.

    Similarly

$$\overline{s}_{\overline{n}|} = (1 + i)^n \, \overline{a}_{\overline{n}|}$$

$$= \frac{(1 + i)^n - 1}{\delta}. \tag{3.20}$$

[c.f. Formula (3.7).]

    We also have

$$\overline{s}_{\overline{n}|} = \int_0^n (1 + i)^t \, dt, \tag{3.21}$$

which has a similar verbal interpretation to that given $\overline{a}_{\overline{n}|}$ as defined by Formula (3.18).

3.6 VARYING ANNUITIES

To this point, all the annuities considered have had a level series of payments. We now remove this restriction and consider annuities with a varying series of payments.

    Any type of annuity can be evaluated by taking the present value or accumulated value of each payment separately and adding the results. There are, however, several types of varying annuities for which relatively simple compact expressions are possible. The only general type we will study is the type where payments vary in arithmetic progression. Specific examples of other types will be considered as well.

First let us assume that payments vary in arithmetic progression. In other words, the first payment is P and payments increase by Q thereafter, continuing for n years.

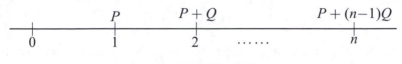

$$\text{FIGURE 3.14}$$

The value of this annuity one year before the first payment is given by

$$A = Pv + (P+Q)v^2 + (P+2Q)v^3 + \cdots + [P+(n-1)Q]v^n. \quad (3.22)$$

Multiplying (3.22) by $1 + i$, we obtain

$$(1+i)A = P + (P+Q)v + (P+2Q)v^2 \\ + \cdots + [P+(n-1)Q]v^{n-1}. \quad (3.23)$$

Subtracting (3.22) from (3.23), we obtain

$$
\begin{aligned}
iA &= P + Q(v + v^2 + \cdots + v^{n-1}) - Pv^n - (n-1)Qv^n \\
&= P(1-v^n) + Q(v + v^2 + \cdots + v^{n-1} + v^n) - nQv^n. \quad (3.24)
\end{aligned}
$$

Hence

$$
\begin{aligned}
A &= P\left[\frac{1-v^n}{i}\right] + Q\left[\frac{a_{\overline{n}|} - nv^n}{i}\right] \\
&= Pa_{\overline{n}|} + Q\left[\frac{a_{\overline{n}|} - nv^n}{i}\right]. \quad (3.25)
\end{aligned}
$$

The accumulated value of these payments at time n is, of course, equal to $A(1+i)^n$, and hence equals

$$Ps_{\overline{n}|} + Q\left[\frac{s_{\overline{n}|} - n}{i}\right]. \quad (3.26)$$

Two special cases often occur in practice. The first of these is the *increasing* annuity where $P = 1$ and $Q = 1$.

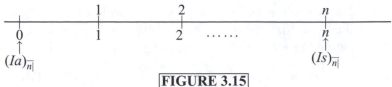

FIGURE 3.15

The value of this annuity at time 0 is denoted by $(Ia)_{\overline{n}|}$, and has the following formula, derived from (3.25) by substituting $P = Q = 1$.

$$
\begin{aligned}
(Ia)_{\overline{n}|} &= a_{\overline{n}|} + \frac{a_{\overline{n}|} - nv^n}{i} \\[2mm]
&= \frac{a_{\overline{n}|}(1+i) - nv^n}{i} \\[2mm]
&= \frac{\ddot{a}_{\overline{n}|} - nv^n}{i}.
\end{aligned}
\tag{3.27}
$$

The value at time n is therefore given by

$$
\begin{aligned}
(Is)_{\overline{n}|} &= (Ia)_{\overline{n}|}(1+i)^n \\[2mm]
&= \frac{\ddot{s}_{\overline{n}|} - n}{i}.
\end{aligned}
\tag{3.28}
$$

The second special case is the *decreasing* annuity where $P = n$ and $Q = -1$.

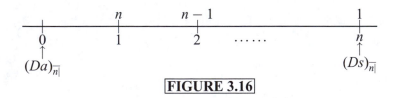

FIGURE 3.16

The present value of this annuity at time 0, derived from (3.25), is given by

$$(Da)_{\overline{n}|} = na_{\overline{n}|} + (-1)\frac{a_{\overline{n}|} - nv^n}{i}$$

$$= \frac{n(1-v^n) - a_{\overline{n}|} + nv^n}{i}$$

$$= \frac{n - a_{\overline{n}|}}{i}. \tag{3.29}$$

The accumulated value at time n is

$$(Ds)_{\overline{n}|} = (Da)_{\overline{n}|}(1+i)^n$$

$$= \frac{n(1+i)^n - s_{\overline{n}|}}{i}. \tag{3.30}$$

Finally, let us consider an increasing perpetuity as shown in Figure

3.17.

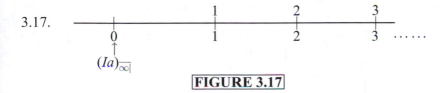

FIGURE 3.17

An appropriate symbol for this would be $(Ia)_{\overline{\infty}|}$, and it is easily seen that $(Ia)_{\overline{\infty}|} = \lim_{n \to \infty} (Ia)_{\overline{n}|}$. Since $\lim_{n \to \infty} \ddot{a}_{\overline{n}|} = 1 + \frac{1}{i}$, and $\lim_{n \to \infty} nv^n = 0$, we obtain

$$(Ia)_{\overline{\infty}|} = \frac{1 + \frac{1}{i}}{i}$$

$$= \frac{1}{i} + \frac{1}{i^2}. \tag{3.31}$$

Alternatively, we could obtain Formula (3.31) from first principles as follows:

$$(Ia)_{\overline{\infty}|} = v + 2v^2 + 3v^3 + \cdots$$

$$= (v + v^2 + v^3 + \cdots) + (v^2 + 2v^3 + \cdots)$$

$$= a_{\overline{\infty}|} + v(v + 2v^2 + 3v^3 + \cdots)$$

$$= \frac{1}{i} + v(Ia)_{\overline{\infty}|}.$$

Solving for $(Ia)_{\overline{\infty}|}$, we obtain $(Ia)_{\overline{\infty}|}(1-v) = \frac{1}{i}$, so that

$$
\begin{aligned}
(Ia)_{\overline{\infty}|} &= \frac{1}{i(1-v)} \\[2mm]
&= \frac{1}{i - \frac{i}{1+i}} \\[2mm]
&= \frac{1+i}{i^2} \\[2mm]
&= \frac{1}{i} + \frac{1}{i^2}, \tag{3.31}
\end{aligned}
$$

as before.

Example 3.13

Find the value, one year before the first payment, of a series of payments 200, 500, 800, ... if $i = .08$ and the payments continue for 19 years.

Solution

Using $P = 200$, $Q = 300$ and $n = 19$, we obtain, from Formula (3.25),

$$
200a_{\overline{19}|} + 300\left[\frac{a_{\overline{19}|} - 19v^{19}}{i}\right] = 1920.72 + 19{,}504.01 = 21{,}424.73. \qquad \square
$$

Example 3.14

Find the present value of an increasing perpetuity which pays 1 at the end of the fourth year, 2 at the end of the eighth year, 3 at the end of the twelfth year, and so on, if $i = .06$.

Solution

This could be done either by first principles or by applying Formula (3.31). If the formula is to be used, we must first compute the effective rate of interest per four-year period. This equals $(1.06)^4 - 1 = .26248$. Hence the answer is $\dfrac{1}{.26248} + \dfrac{1}{(.26248)^2} = 18.32$. $\qquad \square$

Example 3.15

Find the value one year before the first payment of an annuity where payments start at 1, increase by annual amounts of 1 to a payment of n, and then decrease by annual amounts of 1 to a final payment of 1 .

Solution

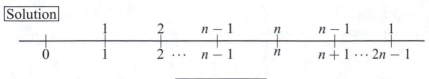

FIGURE 3.18

A time diagram for this is shown in Figure 3.18. Note that the final payment occurs at time $2n - 1$. The present value is

$$(Ia)_{\overline{n}|} + v^n(Da)_{\overline{n-1}|} = \frac{\ddot{a}_{\overline{n}|} - nv^n + (n-1)v^n - v^n a_{\overline{n-1}}}{i}$$

$$= \frac{1 + a_{\overline{n-1}|} - v^n - v^n a_{\overline{n-1}|}}{i}$$

$$= \left[\frac{1 - v^n}{i}\right](1 + a_{\overline{n-1}|})$$

$$= a_{\overline{n}|}(1 + a_{\overline{n-1}|})$$

$$= a_{\overline{n}|} \cdot \ddot{a}_{\overline{n}|}. \qquad (3.32)$$

□

Example 3.16

Show both algebraically and verbally that $(Da)_{\overline{n}|} = (n+1)a_{\overline{n}|} - (Ia)_{\overline{n}|}$.

Algebraic Solution

$$(n+1)a_{\overline{n}|} - (Ia)_{\overline{n}|} = (n+1)\left[\frac{1-v^n}{i}\right] - \left[\frac{\ddot{a}_{\overline{n}|} - nv^n}{i}\right]$$

$$= \frac{n + 1 - nv^n - v^n - \ddot{a}_{\overline{n}|} + nv^n}{i}$$

$$= \frac{n + 1 - v^n - \ddot{a}_{\overline{n}|}}{i}$$

$$= \frac{n - (\ddot{a}_{\overline{n}|} + v^n - 1)}{i}$$

$$= \frac{n - a_{\overline{n}|}}{i}$$

$$= (Da)_{\overline{n}|}.$$

Verbal Solution

Here is a diagram for $(n+1)a_{\overline{n}|}$:

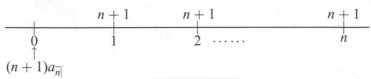

FIGURE 3.19

Here is a diagram for $(Ia)_{\overline{n}|}$:

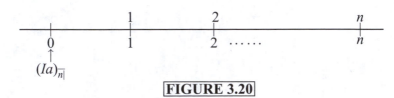

FIGURE 3.20

Subtracting the second diagram from the first, we obtain the following:

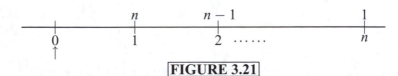

FIGURE 3.21

This is $(Da)_{\overline{n}|}$, as required. □

Example 3.17

An annuity provides for 15 annual payments.   The first of these payments is 200, and each subsequent payment is 5% less than the one preceeding it. Find the accumulated value of this annuity at the time of the final payment if $i = .09$.

Solution

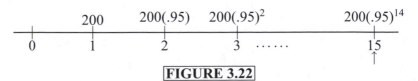

FIGURE 3.22

We want to find the value of this annuity at time 15. Observe that the payments are in geometric, rather than arithmetic sequence, so our earlier formulae cannot be applied. From first principles the value is $S = 200(.95)^{14} + 200(.95)^{13}(1.09) + 200(.95)^{12}(1.09)^2 + \cdots + 200(1.09)^{14}$. This is just the sum of the first 15 terms of a geometric sequence with $a = 200(.95)^{14}$ and $r = \frac{1.09}{.95}$. The formula developed in Theorem 3.2(b) tells us that $S_{15} = 200(.95)^{14} \left[\dfrac{1 - \left[\frac{1.09}{.95}\right]^{15}}{1 - \frac{1.09}{.95}} \right] = 4541.70.$ □

Example 3.18

In settlement of a lawsuit, the provincial court ordered Frank to make 8 annual payments to Fred. The first payment of 10,000 is made immediately, and future payments are to increase according to an assumed rate of inflation of .04 per year. Find the present value of these payments assuming $i = .07$.

Solution

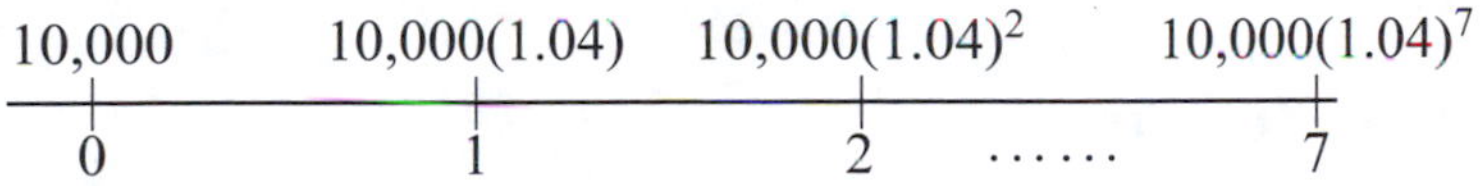

$$
\begin{array}{ccccc}
10{,}000 & 10{,}000(1.04) & 10{,}000(1.04)^2 & & 10{,}000(1.04)^7 \\
| & | & | & & | \\
0 & 1 & 2 & \cdots\cdots & 7
\end{array}
$$

FIGURE 3.23

The required present value is

$$P = 10{,}000 + 10{,}000\left(\frac{1.04}{1.07}\right) + \cdots + 10{,}000\left(\frac{1.04}{1.07}\right)^7$$

$$= 10{,}000 \left(\frac{1 - \left(\frac{1.04}{1.07}\right)^8}{1 - \frac{1.04}{1.07}} \right)$$

$$= 72{,}574.66.$$ □

Note that an alternative way of solving Example 3.18 is to realize that the expression for P is just $10{,}000\ddot{a}_{\overline{8|}}$ at a rate of interest i such that $1 + i = \frac{1.07}{1.04}$. This is often called the *real rate of interest*, and can be calculated in any problem where inflation is involved.

EXERCISES

3.1 Arithmetic and Geometric Sequences

3-1. Find the 17th term and the sum of the first 11 terms of each of the following:
  (a) The arithmetic sequence 2, 7, 12, 17, ...
  (b) The arithmetic sequence with $a = 71$ and $d = -3$.
  (c) The arithmetic sequence whose 5th term is 19 and whose 9th term is 47.
  (d) The geometric sequence 5, 15, 45, ...
  (e) The geometric sequence $3, -\frac{3}{4}, \frac{3}{16}, -\frac{3}{64}, \ldots$
  (f) The geometric sequence whose 5th term is $\frac{2}{9}$ and whose 8th term is $\frac{3}{32}$.

3-2. Prove Theorems 3.1(a), 3.1(b), 3.2(a) and 3.2(b) using mathematical induction.

3.2 Basic Results

3-3. Henrietta borrows 6500 in order to buy furniture. She wishes to pay the loan back by means of 12 annual payments, the first to be made one year after the loan is taken out. If $i = .13$, find the amount of each payment.

3-4. Answer Question 3 if the loan is to be paid back with 144 monthly payments, the first one due one month after the loan is taken out.

3-5. Alphonse deposits 450 in a bank account at the beginning of each year, starting in 1977 and continuing for 20 years. If $i = .08$, find the amount in his account at the end of 1996.

3-6. An annuity pays 1000 a year for 8 years. If $i = .08$, find each of the following:
  (a) The value of the annuity one year before the first payment.
  (b) The value of the annuity one year after the last payment.
  (c) The value of the annuity at the time of the fifth payment.
  (d) The number of years the annuity would have to run in order that its current present value be doubled.
  (e) The number of years the annuity would have to run in order that its current present value be tripled.

3-7. Prove each of the following identities:
    (a) $a_{\overline{m+n}|} = a_{\overline{m}|} + v^m a_{\overline{n}|}$
    (b) $a_{\overline{m-n}|} = a_{\overline{m}|} - v^m s_{\overline{n}|}$
    (c) $s_{\overline{m+n}|} = s_{\overline{m}|} + (1+i)^m s_{\overline{n}|}$
    (d) $s_{\overline{m-n}|} = s_{\overline{m}|} - (1+i)^m a_{\overline{n}|}$

3-8. Give verbal interpretations for each of the identities in Question 7.

3-9. Prove that $\dfrac{1}{a_{\overline{n}|}} = \dfrac{1}{s_{\overline{n}|}} + i$.

3-10. Prove each of the following identities:
    (a) $\ddot{a}_{\overline{n}|} = 1 + a_{\overline{n-1}|}$
    (b) $\ddot{s}_{\overline{n}|} = s_{\overline{n+1}|} - 1$

3-11. Give verbal interpretations for the identities in Question 10.

3-12. Rank n, $a_{\overline{n}|}$ and $s_{\overline{n}|}$ in increasing order of magnitude. Under what conditions will equality hold for all n?

3-13. Harriet wishes to accumulate 85,000 in a fund at the end of 25 years. If she deposits 1000 in the fund at the end of each of the first 10 years, and $1000 + x$ at the end of each of the last 15 years, find x if the fund earns 7% effective.

3-14. Show that $\dfrac{s_{\overline{2n}|}}{s_{\overline{n}|}} + \dfrac{s_{\overline{n}|}}{s_{\overline{2n}|}} - \dfrac{s_{\overline{3n}|}}{s_{\overline{2n}|}} = 1$.

3-15. Prove each of the following identities:
    (a) $\ddot{a}_{\overline{n}|} = a_{\overline{n}|} + 1 - v^n$
    (b) $\ddot{s}_{\overline{n}|} = s_{\overline{n}|} - 1 + (1+i)^n$

3-16. Give verbal interpretations for the identities in Question 15.

3-17. Show that $\displaystyle\sum_{t=a}^{b} (\ddot{s}_{\overline{t}|} - s_{\overline{t}|}) = s_{\overline{b+1}|} - s_{\overline{a}|} - (b+1-a)$.

3-18. An annuity runs for 25 years as follows: at the end of each of the
       first ten years 500 is paid, and then at the end of each of the last 15
       years 300 is paid.   If $i = .08$, find the value of this annuity three
       years before the first payment.

3-19. Edward buys a new house and takes out a mortgage of 60,000. To
       pay off the mortgage, he will make monthly payments with the
       first payment due in one month. Given $i^{(2)} = .12$, find the amount
       of his payment if (a) the payments will continue for the next 25
       years; (b) the payments will continue for the next 20 years; (c) the
       payments will continue for the next 10 years.

3-20. Rework Question 19 if the nominal rate of interest convertible
       semiannually is 16% instead of 12%.

3-21. A man wishes to accumulate a small pension by depositing 2500 at
       the beginning of each year for 25 years. Starting at the end of the
       year in which the final deposit is made, he will make 20 annual
       withdrawals.   Find the amount of each withdrawal, if $i = .07$
       during the first 25 years and $i = .11$ thereafter.

3-22. A series of $n + 1$ payments are made as follows: 1 at the end of
       the first year, 2 at the end of each of the next $n - 1$ years, and 1 at
       the end of year $n + 1$. Show that the value of these payments at
       $t = 0$ is $a_{\overline{n}|} \cdot \ddot{a}_{\overline{2}|}$.

3-23. Give a verbal explanation of why the formula in Question 22 is
       correct.

3-24. An annuity consists of n payments of 1, the first to be made at the
       end of 7 years and the other payments to be made at three year
       intervals thereafter. Show that the present value of the annuity is
       $$\frac{a_{\overline{3n+7}|} - a_{\overline{7}|}}{a_{\overline{3}|}}.$$

3-25. Albert Glover, star third baseman with the Blue Jays, is given a choice of contracts:
 (a) 3,200,000 per year for the next five years, payable at the end of each year.
 (b) 3,000,000 per year for the next five years, payable at the beginning of each year.
 (c) 1,800,000 per year for the next ten years, payable at the end of each year.
 If $i = .04$, find the value of each of these contracts at the beginning of the first year. Repeat for $i = .06$.

3-26. Find the range of interest rates for which each of the contracts in Question 25 has a higher present value then the other two.

3-27. Consider an annuity where $\frac{n}{k}$ payments of 1 are made, the first occurring k years from now with the payments continuing at k-year intervals thereafter, until a period of n years has passed. Prove that the present value of these payments is equal to $\frac{a_{\overline{n}|}}{s_{\overline{k}|}}$.

3-28. Show that the accumulated value of the annuity in Question 27 immediately after the last payment is $\frac{s_{\overline{n}|}}{s_{\overline{k}|}}$.

3-29. Give verbal interpretations for the formulae in Question 27 and Question 28.

3-30. Prove that the present value of an annuity which pays $\frac{1}{m}$ at the end of each mth of a year for the next n years is equal to $\frac{1 - v^n}{i^{(m)}}$. This present value is denoted by $a_{\overline{n}|}^{(m)}$.

3-31. Prove that the accumulated value of the annuity in Question 30 at the time of the last payment is $\frac{(1+i)^n - 1}{i^{(m)}}$. This accumulated value is denoted by $s_{\overline{n}|}^{(m)}$.

3-32. Derive an expression for the present value of an annuity under which payments are 2, 1, 2, 1, ... at the end of every year for the next 25 years.

3-33. If $a_{\overline{n}|} = x$ and $a_{\overline{2n}|} = y$, express d as a function of x and y.

3-34. A loan of 25,000 is to be repaid by annual payments at the end of each year for the next 20 years. During the first 5 years the payments are k per year; during the second 5 years the payments are $2k$ per year; during the third 5 years, $3k$ per year; and during the fourth 5 years, $4k$ per year. If $i = .12$, find k.

3-35. Given $a_{\overline{n}|} = 12$ and $a_{\overline{2n}|} = 21$, find $a_{\overline{4n}|}$.

3-36. Given $\ddot{a}_{\overline{t}|} = 9.370$ and $\ddot{a}_{\overline{t+1}|} = 9.499$, find the effective rate of interest.

3-37. An injured worker submits a Workers Compensation claim. It is decided that she is entitled to annual medical payments of 20,000 for the next 10 years and equal annual indemnity payments for the next 20 years. The medical payments will begin immediately, and the indemnity payments will begin in one year's time. The insurance company has established a fund of 680,000 to support these payments. Find the amount of each annual indemnity payment assuming $i = .07$.

3.3 Perpetuities

3-38. Prove identities (3.14), (3.15) and (3.16).

3-39. Given $i = .15$, find the present value of an annuity of 100 per year continuing forever if (a) the first payment is due in one year; (b) the first payment is due immediately; (c) the first payment is due in 5 years.

3-40. A perpetuity of 500 per year, with the first payment due one year hence, is worth 2500. Find i.

3-41. Deposits of 1000 are placed into a fund at the end of each year for the next 25 years. Five years after the last deposit, annual payments commence and continue forever. If $i = .09$, find the amount of each payment.

3-42. A loan of 5000 is repaid by annual payments continuing forever, the first one due one year after the loan is taken out. If the payments are $X, 2X, X, 2X, \ldots$ and $i = .16$, find X.

3-43. At what effective rate of interest is the present value of a series of payments of 1 at the end of every two years, forever, equal to 10?

3-44. Albert Glover has just signed a contract with the Blue Jays which will pay him 3,000,000 at the beginning of each year for the next five years. To finance his retirement, the player decides to put a part of each year's salary (the same amount each year) into a fund which will pay him, or his estate, 400,000 a year forever, the first payment coming one year after his last salary cheque. If $i = .08$, how much salary does the player have left each year?

3-45. Wilbur leaves an inheritance to four charities, A, B, C and D. The total inheritance is a series of level payments at the end of each year forever. During the first 20 years, A, B and C share each payment equally. All payments after 20 years revert to D. If the present value of the shares of A, B, C and D are all equal, find i.

3-46. A scholarship fund is accumulated by deposits of 400 at the end of each year. The fund is to be used to pay out one annual scholarship of 2000 in perpetuity, with the first scholarship being paid out one year after the last deposit. Assume $i = .08$.
   (a) Find the minimum number of deposits which must be made in order to support such a fund.
   (b) Assume 25 deposits are made. Show that is is possible to pay out one scholarship as described above, but not possible to pay out two such scholarships.
   (c) Despite the result in (b), and again assuming 25 deposits are made, it is desired to pay out a second scholarship of 2000 on a regular basis as often as possible. Find the minimum integer value of t such that a second scholarship could be paid out every t years, starting t years after the last deposit.

3.4   Unknown Time and Unknown Rate of Interest

3-47. Joan takes out a loan of 6000 from her local bank. She wishes to pay it back by means of yearly payments of amount 800 for as long as necessary, with a smaller payment one year later. If the first payment of 800 is due in one year and $i = .11$, find the number of payments required and the amount of the smaller payment.

3-48. Do Question 47 if the payments are 70 monthly, with the first payment due in one month, and i is still 11% per year. Assume the smaller payment is to be made one month after the last regular payment.

3-49. Do Question 47 if the first payment isn't due until two years after the loan is taken out.

3-50. A fund of 5000 is to be accumulated by n annual payments of 50 followed by another n annual payments of 100, plus a final payment, as small as possible, made one year after the last regular payment. If $i = .08$, find n and the amount of the final payment.

3-51. At what effective monthly rate of interest will payments of 200 at the end of every month for the next 3 years be sufficient to repay a loan of 6500?

3-52. Write a computer program which will solve Question 51 by successive approximation. Print out answers which are correct to 3 decimal places, then to 4 decimal places, then to 5 decimal places.

3-53. Write a general computer program which will solve any problem like Question 51 to any required degree of accuracy.

3-54. A fund of 25,000 is to be accumulated at the end of 20 years by annual payments of 500 at the end of each year. Find i.

3-55. A fund of 2200 is to be accumulated at the end of 10 years, with payments of 100 at the end of each of the first 5 years and 200 at the end of each of the second 5 years. Find the effective rate of interest earned by the fund.

3.5 Continuous Annuities

3-56. Prove each of the following identities:

    (a) $\overline{a}_{\overline{n}|} = \frac{i}{\delta} a_{\overline{n}|} = \overline{s}_{\overline{1}|} a_{\overline{n}|}.$

    (b) $\overline{a}_{\overline{n}|} = \dfrac{1 - e^{-n\delta}}{\delta}.$

    (c) $\overline{s}_{\overline{n}|} = \dfrac{e^{n\delta} - 1}{\delta}.$

3-57. (a)   Show that $\dfrac{d}{dn} \overline{s}_{\overline{n}|} = 1 + \delta \cdot \overline{s}_{\overline{n}|}.$

    (b)   Verbally interpret the result obtained in part (a).

3-58. Redo Question 3-6(a), assuming the annuity is continuous.

3.6 Varying Annuities

3-59. Rank the following in increasing order of magnitude, and give a verbal explanation for your ranking.

    (a) $3a_{\overline{2}|}$ (b) $(Ia)_{\overline{2}|} + (Da)_{\overline{2}|}$ (c) $2(Ia)_{\overline{2}|}$ (d) $2a_{\overline{3}|}$ (e) 6

3-60. A man borrows money from a bank. He receives the money in 5 annual installments, taking X each time. He repays the loan with 20 annual payments, the first one equal to 100 and the payments increasing by 100 each year. If the first payment is due one year after the last installment is given out, and if $i = .132$, find X.

3-61. A loan is repaid by annual payments continuing forever, the first one due one year after the loan is taken out. Assume that the effective rate of interest is i.

    (a)   Find a formula for the amount of the loan if the payments are 1, 2, 1, 2, ...

    (b)   Find a formula for the amount of the loan if the payments are $1, 2, \ldots, n, 1, 2, \ldots, n, \ldots$

    (c)   If A_n is your answer to part (b), find $\lim\limits_{n \to \infty} A_n$. Have you seen this before? Where?

3-62. Under an annuity, the first payment of n is made after one year, the second payment of $n-1$ after two years, and so forth, until a payment of p is made, after which payments cease. Show that the present value of this annuity is given by

$$p \cdot a_{\overline{n-p+1|}} + \tfrac{1}{i}(n-p-a_{\overline{n-p|}}).$$

3-63. Find the present value of a perpetuity under which a payment of 100 is made after one year, 200 after 2 years, increasing until a payment of 1500 is made, after which payments are level at 1500 per year forever. Assume $i = .075$.

3-64. Find the present value at 11% effective of an annuity lasting 20 years in which the first payment of 1,000 is due immediately, and in which each successive payment is 10% more than the payment for the preceeding year.

3-65. Find an expression for the present value of an annuity in which the first payment is due six years from now, and in which the payments follow the pattern $n, n-1, n-2, \ldots, 2, 1, 2, \ldots, n-1, n$.

3-66. Find the present value at 9% effective of a 20-year annuity, with the first payment due immediately, in which the payments follow the pattern $1, 4, 9, 16, \ldots, 400$.

3-67. (a)   Show that $\dfrac{d}{di}\, a_{\overline{n|}} = -v\,(Ia)_{\overline{n|}}$.

    (b)   Find $\dfrac{d}{di}\, a_{\overline{n|}}$ evaluated at $i = 0$.

3-68. There are two perpetuities. The first has level payments of p at the end of each year. The second is increasing such that the payments are $q, 2q, 3q, \ldots$. Find the rate of interest which will make the difference in the present values of these perpetuities (a) zero; (b) a maximum.

CHAPTER FOUR
AMORTIZATION AND SINKING FUNDS

4.1 AMORTIZATION

To pay back a loan by the *amortization method* is to repay the loan by means of installment payments at periodic intervals. In Chapter 3 we saw how to calculate the amount of such a payment. In this section we will see how to find the outstanding principal on a loan at any given point in time, and in the next section we will see how to divide payments into their principal and interest portions and how to construct amortization schedules for repayment of loans.

First, let us consider the problem of finding the outstanding principal. This is of crucial importance, for if you want to pay off a loan early, or change your loan payments in any way at all, it is important to know the amount of the outstanding loan. Mortgage statements typically give the outstanding principal at the time of the statement.

There are two approaches which can be used, and one may be preferable to the other depending on the situation. According to the *prospective method*, the outstanding principal at any point in time is equal to the present value at that date of all remaining payments. According to the *retrospective method*, the outstanding principal is equal to the original principal accumulated to that point in time, minus the accumulated value of all payments previously made.

Some examples will illustrate the two methods, and will also demonstrate when one method is preferable to the other.

Example 4.1
A loan is being paid off with payments of 500 at the end of each year for the next 10 years. If $i = .14$, find the outstanding principal, P, immediately after the payment at the end of year 6.

Solution

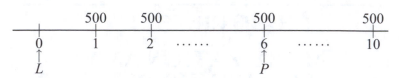

FIGURE 4.1

Here, the prospective method is easier, although both methods will work. Prospectively, there are 4 payments still to come so the outstanding principle is $P = 500a_{\overline{4}|} = 1456.86$. Retrospectively, we would first have to find the amount of the loan $L = 500a_{\overline{10}|}$. Once that is done, we would then have $P = L(1.14)^6 - 500s_{\overline{6}|}$. The reader should verify that this approach also produces $P = 1456.86$.   □

Example 4.2

A 7000 loan is being paid off with payments of 1000 at the end of each year for as long as necessary, plus a smaller payment one year after the last regular payment. If $i = .11$ and the first payment is due one year after the loan is taken out, find the outstanding principal, P, immediately after the ninth payment.

Solution

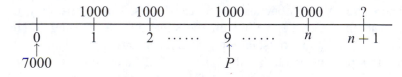

FIGURE 4.2

In this case the retrospective method is more convenient, since it avoids the necessity of finding the number of payments and the amount of the smaller payment. We obtain $P = 7000(1.11)^9 - 1000s_{\overline{9}|} = 3742.29$.   □

   By this point in the text, the reader is certainly aware of the importance of being able to convert a given interest rate to an equivalent rate with a different conversion frequency. The following example illustrates this point with respect to a mortgage loan.

Example 4.3

John takes out a 50,000 mortgage on a home at $12\frac{1}{2}\%$ convertible semi-annually. He pays off the mortgage with monthly payments for 20 years, the first one due one month after the mortgage is taken out. Immediately after his 60th payment, John renegotiates the loan. He agrees to repay the remainder of the mortgage by making an immediate cash payment of 10,000 and repaying the balance by means of monthly payments for ten years at 11% convertible semiannually. Find the amount of his new payment.

Solution

First we have to find the old payment X. To do that, we need a monthly rate of interest j equivalent to the nominal rate $i^{(2)} = .125$. Thus $(1+j)^6 = 1 + \frac{.125}{2}$, so that $j = (1.0625)^{1/6} - 1$. Then we have $X = \frac{50,000}{a_{\overline{240}|}} = 557.05$. Next, we will find the outstanding principal P, immediately after the 60th payment. Either method will work, but the prospective method is easier. Since 180 payments remain, we have $P = 557.05 a_{\overline{180}|} = 45,954.19$. Now we just consider this as a new loan of amount P. Actually, the amount to be repaid is 10,000 less, namely 35,954.19. The new monthly rate is $j = (1.055)^{1/6} - 1$. Note that the new payment is made for only 120 months, so it is equal to $\frac{35,954.19}{a_{\overline{120}|}} = 490.32$. $\qquad\square$

4.2 AMORTIZATION SCHEDULES

To begin with, let us study how a payment can be divided up into its interest and principal parts. As an example, say a payment of X is made at a certain time t. First, we must know the amount of outstanding principal, P, at time $t - 1$, one period before the time we are interested in.

FIGURE 4.3

The amount of interest earned on the loan during this period is equal to iP, so that is the interest portion of X. Hence the other portion, $X - iP$, goes toward repayment of principal.

| Example 4.4 |

A 1000 loan is repaid by annual payments of 150, plus a smaller final payment. If $i = .11$, and the first payment is made one year after the time of the loan, find the amount of principal and interest contained in the third payment.

| Solution |

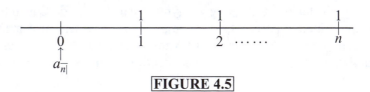

| FIGURE 4.4 |

The outstanding principal at $t = 2$ is, by the retrospective method, equal to $1000(1.11)^2 - 150s_{\overline{2}|} = 915.60$. Hence the interest portion at $t = 3$ is equal to $(915.60)(.11) = 100.72$, and the principal portion at $t = 3$ is equal to $150 - 100.72 = 49.28$. $\square$

For certain types of problems, it is convenient to use some easily developed formulae for dividing payments into principal and interest portions. The reader should be careful, however, to use these formulae only in situations where they are applicable.

Consider a loan which is being repaid by equal annual payments of 1 for n years.

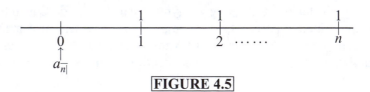

| FIGURE 4.5 |

Such a loan has a value of $a_{\overline{n}|}$ one year before the first payment. The outstanding principal at time t is (prospectively) equal to $a_{\overline{n-t}|}$. Therefore the interest portion of the $(t + 1)^{st}$ payment is equal to

$$ia_{\overline{n-t}|} = 1 - v^{n-t}, \tag{4.1}$$

and the principal part is

$$1 - (1 - v^{n-t}) = v^{n-t}. \tag{4.2}$$

More generally, if a loan is being repaid by equal payments of X for n years, then the interest part of the kth payment will be

$$X(1 - v^{n-k+1}), \tag{4.3}$$

and the principal part will be

$$X \cdot v^{n-k+1}. \tag{4.4}$$

Now let us see how to construct an amortization schedule for repayment of a loan, such a schedule being simply a table which shows how each payment is divided into principal and interest. Amortization schedules can be very useful pictorial tools, as they visibly demonstrate how the interest portion decreases and the principal portion increases as time goes on. They also show how the outstanding balance decreases to zero as payments are made.

As an example, consider a loan of 5000 at 12% per year to be repaid by 5 annual payments, the first due one year hence. We know that the amount X of each payment is given by $Xa_{\overline{5}|} = 5000$, so that $X = 1387.05$. Here is an amortization schedule for this loan.

TABLE 4.1

Duration	Payment	Interest	Principal Repaid	Outstanding Principle
0				5000.00
1	1387.05	600.00	787.05	4212.95
2	1387.05	505.55	881.50	3331.45
3	1387.05	399.77	987.28	2344.17
4	1387.05	281.30	1105.75	1238.42
5	1387.05	148.61	1238.44	0

It is easy to see how such a table was constructed. The outstanding principal at time 0 is 5000, the amount of the loan. The amount of each payment is listed in Column 2 opposite the appropriate duration. The entry of 600 at the top of Column 3 is obtained by multiplying 5000 by .12. We then subtract 600 from 1387.05 to obtain 787.05, and then 787.05 is subtracted from 5000 to obtain the new outstanding principal,

4212.95. The procedure is now repeated (using 4212.95 as the out-standing loan balance) to obtain the next row. This continues until the outstanding principal is zero; notice in our example that rounding off the second decimal place has led to a small imbalance at the last stage.

In general the rules to obtain an amortization schedule are as follows:

I.   Take the entry from Column 5 of the previous row, multiply it by i, and enter the result in Column 3.
II.   Column 2 − Column 3 = Column 4.
III. Column 5 of previous row − Column 4 = Column 5.
IV.   Continue.

Example 4.5

Construct an amortization schedule for the loan described in Example 4.4.
Solution
One way to solve this would be to first find the duration and amount of the smaller final payment and to proceed as above. Alternatively, we can just start forming the amortization schedule and worry about the final payment later! Here are the first 12 rows of this schedule.

TABLE 4.2

Duration	Payment	Interest	Principal Repaid	Outstanding Principle
0				1000.00
1	150	110.00	40.00	960.00
2	150	105.60	44.40	915.60
3	150	100.72	49.28	866.32
4	150	95.30	54.70	811.62
5	150	89.38	60.72	750.90
6	150	82.60	67.40	683.50
7	150	75.19	74.81	608.69
8	150	66.96	83.04	525.65
9	150	57.82	92.18	433.47
10	150	47.68	102.32	331.15
11	150	36.43	113.57	217.58
12	150	23.93	126.07	91.51

Note that at this point the outstanding principal is 91.51, so the interest required in the next payment is $(91.51)(.11) = 10.07$. The principal required in the 13th payment is 91.51, in order that the balance be brought to 0. Hence the final payment is $10.07 + 91.51 = 101.58$, and row 13 of the schedule would be

| 13 | 101.58 | 10.07 | 91.51 | 0 |

☐

Of course, as we have seen earlier, it is not necessary to construct the entire amortization schedule if one simply wants to divide any one particular payment into principal and interest portions. In that case one should follow the method demonstrated in Example 4.4.

4.3 SINKING FUNDS

Instead of amortization, an alternate way of repaying a loan is for the borrower to pay the interest on the loan as it comes due, keeping the amount of the loan constant, and then repaying the principal by a single lump-sum payment at some point in the future. This method is demonstrated in Figure 4.6, for a loan of amount L with interest at rate i.

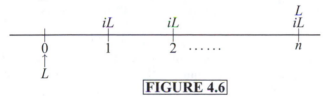

FIGURE 4.6

This lump-sum payment of principle is often accumulated by periodic deposits into a separate fund, called the *sinking fund*. Usually the sinking fund will accumulate at a rate of interest different from (usually smaller than) that charged by the lender. From the borrower's point of view, the total outlay at any point of time is the sum of the interest payment, made directly to the lender, and the sinking fund payment. Observe, however, that the lender is oblivious to the sinking fund; she only cares that she receives her regular interest payments and her principal back at the end of the period.

If the borrower is able to obtain a *higher* rate of interest on the sinking fund than that charged on the loan, then his total annual outlay will be less than if he were repaying this loan by the amortization method. On the other hand, a lower rate of interest in the sinking fund implies a higher annual outlay for the borrower.

Let us consider some examples.

| Example 4.6 |

John borrows 15,000 from a trust company at 17% effective annually. He agrees to pay the interest annually, and to build up a sinking fund which will repay the loan at the end of 15 years. If the sinking fund accumulates at 12% annually, find (a) the annual interest payment; (b) the annual sinking fund payment; (c) his total annual outlay; (d) the annual amortization payment which would pay off this loan in 15 years.

| Solution |

(a)   The annual interest payment is $15,000(.17) = 2550$.
(b)   The annual sinking fund payment X is given by the equation $Xs_{\overline{15}|.12} = 15,000$, so $X = 402.36$.
(c)   His total annual outlay is, therefore, $T = 2952.36$.
(d)   The amortization payment K would be given by the equation $Ka_{\overline{15}|.17} = 15,000$, so that $K = 2817.33$.

Observe that $K < T$, which is not surprising since the interest rate on the loan is 17%, whereas the sinking fund only earns interest at 12% annually.   □

| Example 4.7 |

Helen wishes to borrow 7000 to buy a car. One lender offers a loan in which the principal is to be repaid at the end of 5 years. In the meantime, interest at 11% effective is to be paid on the loan, and the borrower is to accumulate her principal by means of annual payments into a sinking fund earning 8% effective. Another lender offers a loan for 5 years in which the amortization method will be used to repay the loan, with the first of the annual payments due in one year. Find the rate of interest, i, that this second lender can charge in order that Helen finds the two offers equally attractive.

| Solution |

Consider the terms offered by the first lender. Helen's annual interest payment is $7000(.11) = 770$, and her annual sinking fund payment X is given by $Xs_{\overline{5}|.08} = 7000$, so that $X = 1193.20$. Hence Helen's total annual outlay is 1963.20. She would find the two offers equally attractive if this were also her amortization payment to the second lender. Hence the rate of interest we want is the rate i for which $7000 = 1963.20a_{\overline{5}|}$. Using our calculator, as described earlier in the text, we find $i = .124425$.   □

We note that this interest rate is higher than *either* rate involved in the first lender's offer. This reflects the fact that the sinking fund is earning interest at a rate less than that of the loan, so Helen's annual outlay is greater than it would be if she were paying the first lender back by the amortization method. Hence, the actual rate of interest she is paying is greater than 11%.

4.4 YIELD RATES

Consider an investor who makes a number of outlays at various points in time, and receives other payments in return. There is (at least) one interest rate for which the value of his expenditures will equal the value of the payments he receives, when all are considered at the same point in time. This rate is called the *yield rate* he earns on his investment.

We have seen a number of examples of yield rates. If a loan company lends Harry 10,000 which he pays back by the amortization method at 15% per year, then the yield rate earned by the company is 15%. Exercises 26(c) and 31(b) in Section 4.3 are examples of yield rates in reverse; we calculate, in those situations, the real rate of interest that a borrower is paying on a loan. Also, in Exercise 2-15, we calculated an investor's yield rate, without using that term.

Here are several examples of problems involving yield rates. The crucial thing to remember is that only the payments made directly to, or directly by, the person involved should be considered in evaluating that person's yield rate.

| Example 4.8 |

Herman borrows 5000 from George and agrees to repay it in 10 equal annual installments at 11%, with first payment due in one year. After 4 years, George sells his right to future payments to Ruth, at a price which will yield Ruth 12% effective.
(a)   Find the price Ruth pays.
(b)   Find George's overall yield rate.

| Solution |

First, we need to find the amount of each installment P. This is given by

$P \cdot a_{\overline{10}|.11} = 5000$, so that $P = \dfrac{5000}{a_{\overline{10}|.11}} = 849.01$.

(a)   As mentioned before, we should concentrate attention on the
       payments involving Ruth. She pays a certain amount of money, X,
       and in return she receives the final 6 payments of 849.01, the first
       due in one year. If she is to earn 12%, we must have
       $X = 849.01a_{\overline{6}|.12} = 3490.63$.

(b)   George pays out 5000 at time 0. In return, he receives 4 payments
       of 849.01, and, at the same time as the last payment, he receives an
       additional 3490.63 from Ruth.

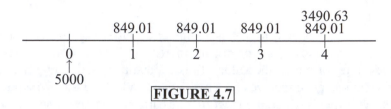

$$\boxed{\text{FIGURE 4.7}}$$

His yield rate is the rate of interest at which these payments
balance, which implies that $5000 = 849.01a_{\overline{4}|} + 3490.63v^4$. This
equation is solved by calculator giving $i = .10526$. We shouldn't
be surprised that the answer is less than 11%; the fact that Ruth is
earning a higher rate of interest than George on the annuity means
that George has to be losing something by selling. Of course,
Herman is oblivious to all the financial wheeling and dealing; he is
paying 11%, pure and simple, until the loan is repaid. Query:
Who is George Herman Ruth?   □

$\boxed{\text{Example 4.9}}$
At what yield rate are payments of 500 now and 600 at the end of 2 years
equivalent to a payment of 1098 at the end of 1 year?
$\boxed{\text{Solution}}$
We wish to solve $500 + 600v^2 = 1098v$, or $300v^2 - 549v + 250 = 0$.
Using the quadratic formula, we find $v = \dfrac{549 \pm \sqrt{1401}}{600}$, which gives
$v = \dfrac{586.43}{600}$ or $\dfrac{511.57}{600}$. Hence $i = .023$ or $.173$. We observe that the
answer to a question like this need not be unique!   □

Example 4.10

Henri buys a 15-year annuity with a present value of 5000 at 9% at a price which will allow him to accumulate a 15-year sinking fund to replace his capital at 7%, and will produce an overall yield rate of 10%. Find the purchase price of the annuity.

Solution

We must be very clear what is going on here. Henri pays a price, P, for this annuity. In return, he gets payments for 15 years. We must first find the amount, X, of each payment. This comes from the equation $Xa_{\overline{15}|.09} = 5000$, so that $X = \dfrac{5000}{a_{\overline{15}|.09}} = 620.29$. We know that the price, P, must be replaced by a 7% sinking fund in 15 years, so the sinking fund deposit is $\dfrac{P}{s_{\overline{15}|.07}} = .0397946247P$. In order that the yield rate be 10%, we need $.1P + .0397946247P = 620.29$. Finally, $P = 4437.15$. $\square$

EXERCISES

4.1 Amortization; 4.2 Amortization Schedules

4-1 A loan of 50,000 is being repaid with semiannual payments for 10 years at 13% convertible semiannually. The first payment is due six months after the loan is taken out.
(a) Find the outstanding loan balance at the end of the sixth year.
(b) Divide the 13th payment into principal and interest.

4-2. A loan is being repaid by 20 annual payments. The first 5 install-ments are 300 each, the next 8 are 400 each, and the last 7 are 600 each. Assume $i = .14$.
(a) Find the loan balance immediately after the tenth payment.
(b) Divide the 11th payment into principal and interest.

4-3. A loan is being repaid by monthly payments of 200, the first due one month after the loan is taken out, along with a smaller final payment. If $i = .11$ and the loan balance at the end of 18 months is 5,000, find the amount of the original loan.

4-4. A loan of 1000 is being repaid by annual installments of 200, the first due in one year, and a smaller final payment made one year after the last regular payment. If $i = .16$, find the outstanding principal immediately after the 4th payment.

4-5. A loan is repaid by level payments at the end of each month. The principal outstanding on May 1, 1996, was Q; on May 1, 1997, was R; on May 1, 1998, was S; on May 1, 1999, was T. Determine whether or not each of the following is true:
  (a) $Q + T < R + S$
  (b) $(Q + R)(S + T) = (R + S)^2$
  (c) $(Q - R)(S - T) = (R - S)^2$

4-6. Garfield is repaying a debt with 20 annual payments of 1000 each. At the end of the fourth year, he makes an extra payment of 2000. He then shortens his remaining payment period by two years, and makes level payments over that time. If $i = .12$, find the revised annual payment.

4-7. A 90,000 mortgage is repaid by payments at the end of each month for the next 25 years. The rate of interest is $11\frac{1}{2}\%$ convertible semiannually.
  (a)   Divide the first payment into principal and interest.
  (b)   Find the outstanding principal immediately after the 75th payment.
  (c)   Divide the 76th payment into principal and interest.
  (d)   Find the total amount of interest paid during the life of the mortgage.
  (e)   The borrower is temporarily unable to make payments 76 through 94 inclusive. He then wishes to increase his payments so that the mortgage will still be paid off at the scheduled time. Find the amount of the new payment.

4-8. A loan of 1000 is being repaid with annual installments for 20 years at 5% effective, with the first installment due one year after the loan is taken out. Show that the amount of interest in the 11th installment is 30.98.

4-9. A loan is being repaid with 30 equal annual installments at $i = .17$. In what installment are the principal and interest portions most nearly equal to each other?

4-10. A loan is repaid by 20 equal annual payments at 11% effective. If the amount of principal in the 4th payment is 150, find the amount of interest in the 12th payment.

4-11. A loan is being repaid with 30 equal annual installments. The principal portion of the 11th payment is 247.13, and the interest portion is 352.87. Find i.

4-12. A loan is being repaid with 20 annual installments of 1. Interest is at effective rate i for the first 10 years, and j for the last 10 years. Find an expression for each of the following:
(a) The amount of principal repaid in the eighth installment.
(b) The amount of interest paid in the last installment.

4-13. In order to pay off a loan of A, Herman makes payments of X at the end of each year. Interest on the first B of the unpaid balance is at rate i, and interest on the excess is at rate j. Find the outstanding balance at the end of the rth year, assuming it to be more than B.

4-14. The original amount of an inheritance was just sufficient at 8% effective to pay 5000 at the end of each year for 10 years. The payments of 5000 were made for the first 5 years even though the fund actually earned 10% effective. How much excess interest was in the fund at the end of 5 years?

4-15. George was making annual payments of X on a 16% 10-year loan. After making 4 payments, he renegotiates to pay off the debt in 3 more years with the lender being satisfied with 14% over the entire period. Find an expression for the new payment.

4-16. Harriet is repaying a loan with payments of 3000 at the end of every two years. If the amount of interest in the 5th installment is 2,982.31, find the amount of principal in the 8th installment. Assume $i = .13$.

4-17. Henry borrows 5000 at 14% per year, and wishes to pay it back with 6 equal annual payments, the first due in one year. Construct an amortization schedule for this loan.

4-18. Construct an amortization schedule for the loan in Question 1.

4-19. Construct an amortization schedule for the loan in Question 2.

4-20. Construct an amortization schedule for the loan in Question 4.

4-21. Consider a loan which is being repaid by n equal annual payments of 1, the first due one year after the loan is taken out.
(a)   Assuming $n > 5$, construct the first 5 rows of the amortization schedule.
(b)   Assuming $n > 20$, construct the 20th row of the amortization schedule.
(c)   Construct the last 3 rows of the amortization schedule (assume $n > 3$).

4-22. Assuming a loan is to be repaid by equal payments, write a computer program which will output an amortization schedule for such a loan. Test your program by redoing Questions 17 and 18.

4-23. Use the program of Question 22 to produce an amortization schedule for Question 7.

4-24. Modify the program of Question 22 so that it can handle problems like Question 19. Test your program by redoing Question 19.

4-25. Modify the program of Question 22 so that it can handle problems like Question 20. Test your program by redoing Question 20.

4.3 Sinking Funds

4-26. A loan of 10,000 is taken out on March 1, 1995, at an effective rate of interest of 8% per year. Interest is paid annually, and a sinking fund is established to repay the principal on March 1, 2002. Payments are made annually into the fund beginning on March 1, 1996, and the fund earns interest at 9% per year.
   (a)   Find the amount of each payment made to the sinking fund.
   (b)   Find the total amount the borrower must pay each year.
   (c)   From the point of view of the borrower, what rate of interest is she really paying each year?

4-27. A loan of 50,000 is taken out at 11% per year effective. Repayment is by the amortization method, with equal payments at the end of each year for the next 20 years. Immediately after the 10th payment, the borrower renegotiates with the lender, and they agree that the remainder of the loan will be repaid by the sinking fund method, where the interest rate on the loan increases to 12% per year and the sinking fund earns interest at 14% per year. Interest payments and sinking fund deposits will still be annual and continue for 10 more years. Find the sinking fund deposit, and compare the borrower's new total payment with his old one.

4-28. A loan of 1000 is to be repaid by the sinking fund method over 10 years. The rates of interest on the loan and the sinking fund are i and i', respectively. The borrower's total payment each year is 125.
   (a)   If $i = i'$, find i.
   (b)   What is the maximum possible value for i?

4-29. Kelly has borrowed 1000 on which she is paying interest at $11\frac{1}{2}\%$ effective per year. She is accumulating a sinking fund at 9% effective to repay the loan. At the end of the eighth year, the borrower makes a total payment of 149.06.
   (a)   How much of the 149.06 pays interest on the loan?
   (b)   How much of the 149.06 goes into the sinking fund?
   (c)   What is the sinking fund balance at the end of the eighth year?
   (d)   In which year will the principal be paid off?

4-30. Walter borrows 5000 for 20 years at 9% effective for the first 10 years and 11% effective for the last 10 years. He wishes to pay interest yearly and to repay the principal by annual payments into a sinking fund earning interest at rate i.

    (a)   If his total annual payment is 570 and $i = .09$, find how much he is short of repaying the loan at the end of 20 years.

    (b)   If his total annual payment is 570, find i such that the loan is exactly repaid after 20 years.

    (c)   If $i = .10$ and his total annual payment is constant, find the amount of that payment in order that the loan be exactly repaid after 20 years.

    (d)   If $i = .10$ and the sinking fund deposit is constant, find the amount of that deposit in order that the loan is completely repaid after 20 years.

4-31. Ashley borrows 3000 for 10 years at 13% effective. She pays the interest yearly, and the principal by means of two sinking funds. One-third of the principal is repaid by a sinking fund earning 16% effective, and the other two-thirds by a sinking fund earning 11% effective.

    (a)   Find Ashley's total annual payment.

    (b)   Determine the rate of interest she is really paying on her loan.

    (c)   Redo (a) if Ashley puts one-third of her total sinking fund deposit in the 16% fund and two-thirds into the 11% fund.

4.4　Yield Rates

4-32. *A* borrows 1000 from *B*, and agrees to repay it in 8 equal installments at 18% effective, with the first payment due in one year. After 3 payments, *B* sells her right to future payments to *C* at a price which yields *C* 19% effective.

    (a)   Find the price which *C* pays to *B*.

    (b)   Find the overall yield rate to *B*.

    (c)   Find the overall yield rate to *C*.

4-33. Consider the transactions described in Question 32. Assume, in addition, that after 3 more payments, C sells his right to future payments back to B at a price which yields B 20% effective on those remaining payments.
  (a) Find the price which B now pays to C.
  (b) Find the overall yield rate to C on the entire set of transactions.
  (c) Find the overall yield rate to B on the entire set of transactions.
  (d) In each of parts (b) and (c), find the real rate of interest earned if the rate of inflation is 5% per year. (See end of Section 3.6.)

4-34. Ellen is repaying Friendly Trust a 10,000 loan with 8 equal annual payments of principal, the first due one year after the loan is taken out. In addition, she pays interest at 11% effective on the outstanding principal each year. An investor wishes to purchase these payments from Friendly Trust at a price which will yield her $11\frac{1}{2}\%$ effective. Find the price.

4-35. Find the price which should be paid for an annuity of 500 per year for the next 10 years, if the yield rate is to be 11% and if the principal can be replaced by a sinking fund earning 8% per year for the next 6 years and 7% per year for the following 4 years after that.

4-36. After having made 6 annual payments of 500 each on a 3000 loan at 11% effective, with first payment one year after the loan was taken out, the borrower decides to repay the balance of the loan over the next 5 years by equal annual payments of principal in addition to the annual interest due on the unpaid balance. If the lender insists on a yield rate of 14% over the final 5-year period, find the total payment, principal plus interest, for the tenth year.

4-37. Seven years ago, Jean took out a 20-year 30,000 loan at 8% effective on which she was making annual payments, with the first payment due one year after the loan was taken out. She now wishes to make a lump-sum payment of 6000, and then pay off the loan in 5 more years. Find the revised annual payment under each of the following situations:

(a)   The lender is satisfied with earning 8% effective.

(b)   The lender is satisfied with 8% effective for the past 7 years, but insists on an 11% yield for the next 5 years.

(c)   The lender insists on an 11% yield for the entire life of the loan.

CHAPTER FIVE
BONDS

5.1 PRICE OF A BOND

When a corporation or government needs to raise money, it issues bonds and sells them to a large number of investors. A bond is a certificate in which, in return for receiving an initial sum of money from the investor, the borrower agrees to pay interest at a specified rate (the *coupon rate*) until a specified date (the *maturity date*), and, at that time, to pay a fixed sum (the *redemption value*). The coupon rate is customarily quoted as a nominal rate convertible semiannually, and is applied to the *face* (or *par*) *value*, which is stated on the front of the bond. Usually the face and redemption values are equal, but this is not always the case.

This may appear complicated at first glance, but there is, in fact, nothing fancy or new going on here. It's really a familiar story: in return for lending the borrower some money, the investor obtains regular interest payments and a final lump sum payment at the end of the term. For example, consider a bond of face amount 500, redeemable at its par value in 10 years with semiannual coupons at rate 11%, compounded semiannually. When an investor buys this bond he receives, in return, 20 half-yearly payments of $(.055)(500) = 27.50$ interest, and a lump sum payment of 500 at the end of the 10 years.

The investor's price for this bond may differ from 500. If she is able to buy it for less than 500, then we know from Section 4.4 that her yield rate (the rate of return on her investment) will be greater than 11%. If she pays more than 500, her yield rate will be less than 11%.

Let us introduce the notation to be used in this section, and also take this opportunity to review some basic terminology:

F = the face value or par value of the bond.

r = the coupon rate per interest period. Throughout this section, the rate quoted will usually be a nominal rate $2r$ convertible semi-annually. Observe that the *amount* of each semiannual interest payment (coupon) is Fr.

C = the redemption value of the bond. Often $C = F$, and the phrase "redeemable at par" describes this situation.

i = the yield rate per interest period.

n = the number of interest periods until the redemption date.

P = the purchase price of the bond to obtain yield rate i.

Our knowledge of annuities easily gives us a formula for P, in terms of the other quantities described above.

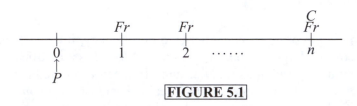

$$\boxed{\text{FIGURE 5.1}}$$

In return for paying out P at time 0, the investor receives n coupons of value Fr each and a final payment of C at time n. Hence, to obtain a yield rate i,

$$P = (Fr)a_{\overline{n}|i} + C(1+i)^{-n}. \tag{5.1}$$

The student will be asked to derive a variation of the above formula in the exercises.

$\boxed{\text{Example 5.1}}$

A bond of 500, redeemable at par after 5 years, pays interest at 13% per year convertible semiannually. Find the price to yield an investor (a) 8% effective per half-year; (b) 16% effective per year.

$\boxed{\text{Solution}}$

(a) We use Formula (5.1) with $F = C = 500$, $n = 10$, $r = .065$, $i = .08$, and obtain $P = 32.5a_{\overline{10}|.08} + 500(1.08)^{-10} = 449.67$.

(b) We use Formula (5.1) with $F = C = 500$, $n = 10$, $r = .065$ and calculate the yield rate $i = (1.16)^{1/2} - 1$. Then we have $P = 32.5a_{\overline{10}|i} + 500(1+i)^{-10} = 459.08$. $\qquad\square$

In each part of the last example, the investor is buying the bond for less than the redemption value (i.e., at a *discount*), because the yield rate is higher than the coupon rate. If the coupon rate were higher, she would have to buy the bond at a *premium*. In that case we would have $P > C$, with $P - C$ being the amount of the premium.

Example 5.2

A corporation decides to issue 15-year bonds, redeemable at par, with face amount of 1000 each. If interest payments are to be made at the rate of 10% convertible semiannually, and if George is happy with a yield of 8% convertible semiannually, what should he pay for one of these bonds?

Solution

FIGURE 5.2

For these bonds we have $F = C = 1000$, $n = 30$, $r = .05$ and $i = .04$.
Then $P = 50a_{\overline{30}|.04} + 1000(1.04)^{-30} = 1172.92$.   □

Example 5.3

A 100 par-value 15-year bond with coupon rate 9% convertible semi-annually is selling for 94. Find the yield rate.

FIGURE 5.3

Solution

We have $94 = 4.50a_{\overline{30}|} + 100v^{30}$, and our calculators give us the value $i = .04885$ effective per half-year. It is interesting to see as well how to solve this problem by successive approximation. In this case we have $P = Fra_{\overline{n}|} + Cv^n$, so $Pi = Fr(1-v^n) + Cv^n i$, and

$i(P - Cv^n) = Fr(1 - v^n)$. Therefore $i = \dfrac{Fr(1 - v^n)}{P - Cv^n}$, and this is the

form we use. We start with $i_0 = .05$ in the right hand side, and obtain

$i_1 = \dfrac{4.50(1 - v^{30})}{94 - 100\, v^{30}} = .04881$. Then using .04881 on the right hand side,

we get $i_2 = .04885$. Next we use .04885, and obtain $i_3 = .04885$, so we are done. Observe how quickly this particular example converges to an answer.   □

5.2 BOOK VALUE

In the same sense that a loan has an outstanding balance at any point in time, we can talk about the *book value* of a bond at any time t. Prospectively the definition is the same, namely that the book value is the present value of all future payments. If we assign the usual meanings to the symbols F, C, r, i and n for a bond, and if we are at a point in time where the tth coupon has just been paid, then the book value at time t is the value of the remaining payments: $n - t$ coupons and a payment of C at time n. Hence the book value is

$$B_t = (Fr)a_{\overline{n-t|}} + Cv^{n-t}. \qquad (5.6)$$

Observe that when $t = 0$ the book value is P, and when $t = n$ the book value is C. For values of t between 0 and n, the book value lies between P and C, and represents a reasonable value to assign to the bond on that date. Book values are often used by investors when preparing financial statements, and are also important in constructing bond amortization schedules, as we shall see in the next section.

| Example 5.4 |

Find the book value immediately after the payment of the 14th coupon of a 10-year 1,000 par-value bond with semiannual coupons, if $r = .05$ and the yield rate is 12% convertible semiannually.

| Solution |

FIGURE 5.4

We have $F = C = 1000$, $n = 20$, $r = .05$ and $i = .06$. At $t = 14$ there are 6 coupons left, so the book value is

$$(1000)(.05)a_{\overline{6|}} + 1000(1.06)^{-6} = 950.83.$$

Observe, as mentioned above, that this is larger than the price $P = 885.30$, but smaller than the redemption value $C = 1000$. $\qquad \square$

|Example 5.5|
Let B_t and B_{t+1} be the book values just after the tth and $(t+1)^{st}$ coupons are paid. Show that $B_{t+1} = B_t(1+i) - Fr$.
|Solution|
We know that $B_t = (Fr)a_{\overline{n-t|}} + Cv^{n-t}$. Hence

$$B_t(1+i) - Fr \quad = \quad (Fr)\left[\frac{1-v^{n-t}}{i}\right](1+i) + Cv^{n-t}(1+i) - Fr$$

$$= \quad \frac{Fr}{i} - \frac{Frv^{n-t}(1+i)}{i} + Cv^{n-t-1}$$

$$= \quad \frac{Fr}{i} - \frac{Frv^{n-t-1}}{i} + Cv^{n-t-1}$$

$$= \quad Fr\left[\frac{1-v^{n-t-1}}{i}\right] + Cv^{n-t-1}$$

$$= \quad (Fr)a_{\overline{n-t-1|}} + Cv^{n-t-1}$$

$$= \quad B_{t+1}. \qquad\qquad\qquad\qquad \square$$

We have now seen how to find the book value at the time a coupon is paid, but what do we do between coupon payment dates? The answer is that we assume simple interest at rate i per period between adjacent coupon payments, just as we did with loans in Chapter 4.

|Example 5.6|
Find the book value of the bond in Example 5.4 exactly 2 months after the 14th coupon is paid.
|Solution|
We know from Example 5.4 that the book value at $t = 14$ is 950.83. Hence the answer is $950.83\left[1 + \left(\frac{2}{6}\right)(.06)\right] = 969.85$. $\qquad\qquad \square$

Observe that if we extend Example 5.6 to 6 months after the 14th coupon, we would obtain a book value of $950.83(1 + i)$. This is, in fact, the book value *just before* the next coupon is paid. After the coupon is paid, however, the value goes down by the amount of the coupon, and becomes $950.83(1+i) - Fr$. This agrees with our result in Example 5.5. The book value calculated in this way is called the *flat price* of a bond.

If instead of allowing the book value to increase from 950.83 to 950.83$(1 + i)$, and then to drop sharply as the coupon is paid, we simply interpolate linearly between successive coupon date book values, we obtain what is called the *market price* (or sometimes the *amortized value*) of the bond. This procedure has the advantage of giving us a smooth progression of book values from $P = B_0$ to $C = B_n$.

In practice, the bond (flat) price is usually quoted as the market price plus accrued interest. However, it is also common bookkeeping procedure for the book value of a bond to be considered equal to the market price. If the latter procedure is used, then any accrued interest in the financial statements must be handled separately.

|| Example 5.7 ||

Find the market price of the bond in Example 5.4 exactly two months after the 14th coupon is paid.

| Solution |

We know that the book value at $t = 14$ is 950.83, and the book value at $t = 15$ equals $950.83(1.06) - 50 = 957.88$. We interpolate between these values to obtain $950.83 + \frac{2}{6}(957.88 - 950.83) = 953.18$.   □

Observe that the answer to Example 5.7 is less than the answer to Example 5.6, demonstrating that the market price is less than the flat price.

5.3 BOND AMORTIZATION SCHEDULES

We saw in the last section how to find the book value of a bond at any point in time, and we also saw that this corresponds to the outstanding balance of a loan. In the same way that amortization schedules were constructed for loans in Section 4.2, we can now construct bond amortization schedules in which the final column gives the book value of the bond. Furthermore, the bond amortization schedule will show us how the book value changes over time from P to C, just as a loan amortization schedule shows us how the outstanding principal decreases to 0 over time.

The basic idea is familiar. The book value is B_t at time t, and the amount of the coupon at time $t + 1$ is Fr. Since the investor is earning a yield rate of i, the amount of interest contained in this coupon is $B_t i$. The difference, $Fr - B_t i$, is therefore the change in the book value of the bond between these dates. This gives us row $t+1$ of the bond amortization schedule, and we continue on. Before presenting a full table, let us give an example.

Example 5.8

Find the amount of interest and change in book value contained in the 15th coupon of the bond discussed in Example 5.4.

Solution

The book value at $t=14$ was seen to be 950.83, so the amount of interest in the 15th coupon is $(950.83)(.06)=57.05$. Horrors! The amount of interest is *greater* than the amount (50) of the coupon itself! However, this is no problem; it just means that the book value is increasing instead of decreasing, and to get the new book value we add 7.05 to obtain $B_{15}=957.88$, as we saw Example 5.7. If the amount of interest were less than the coupon, that would tell us that $P>C$ and the book value was decreasing. In particular, the excess of the coupon over the amount of interest would be the size of decrease in the book value. $\square$

We will now proceed to construct a complete amortization schedule. As was true in the case of loans, this can be constructed from time 0 without knowledge of intermediate book values. However, if only part of a schedule is required, the method to be followed should be that of Example 5.8.

Example 5.9

Construct a bond amortization schedule for a 1000 par value two-year bond which pays interest at 8% convertible semiannually, and has a yield rate of 6% convertible semiannually.

Solution

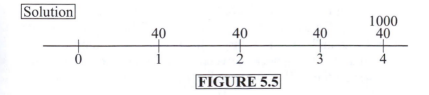

FIGURE 5.5

We have $F = C = 1000$, $n = 4$, $r = .04$ and $i = .03$. Hence the price is $P = 1000(.04)a_{\overline{4}|} + 1000(1.03)^{-4} = 1037.17$. This means that over the two-year period the book value of this bond will decrease from 1037.17 to 1000.00.

At $t = 0$, the book value is 1037.17. When $t = 1$ (measured in half-years), the first coupon of $(1000)(.04) = 40$ is paid. From the investor's point of view, the amount of interest in this coupon is $(1037.17)(.03) = 31.12$. Hence the amount of principal adjustment (change in book value) is $40 - 31.12 = 8.88$. Noting that book values are decreasing, the new book value will be $1037.17 - 8.88 = 1028.29$.

The first two columns of the bond amortization schedule are as follows:

TABLE 5.1

Time	Coupon	Interest	Principal Adjustment	Book Value
0				1037.17
1	40	31.12	8.88	1028.29

This procedure is now continued, using the new book value to construct the $t = 2$ row. The complete schedule is shown in Table 5.2; the student should verify the entries in this table.

TABLE 5.2

Time	Coupon	Interest	Principal Adjustment	Book Value
0				1037.17
1	40	31.12	8.88	1028.29
2	40	30.85	9.15	1019.14
3	40	30.57	9.43	1009.71
4	40	30.29	9.71	1000.00

Observe how nicely this tells us what happens to the value of the bond as time goes on.   □

If the bond in Example 5.9 were bought at a discount instead of at a premium, exactly the same procedure would be followed, except that the entries in Column 3 would be larger than those in Column 2. This would tell us that the differences between the columns should be added to Column 5, so that the book values would increase as time goes on.

5.4 OTHER TOPICS

In this section we will deal with a number of different problems related
to bonds.

Example 5.10

Find the price of a 1000 par-value 10-year bond which has quarterly 2%
coupons and is bought to yield 9% per year convertible semiannually.

Solution

FIGURE 5.6

In this problem, the coupon period and yield rate conversion period do
not coincide, so we must first find the equivalent quarterly yield rate i.
We have $1 + i = (1.045)^{1/2}$. Now we proceed with $F = C = 1000$,
$r = .02$, $i = (1.045)^{1/2} - 1$, $n = 40$, and obtain

$$P = 20a_{\overline{40}|} + 1000 \left[\frac{1}{(1.045)^{1/2}} \right]^{40} = 940.75. \qquad \square$$

Example 5.11

Find the price of a 1000 par-value 10-year bond which has semiannual
coupons of 10 the first half-year, 20 the second half-year, ..., 200 the
last half-year, bought to yield 9% effective per year.
Solution

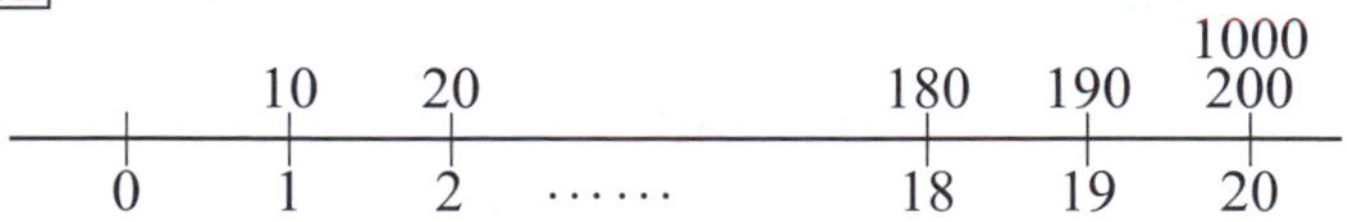

$$
\begin{array}{ccccccc}
 & 10 & 20 & & 180 & 190 & \overset{\displaystyle 1000}{\overset{\displaystyle 200}{|}} \\
\hline
0 & 1 & 2 & \cdots\cdots & 18 & 19 & 20
\end{array}
$$

FIGURE 5.7

The yield rate i, effective per half-year, is given by $1 + i = (1.09)^{1/2}$.
The price is then given by

$$P = 10(Ia)_{\overline{20}|} + 1000\,(1+i)^{-20} = 10 \left[\frac{\ddot{a}_{\overline{20}|} - 20v^{20}}{i} \right] + 1000v^{20}$$

$$= 1614.14. \qquad \square$$

Example 5.12

Find the price of a 1000 par-value 10-year bond with coupons at 11% convertible semiannually, and for which the yield rate is 5% per half-year for the first 5 years and 6% per half-year for the last 5 years.

Solution

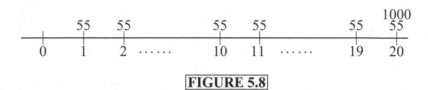

FIGURE 5.8

For the first 10 coupons, we have a value at time 0 of $55a_{\overline{10}|.05} = 424.70$. The value of the last 10 coupons at $t = 0$ is $(55a_{\overline{10}|.06})(1.05)^{-10} = 248.51$. The present value of the redemption amount at $t = 0$ is given by $1000(1.05)^{-10}(1.06)^{-10} = 342.81$. The price equals the sum of these three present values, which is $424.70 + 248.51 + 342.81 = 1016.02$. $\square$

Let us now consider a type of bond which differs somewhat from those studied so far.

A *callable bond* is one for which the borrower has the right to redeem the bond at any of several time points, the earliest possible date being named the *call date* and the latest possible date being the usual date of maturity of the bond. Once the bond is redeemed, no more coupons will be paid.

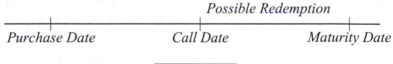

FIGURE 5.9

Calculating prices and yield rates gets tricky here because of the uncertainty concerning the date of redemption. Complicating the matter is the fact that sometimes the redemption values will differ, depending on the date chosen. Two examples should help clarify the situation.

Example 5.13

Consider a 1000 par-value 10-year bond with semiannual 5% coupons. Assume this bond can be redeemed at par at any of the last 4 coupon dates. Find the price which will guarantee an investor a yield rate of (a) 6% per half-year; (b) 4% per half-year.

Solution

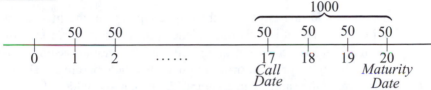

FIGURE 5.10

(a)   Since the yield rate is greater than the coupon rate, the investor will be buying this bond at a discount. If the redemption date were known to be the *last* coupon date, the investor's price would be equal to $50a_{\overline{20}|} + 1000(1.06)^{-20} = 885.30$. If the redemption date is any earlier, he should pay more, but, since the redemption date is uncertain at the time of purchase, if he pays 885.30, he will be guaranteed of earning at least 6%.

(b)   Here the yield rate is less than the coupon rate, so the price will be greater than 1000. If the redemption date were known to be 4 coupon dates earlier than the maturity date, the price would be $50a_{\overline{17}|} + 1000(1.04)^{-17} = 1121.66$. If the redemption date is any later, then he should pay more, so this price will guarantee him a return of at least 4%.   □

Example 5.14

Consider a 1000 par-value 10-year bond with 5% semiannual coupons. This bond can be redeemed for 1100 at the time of the 18th coupon, for 1050 at the time of the 19th coupon, or for 1000 at the time of the 20th coupon. What price should an investor pay to be guaranteed a yield rate of (a) 6% per half-year? (b) 4% per half-year?

$$\text{FIGURE 5.11}$$

(a)   Since the yield rate is greater than the coupon rate, the investor is buying this bond at a discount. Hence the worst scenario for him is if the bond is redeemed at $t = 20$, and he should assume this case in fixing his price in order to guarantee the 6% return. Hence the answer is the same as in Example 5.13(a), namely 885.30.

(b)   Here we have a trickier situation. In Example 5.13, assuming an earliest possible redemption date gave the answer, but the different possible values for C cause trouble in this example. All we can do here is work out the three cases separately, and pick the lowest of the prices. If redemption occurs at $t = 18$, the price should be $50a_{\overline{18}|} + 1100(1.04)^{-18} = 1175.96.$ If redemption occurs at $t = 19$, the price should be $50a_{\overline{19}|} + 1050(1.04)^{-19} = 1155.07.$ If redemption occurs at $t = 20$, the maturity date, then the price should be $50a_{\overline{20}|} + 1000(1.04)^{-20} = 1135.90.$ Hence he should pay 1135.90 to be sure of earning 4%. Then, if redemption occurs earlier, his yield will turn out to be larger.   □

In Example 2.4 of Section 2.1, we saw how to find a point in time where a single payment was equivalent to a series of payments made at different times. We remarked that there is an approximate method, called the method of equated time, also available for such problems.

These approaches work just as well for bonds as they did in the earlier examples. In addition, two other concepts are introduced here with particular application to bonds. As with the Chapter 2 concepts, they are generally used to provide indices of the average length of an investment.

Let $R_1, R_2, \ldots, R_n$ be a series of payments made at times $t_1, t_2, \ldots, t_n$. The *duration* of the investment, denoted $\overline{d}$, is defined by

$$\overline{d} = \frac{\displaystyle\sum_{j=1}^{n} t_j \, v^{t_j} R_j}{\displaystyle\sum_{j=1}^{n} v^{t_j} R_j}, \tag{5.7}$$

and the *modified duration*, denoted $\bar{v}$, is defined by

$$\bar{v} = \frac{\bar{d}}{1+i}. \tag{5.8}$$

The term *volatility* is sometimes used for modified duration

| Example 5.15 |

Find $\bar{d}$ and $\bar{v}$ for the bond of Example 5.10.

| Solution |

$$\bar{d} = \frac{\sum_{j=1}^{40} j v^j (20) + 40 v^{40}(1000)}{\sum_{j=1}^{40} v^j (20) + v^{40}(1000)}$$

$$= \frac{(Ia)_{\overline{40|}} + 2000 v^{40}}{a_{\overline{40|}} + 50 v^{40}}$$

$$= 27.48,$$

by evaluating at effective rate $i = (1.045)^{1/2} - 1$ per quarter. Then

$$\bar{v} = \frac{\bar{d}}{1+i} = 26.88.$$

Note in this example that times are given in quarters of a year. □

EXERCISES

5.1 Price of a Bond

5-1. A 10-year 1000 face value bond, redeemable at par, earns interest at 9% convertible semiannually. Find the price to yield an investor 8% convertible semiannually.

5-2. A 1000 par value bond, with $r = .055$, has coupons payable on January 1 and July 1, and will be redeemed July 1, 2001. The bond is bought January 1, 1999, to yield 12% convertible semiannually. Find the price.

5-3. Derive the alternate price formula

$$P = C + (Fr - Ci)a_{\overline{n}|}. \tag{5.2}$$

5-4. One bond of face value 100 with semiannual coupons and $r = .025$ costs 75.74. A similar bond with semiannual coupons and $r = .04$ costs 112.13. Both are redeemable at par in n years and have the same yield rate i.
   (a)   Find i
   (b)   Find n.

5-5. Two 1000 face value bonds, redeemable at par at the end of the same period, are bought to yield 12% convertible semiannually. One bond costs 879.58 and pays coupons at 10% per year convertible semiannually. The other bond pays coupons at 7% per half-year. Find the price of the second bond.

5-6. Two 10-year 100 face value bonds, each redeemable at par, have 8% and 10% semiannual coupons and are priced at A_1 and A_2, respectively, to give the same yield. Prove that the price of a 10-year 100 face value bond, with a redemption value of 110 and 9% semiannual coupons, is, at the same yield rate, equal to $A_1 + .10A_2$.

5-7. For a bond of face value 1, $r = \frac{3}{2}i$ and the price is $1 + p$. Find the price of a similar bond with the same number of coupons and the same yield rate, but for which $r = \frac{3}{4}i$. Assume both bonds are redeemable at par.

5-8. A 100 par-value 10-year bond with semiannual coupons and $r = .035$ is selling for 103 . Find the yield rate.

5-9.   A 100 par-value bond with semiannual coupons is redeemable at the end of 4 years. At a purchase price of 105.91, the yield rate per half-year is exactly 1% less than the coupon rate per half-year. Find the yield rate.

5-10.   A corporation issues par-value bonds with annual 6% coupons maturing in 5 years, and sells them at a price yielding 4% effective. It is proposed to replace them with 5% bonds having annual coupons. How long must the new bonds run so that investors will still realize a yield which is at least 4%?

5-11.   A 6% 100 face value bond with annual coupons, redeemable at the end of n years at 105, sells at 93.04 to yield $7\frac{1}{2}\%$ effective per year. Find the price of a 5% 100 face value bond with annual coupons, redeemable at the end of $2n$ years at 104, to yield $7\frac{1}{2}\%$ effective per year.

5-12.   In addition to the notation already introduced in this section, let
$$k = \frac{P-C}{C} \text{ and } g = \frac{Fr}{C}.$$

(a)   Derive Makeham's Formula, which is
$$P = Cv^n + \frac{g}{i}\left(C - Cv^n\right). \tag{5.3}$$

(b)   Show that $i = g - \dfrac{k}{a_{\overline{n}|}}$.

(c)   Show that $\dfrac{1}{a_{\overline{n}|}} = \dfrac{1}{n}\left[1 + \dfrac{n+1}{2}i + \dfrac{n^2-1}{12}i^2 + \cdots\right]$.

(d)   Using the first two terms of part (c), derive the approximation $i \approx g - \dfrac{k}{n}\left[1 + \dfrac{n+1}{2}i\right]$.

(e)   Conclude from (d) that
$$i \approx \frac{g - \frac{k}{n}}{1 + \left(\frac{n+1}{2n}\right)k}. \tag{5.4}$$

(f)   Approximating $\dfrac{n+1}{2n}$ by $\dfrac{1}{2}$ in (e), obtain the *bond salesman's* approximation
$$i \approx \frac{g - \frac{k}{n}}{1 + \frac{1}{2}\cdot k}. \tag{5.5}$$

(g)   Apply Formula (5.5) to find the yield rate in Question 8.

5.2   Book Value

5-13. For the bond in Question 1, find the book value at each of the
following times:
(a)   Just after the 7th coupon has been paid.
(b)   4 months after the 7th coupon has been paid.
(c)   Just before the 8th coupon has been paid.

5-14. For the bond in Question 2, find the book and market values on
each of the following dates:
(a)   June 30, 1999 (11:59 p.m.).
(b)   July 1, 2000 (12:01 a.m.).
(c)   March 1, 2001.
(d)   June 23, 2001.

5-15. Give a verbal argument for the result shown in Example 5.5.

5.3   Bond Amortization Schedules

5-16. Construct a bond amortization schedule for a 3-year bond of 1000
face amount, redeemable at par with semiannual coupons, if
$r = .035$ and $i = .025$.

5-17. Do Question 16 if $r = .035$ and $i = .04$.

5-18. Construct the $t = 8$ and $t = 17$ rows of the amortization schedule
for the bond given in Question 1.

5-19. Write a computer program which will construct bond amortization
schedules.   Test your program on Question 16.   If it works,
construct the entire bond amortization schedule for Question 1.

5-20. A 5000 par-value bond with semiannual coupons and $r = .03$ has a
yield rate of 5%, convertible semiannually. Find the book value of
this bond one year before the redemption date.

5-21. A 10-year bond of 1000 face amount with semiannual coupons, redeemable at par, is bought at a discount to yield 12% convertible semiannually. If the book value six months before the redemption date is 985.85, find the total amount of discount in the original purchase price.

5-22. A 1000 par-value 10-year bond with semiannual coupons at 8% convertible semiannually is bought to yield 9% convertible semiannually. Find the total of the interest column in the bond amortization schedule.

5-23. A 10,000 par-value 20-year bond with semiannual coupons is bought at a premium to yield 12% convertible semiannually. If the amount of principle adjustment in the 18th coupon is 36, find the amount of principle adjustment in the 29th coupon.

5.4   Other Topics

5-24. Find the price of a 1000 par-value 10-year bond with coupons at 10% convertible semiannually if the buyer wishes a yield rate of (a) 12% per year; (b) 1% per month.

5-25. (a)   Find the duration and modified duration for the bond in Question 5.24(a).

(b)   Using the same notation as in the text, the *method of equated time* gives a single-time value of

$$\bar{t} = \frac{\sum\limits_{j=1}^{n} t_j R_j}{\sum\limits_{j=1}^{n} R_j}. \tag{5.9}$$

Find $\bar{t}$ for the bond in Question 5.24(a).

5-26. A 1000 par-value 10-year bond has semiannual coupons of 6% for the first 5 years and 7% for the last 5 years. Find the price an investor should pay if she wishes to earn (a) 7% per half-year; (b) 14% per year.

5-27. A 10-year par-value bond of 1000 face amount has annual coupons which start at 200 and decrease by 20 each year to a final coupon of 20.
   (a)   Find the price to yield 12% per year.
   (b)   Find the yield rate if the bond is purchased at its face value.

5-28. A 1000 par-value 15-year bond has semiannual coupons of 60 each. This bond is callable at any of the last 10 coupon dates. Find the price an investor should pay to guarantee a semiannual yield rate of (a) 7%; (b) 5%; (c) 6%.

5-29. In Example 5.13(a), we saw that an investor should pay 885.30 to guarantee himself a return of 6% on the bond described. What yield rate would the investor actually earn if this bond were redeemed at $t = 18$ instead of at the last possible date?

5-30. Consider a 100 par-value 15-year bond with semiannual 2% coupons. Assume that this bond is callable at 109 at any coupon date from $t = 10$ to $t = 20$ inclusive, at 104.50 from $t = 21$ to $t = 29$ inclusive, and at 100 at the time of the final coupon. What price should the investor pay to guarantee himself a yield of
   (a) $2\frac{1}{2}\%$ semiannually? (b) $1\frac{1}{2}\%$ semiannually?

5-31. Ten 1000 par-value bonds with semiannual coupons of 50 are issued on January 1, 1992. One bond is redeemed on January 1, 2003, another on January 1, 2004, and so on until the last one is redeemed on January 1, 2012. What price should an investor pay for all ten bonds on January 1, 1992, in order to earn 11% convertible semiannually? [Bonds like these are called *serial bonds*. The student will find that Formula (5.3), Makeham's Formula given in Question 5-12, is more convenient than Formula (5.1) for finding the price of a serial bond.]

5-32. A preferred stock can be thought of as a bond in which the coupons (dividends) continue forever and for which there is no redemption date.

    (a)   Find the price of a preferred stock which pays semiannual dividends of 3, if the purchaser wishes to earn 12% per year convertible semiannually.

    (b)   State a general formula for the price of a preferred stock paying a yearly dividend of X, if the desired yield rate is i per year.

    (c)   State a general formula for the price of a preferred stock paying a quarterly dividend of X, if the desired yield rate is i per year.

5-33. Common stock differs from preferred stock in that the amount of the dividend paid is not constant. In theory, however, the price of a common stock should be equal to the present value of all future dividends, and one would try to settle on a price by estimating what these dividends are likely to be. In practice, however, prices vary widely in the market because of the influence of investors buying and selling various stocks, and we have not taken any of this into account. However, let us try one problem in this area.

Deepwater Oil Inc. has a policy of paying out 25% of its earnings as quarterly dividends. It is estimated that Deepwater will earn 2 per share during the next quarter, and that earnings will increase at a rate of 2% per quarter thereafter. Find the theoretical price an investor should pay to earn (a) 10% per year convertible quarterly; (b) 6% per year convertible quarterly.

5-34. Let $f(i) = \sum\limits_{j=1}^{n} v^{t_j} R_j$ denote the denominator of Equation (5.7).

    (a)   Show that $\bar{v} = -\dfrac{f'(i)}{f(i)}$.

    (b)   Another concept sometimes encountered is the *convexity*, defined by $\bar{c} = \dfrac{f''(i)}{f(i)}$. Show that the derivative of $\bar{v}$ with respect to i is equal to $\bar{v}^2 - \bar{c}$.

CHAPTER SIX
PREPARATION FOR LIFE CONTINGENCIES

6.1 INTRODUCTION

Mary takes out a loan of 5000 from Friendly Trust and agrees to pay it back by the amortization method. Unfortunately, Mary runs short of cash and is not able to make all her payments.

The All-Mighty Bank lends a large sum of money to a small Central American country. Due to an extremely high rate of inflation, the country defaults on its loan.

The above situations are common in real life, and any financial institution has to take them into account when lending money. However, these possibilities were ignored in the first five chapters of this book; we always assumed that all payments were made. It is the uncertainty of events in the real world which forces interest rates on most loans to be higher than the prime rate, and also forces rates on loans to high-risk borrowers to be higher than those on loans to others. We are continually reading in the news how a certain country has an AAA credit rating, whereas another country might have an AA, A or a B rating. Lower ratings indicate a higher risk and, consequently, a higher rate of interest will have to be paid.

The mathematical discipline which deals with uncertainty is probability and statistics. In this and subsequent chapters, we will see how elementary probability theory can be combined with the theory of interest to produce the important area of mathematics called *life contingencies*. In Section 6.2 we lay the foundation for later work and then indicate, in Section 6.3, the basic approach to solving life contingencies problems.

6.2 PROBABILITY AND EXPECTATION

Let us briefly highlight some of the basic concepts of probability which will be needed in the rest of the book. (A reader with no previous experience with probability theory may need to consult a standard text on the subject, since this section is intended primarily as a review.)

Assume that a certain event X can happen in a different ways and fail to happen in b different ways, all of which are equally likely. The *probability* that X occurs is defined by

$$Pr(X) = \frac{a}{a+b}. \tag{6.1}$$

Formula (6.1) says that the probability equals the number of ways in which X can occur, divided by the total number of possibilities. We stress that, in order for this formula to be valid, all the possibilities have to be equally likely. Later examples will show how crucial this requirement is.

The probability that X does *not* occur is equal to

$$Pr(\overline{X}) = 1 - \frac{a}{a+b} = \frac{b}{a+b}. \tag{6.2}$$

In general, if X is any event, we will always have $0 \leq Pr(X) \leq 1$, and $Pr(\overline{X}) = 1 - Pr(X)$. If $Pr(X) = 0$, then X never occurs, whereas if $Pr(X) = 1$, then X is certain to occur. We now give several examples.

| Example 6.1 |
Find the probability that one card drawn from a deck of 52 is a Jack.
| Solution |
Since there are 52 cards, 4 of which are Jacks, the answer is $\frac{4}{52} = \frac{1}{13}$. □

| Example 6.2 |
Find the probability that two cards drawn from a deck are both Jacks.
| Solution One |
Imagine drawing the cards one at a time. The probability that the first card is a Jack is $\frac{1}{13}$. After that, there are 51 cards left of which 3 are Jacks. Hence the probability that the second card is a Jack is $\frac{3}{51} = \frac{1}{17}$. The answer is $\frac{1}{13} \times \frac{1}{17} = \frac{1}{221}$, where we multiply the separate probabilities to obtain the probability of both events occurring.

Solution Two

There are $\binom{52}{2}$ ways of choosing 2 cards, and there are $\binom{4}{2}$ ways of choosing 2 Jacks out of the 4 in the deck. Hence the answer is given by

$$\frac{\binom{4}{2}}{\binom{52}{2}} = \frac{4 \cdot 3}{52 \cdot 51} = \frac{1}{221}, \text{ where } \binom{n}{r} = \frac{n!}{r!(n-r)!} \text{ is the number of ways}$$

of choosing r items out of n. $\square$

Example 6.3

A fair die is thrown. Find the probability of getting a 5.

Solution

There are six possible outcomes, so clearly the answer is $\frac{1}{6}$. $\square$

Example 6.4

A fair die is thrown twice. Find the probability that the total of the numbers obtained is 9.

Solution

This is more interesting. The beginner might be tempted to think that the answer is $\frac{1}{11}$, since there are 11 possible totals. However this is false because the different totals are not all equally likely. Instead we should concentrate on the 36 different possible pairs of numbers we could obtain from the two throws. Of these, 4 pairs add up to 9 ($3 + 6$, $4 + 5$, $5 + 4$, $6 + 3$). Hence the answer is $\frac{4}{36} = \frac{1}{9}$. $\square$

Example 6.5

A fair die is thrown twice. Find the probability that the total of the numbers obtained is 4 or larger.

Solution

We could just list all the possibilities, but there is an easier approach. Observe that the probability that the total equals 2 is $\frac{1}{36}$, and the probability that the total equals 3 is $\frac{2}{36}$ ($1 + 2$ or $2 + 1$). Hence the probability that the total equals 2 or 3 is $\frac{1}{36} + \frac{2}{36} = \frac{1}{12}$, and the probability that the total is 4 or more is equal to $1 - \frac{1}{12} = \frac{11}{12}$. $\square$

Example 6.6

A bag contains 4 white, 5 black and 3 green balls. Determine the probability of each of the following:
(a)   Drawing a green ball
(b)   Drawing a white or a black ball.
(c)   Drawing two white balls (no replacement).
(d)   Drawing two white balls (with replacement).
(e)   Drawing a green ball followed by a black ball (no replacement).
(f)   Drawing a green ball, then a black ball (with replacement).

Solution

(a)   The answer is $\frac{3}{12} = \frac{1}{4}$.

(b)   The answer is $\frac{9}{12} = \frac{3}{4}$.

(c)   The probability that the first ball is white is $\frac{4}{12} = \frac{1}{3}$. Since there is no replacement, the second ball has probability $\frac{3}{11}$ of being white. Hence, the answer is $\frac{1}{3} \times \frac{3}{11} = \frac{1}{11}$.

(d)   The answer is $\frac{1}{3} \times \frac{1}{3} = \frac{1}{9}$.

(e)   We obtain $\frac{3}{12} \times \frac{5}{11} = \frac{5}{44}$.

(f)   The answer is $\frac{1}{4} \times \frac{5}{12} = \frac{5}{48}$.   □

Example 6.7

A life insurance company determines that the probability of surviving for ten years is 0.9, 0.8, 0.6 and 0.4 for persons aged 40, 50, 60 and 70, respectively. Determine each of the following:
(a)   The probability of dying in the next ten years for each group.
(b)   The probability that a 40-year-old lives to age 80.
(c)   The probability that a 50-year-old dies between ages 70 and 80.

Solution

(a)   We use $Pr(\bar{X}) = 1 - Pr(X)$ to obtain the following results:
      Pr(40-year-old dies in next 10 years) $= 1 - 0.9 = 0.1$.
      Pr(50-year-old dies in next 10 years) $= 1 - 0.8 = 0.2$.
      Pr(60-year-old dies in next 10 years) $= 1 - 0.6 = 0.4$.
      Pr(70-year-old dies in next 10 years) $= 1 - 0.4 = 0.6$.

(b)   In order for a 40-year-old to reach age 80, he must live through each of the intervals. Hence the required probability is $(0.9)(0.8)(0.6)(0.4) = 0.1728$.

(c)   In order that a 50-year-old dies between age 70 and 80, she must first live to 70 and then die between 70 and 80. The answer is $(0.8)(0.6)(1 - 0.4) = 0.288$. □

Another topic that we need to explore at this time is *mathematical expectation* or *expected value*. If a particular game or experiment has the several possible outcomes $x_1, x_2, \ldots$, and the corresponding probability for each of these outcomes is $f(x_1), f(x_2), \ldots$, then we define the expected value to be

$$E = x_1 f(x_1) + x_2 f(x_2) + x_3 f(x_3) + \cdots . \tag{6.3}$$

That is, the expected value is the sum of terms $x_i f(x_i)$, where x_i is one possible outcome and $f(x_i)$ is its probability. In all of our examples, there will be only finitely many possible outcomes, so the expected value is equal to $\sum_{i=1}^{n} x_i f(x_i)$. Expected value should be thought of as the *average value* to be obtained in a particular game or experiment.

Example 6.8

If you throw a single die, what is the expected value of the number of dots which appears on the die's upward face?

Solution

There are six possible values which could appear, and each has probability $\frac{1}{6}$. Making use of Formula (6.3) we find the answer to be $(1)(\frac{1}{6}) + (2)(\frac{1}{6}) + (3)(\frac{1}{6}) + (4)(\frac{1}{6}) + (5)(\frac{1}{6}) + (6)(\frac{1}{6}) = 3\frac{1}{2}$. Note that this is just an average value; we shouldn't be bothered by the fact that $3\frac{1}{2}$ dots cannot actually appear in one throw! □

Example 6.9

Henry enters a betting game involving a fair coin. If he can get 4 tails in a row, he wins 15 dollars. Otherwise, he loses 1 dollar. What is his expected value?

Solution

The probability of getting 4 tails in a row is $\left(\frac{1}{2}\right)^4 = \frac{1}{16}$, so the probability of losing is $1 - \frac{1}{16} = \frac{15}{16}$. Thus we have an expected value of $15(\frac{1}{16}) + (-1)(\frac{15}{16}) = 0$. Therefore, in the long run, Henry should expect to neither win nor lose. □

Example 6.10

Consider the data in Example 6.7. Assume, in addition, that the probability that a person aged 80 will survive ten years is 0. As a rough estimate, we will also assume that all deaths occur exactly halfway between the endpoints of an interval (i.e., at age 45, 55, 65, 75 or 85). What is the expected life span of a 40-year-old?

Solution

We have the following for a 40-year-old:

$$Pr(\text{dying at age } 45) = 0.1$$
$$Pr(\text{dying at age } 55) = (0.9)(0.2) = 0.18$$
$$Pr(\text{dying at age } 65) = (0.9)(0.8)(0.4) = 0.288$$
$$Pr(\text{dying at age } 75) = (0.9)(0.8)(0.6)(0.6) = 0.2592$$
$$Pr(\text{dying at age } 85) = (0.9)(0.8)(0.6)(0.4) = 0.1728$$

Then the expected value, using Formula (6.3), is
$$45(0.1) + 55(0.18) + 65(0.288) + 75(0.2592) + 85(0.1728) = 67.248.$$
□

Example 6.11

In a certain lottery, 5 million 1-dollar tickets are sold each week. The following prizes are awarded:

5 prizes of 100,000 each
20 prizes of 25,000 each
45 prizes of 5,000 each
100 prizes of 1,000 each
1950 prizes of 100 each
24,500 prizes of 10 each

Find the expected value of a single ticket.

Solution

Since 5 million tickets are sold, the probability of winning 100,000 is $\frac{5}{5,000,000} = \frac{1}{1,000,000}$. Similarly, the probabilities of winning the other prizes are easily calculated. Hence the expected value is

$$100,000\left(\frac{5}{5,000,000}\right) + 25,000\left(\frac{20}{5,000,000}\right) + 5000\left(\frac{45}{5,000,000}\right)$$
$$+ 1000\left(\frac{100}{5,000,000}\right) + 100\left(\frac{1950}{5,000,000}\right) + 10\left(\frac{24,500}{5,000,000}\right) = .353.$$

This means that the expected return on a 1 dollar ticket is 35 cents. □

Example 6.12

Take the data from Example 6.11 and assume, in addition, that 1,250,000 prizes of 1 free ticket on the next draw are awarded. Find the expected value in this case.

Solution

This means that, on any draw, 1,250,000 tickets have the same expectation as the ticket you purchase. So, if E is the expectation, we obtain

$$E = (\text{previous expectation}) + E\left(\frac{1,250,000}{5,000,000}\right). \quad \text{Then } E = .353 + .25E,$$

so that $.75E = .353$, and $E = .471$. The expected return is now 47 cents.

□

6.3 CONTINGENT PAYMENTS

Henry borrows 1000 from Amicable Trust and agrees to repay the loan in one year. If repayment were certain, the trust company would charge 13% interest. From prior experience, however, it is determined that there is a 5% chance that Henry will not repay any money at all. What should Amicable Trust ask Henry to repay?

This situation is a good example of a contingent payment. To solve the problem, the finance company first determines their expected value to be $(.95)X + (.05)(0)$, where X is the amount to be repaid. This is just a very special case of the type of calculation done in the last section, since there is a .95 chance that X will be repaid and a .05 chance that the company will receive nothing.

The present value of this expected value at the time of the loan is $.95X(1.13)^{-1}$, so we have $.95(X)(1.13)^{-1} = 1000$, from which we find $X = 1000(1.13)(.95)^{-1} = 1189.47$. We observe that the rate of interest the trust company charges Henry is 18.947%, considerably higher than the 13% originally given. This does not mean, however, that Amicable Trust is making a fortune; if they were to lend money to 100 people of whom only 95 actually repay, then the company would make 13% on its investments.

Let us look at some more examples.

Example 6.13

The All-Mighty Bank lends 50,000,000 to a small Central American country, with the loan to be repaid in one year. It is felt that there is a 20% chance that a revolution will occur and that no money will be repaid, a 30% chance that due to soaring inflation only half the loan will be repaid, and a 50% chance that the entire loan will be repaid.   If repayment were certain, the bank would charge 9%.   What rate of interest should the bank charge?

Solution

Let X be the amount to be repaid. Then the expected value is

$(.5)X + (.3)(\frac{1}{2}X) + (.2)(0) = .65X,$ and $.65X(1.09)^{-1} = 50,000,000,$

which gives $X = 83,846,153.85$. The rate of interest charged is therefore $\frac{33,846,153.85}{50,000,000} = .677$, so the country must pay 67.7% on its loan! $\square$

Example 6.14

Mrs. Rogers receives 1000 at the end of each year as long as she is alive. The probability is 80% she will survive one year, 50% she will survive 2 years, 30% she will survive 3 years, and negligible that she will survive longer than 3 years. If the yield rate is 15%, what value should Mrs. Rogers place on these payments now?

Solution

We solve this by finding the expected value of Mrs. Rogers' payments for each year, and then bring them back to the present. The answer is

$1000(.8)(1.15)^{-1} + 1000(.5)(1.15)^{-2} + 1000(.3)(1.15)^{-3} = 1,270.98.$ $\square$

Example 6.15

An insurance company issues a policy which pays 50,000 at the end of the year of death, if death should occur during the next two years. The probability that a 25-year-old will live for one year is .99936, and the probability he will live for two years is .99858. What should the company charge such a policyholder to earn 11% on its investment?

Solution

We have to be a little more careful here. The probability that death will occur in the first year is .00064, so the expected value of that payment is (.00064)(50,000). To find the expected value of the second payment, we must calculate the probability that death occurs during the second year. The probability that death occurs within the first two years is .00142. Hence the probability we want is $.00142 - .00064 = .00078$, and the expected value is (.00078)(50,000). Thus the company should charge

$(.00064)(50,000)(1.11)^{-1} + (.00078)(50,000)(1.11)^{-2} = 60.48.$ $\square$

Example 6.16

Alphonse wishes to borrow some money from Friendly Trust. He promises to repay 500 at the end of each year for the next 10 years, but there is a 5% chance of default in any year. Assume that once default occurs, no further payments will be received. How much can Friendly Trust lend Alphonse if it wishes to earn 9% on its investment?

Solution

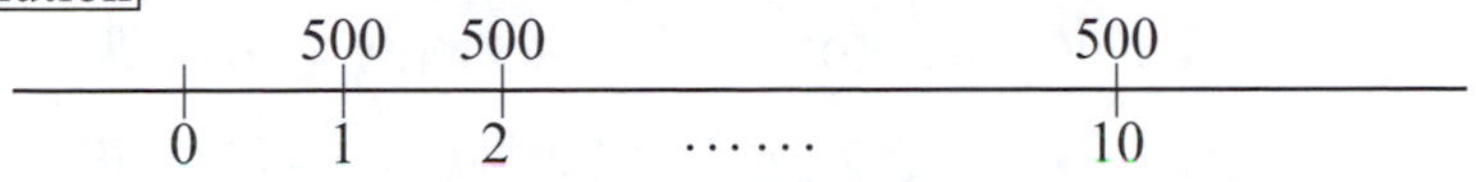

	500	500		500
0	1	2	......	10

FIGURE 6.1

Note that unlike examples given in earlier chapters, here the payments of 500 each are not all guaranteed. We must find the expected value of each payment and then discount these values to the point where the loan is taken out. The fact that there is a 5% chance of default in any year means that there is a 95% probability of receiving the first payment, 90.25% $\left(\text{i.e., } (.95)^2\right)$ of receiving the second payment, and so on. Hence the answer is given by

$$500(.95)(1.09)^{-1} + 500(.95)^2(1.09)^{-2} + \cdots + 500(.95)^{10}(1.09)^{-10}$$
$$= 500\left(\frac{.95}{1.09}\right) + \cdots + 500\left(\frac{.95}{1.09}\right)^{10}.$$

Summing this series we obtain $500\left(\frac{.95}{1.09}\right)\left(\frac{1 - (\frac{.95}{1.09})^{10}}{1 - \frac{.95}{1.09}}\right) = 2534.76.$

$\square$

Let us note one thing about the previous example. We solved the problem by using the formula for the sum of n terms of a geometric sequence, developed in Chapter Three. Alternatively we could have noted that our expression is just the value at time 0 of a 10-year annuity of 500 per year, where the rate of interest is $j = \frac{1}{.95/1.09} - 1$. The formula for $a_{\overline{n}|}$ could now be used to solve the problem. We note that this method is quite illuminating, since j (roughly .147) is, in fact, the rate of interest which Alphonse pays on his loan.

The reader should also be aware that the fact of no further payments once default occurs is necessary for our calculations to work.

Example 6.17

Redo Example 6.16, without the restriction that once default occurs, no further payments will be received.

Solution

In this case, there is simply a 95% chance that each payment is made. Then

$$500(.95)(1.09)^{-1} + 500(.95)(1.09)^{-2} + \cdots + 500(.95)(1.09)^{-10}$$
$$= (500)(.95)a_{\overline{10}|.09} = 3048.39. \qquad \square$$

Example 6.18

A 20-year 1000 face value bond has coupons at 14% convertible semi-annually and is redeemable at par. Assume a 2% chance that, in any given half-year, the coupon is not issued, and that once default occurs, no further payments are made. Assume as well that a bond can be redeemed only if all coupons have been paid. Find the purchase price to yield on investor 16% convertible semiannually.

Solution

FIGURE 6.2

The same considerations as in Example 6.16 tell us that the price is

$$70[(.98)(1.08)^{-1} + (.98)^2(1.08)^{-2} + \cdots + (.98)^{40}(1.08)^{-40}]$$
$$+ 1000(.98)^{40}(1.08)^{-40}$$

$$= 70\left(\frac{.98}{1.08}\right)\left[\frac{1 - \left(\frac{.98}{1.08}\right)^{40}}{1 - \frac{.98}{1.08}}\right] + 1000\left(\frac{.98}{1.08}\right)^{40} = 692.44. \qquad \square$$

EXERCISES

6.1 Introduction;   6.2 Probability and Expectation

6-1. Given a normal deck of 52 cards, determine the following probabilities:
  (a)   Drawing the 2 of hearts.
  (b)   Drawing a heart.
  (c)   Drawing a 2 *or* a heart.
  (d)   Drawing the 2 of hearts in 2 draws (without replacement).
  (e)   Drawing the 2 of hearts in 2 draws (with replacement).

6-2. Given a fair die, determine the following probabilities:
  (a)   Throwing a 3.
  (b)   Throwing a number 3 or larger.
  (c)   In two rolls, throwing a total of 8.
  (d)   In two rolls, throwing a number smaller than 3 each time.
  (e)   In two rolls, throwing a total of 15.

6-3. Given a fair coin, determine the following probabilities:
  (a)   Throwing 2 consecutive heads.
  (b)   Throwing 2 heads and then a tail.
  (c)   Throwing exactly 2 heads in 3 tosses.
  (d)   Throwing at least 2 heads in 3 tosses.

6-4. The probability of a 45-year-old surviving to age 80 is $\frac{1}{4}$.   The
probability of a 45-year-old dying between 60 and 80 is $\frac{2}{5}$.   Find
the probability of a 45-year-old surviving to age 60.

6-5. A single die is thrown. If a 1, 2 or 3 turns up, player A wins that
amount of money (1, 2 or 3). If a 4, 5 or 6 turns up, player B wins
the amount of money showing. Find the expected value for each
player.

6-6. A box contains 3 10-dollar bills, 6 5-dollar bills, and 4 1-dollar bills. You are allowed to pull two bills (without replacement) from the box. If both bills are of the same denomination you can keep them. Otherwise, you lose 3 dollars. What is your expected value?

6-7. For a 1-dollar ticket, a lottery offers the following prizes:

1 prize of 25,000;
20 prizes of 1,000 each;
50 prizes of 100 each;
100 prizes of 25 each;
1500 prizes of 5 free tickets.

If 100,000 tickets are sold, find the expectation per ticket.

6-8. A current quiz program gives the contestants 5 true/false statements and awards 5 for each correct answer. If all 5 are answered correctly, the contestant gets 1,000 extra. Find the expected value for someone who guesses at each answer.

6-9. A perishable product is purchased by a retailer for 5 and sold for 9. Based on past experience, it is estimated that $\frac{1}{4}$ of the time 10 items can be sold, $\frac{1}{2}$ of the time 11 items are sold, and $\frac{1}{8}$ of the time 12 items are sold. There is also a $\frac{1}{8}$ probability that a strike will occur and no items can be sold at all. If an item is not sold, the retailer will lose 5. Find the number of items he should purchase in order to maximize profit.

6.3   Contingent Payments

6-10. The Trustworthy Trust Company would like to obtain a yield of 16% on their loans. Past experience indicates that 5% of all loans are not paid. What rate of interest should Trustworthy Trust charge?

6-11. Mr. Hill wishes to borrow 5000. He will repay the loan with a single payment at the end of one year. The lending agency has a "risk-free" rate of interest of 13%, but estimates there is an 8% chance that Mr. Hill will not repay the loan. How much should they ask Mr. Hill to repay?

6-12. Mrs. Kelly wants to borrow some money. She wishes to repay the loan with a single payment of 3000 in two years' time. It is felt that there is a 5% chance she will not repay the loan. How much will the lending agency lend to Mrs. Kelly if they wish a yield of 14%? If she repays the loan in full, what yield rate was actually realized?

6-13. Friendly Finance Company wishes a yield rate of 15%, but charges 22% on loans repayable with a single payment at the end of one year. What default rate is being assumed?

6-14. Mrs. Trudeau is interested in ensuring that her newborn son will have sufficient funds for higher education. A certain plan will award a 5000 scholarship if her son survives to age 18 and enters a university. The cost for this plan at time of birth is 200. The probability that a newborn male survives to age 18 is .9821. If Mrs. Trudeau feels she can make 17% on her money, what probability must she assign to her son entering university for this scheme to be worthwhile?

6-15. How much would you lend a person today if he promised to repay 2000 at the end of each year for the next 10 years? Assume there is a 3% chance of default in any year and you wish to earn 11% on your money. Also assume that once there is a default, no further payments are forthcoming.

6-16. The All-Mighty Bank wishes to lend 100,000,000 to a South American country and would like to earn 12% on its investment. Repayment of the loan will be by two equal annual payments, the first due in one year. It is estimated that, in any given year, there is a 20% chance that no payment will be made. There is also a 40% chance that half the payment will be made, and a 40% chance of payment in full. If no payment is made the first year, it is assumed that there will be no payment the second year. It is considered possible, however, that there might be partial payment the first year and full, partial or no payment the second year. How much will the bank ask the country to repay each year?

6-17. An insurance company sells an annuity to a person whose probability of surviving 1 year is .65, of surviving 2 years is .45, and whose probability of surviving 3 years is negligible. If the annuity pays 3000 at the end of each year, and if the company wishes to earn 14%, what is a fair price for this annuity?

6-18. Do Question 17 for a perpetuity of 3000 if the probability of surviving t years is estimated to be $\frac{1}{2^t}$.

6-19. A 20-year 100 face value bond, redeemable at par, is offered for sale. The coupon rate is 12% convertible semiannually. Find the purchase price to yield 8% convertible semiannually, if the probability of default in any 6-month period is 1%. Assume that once default occurs, no further payments are received.

6-20. The Happy Finance Company experiences a 10% default rate on one-year loans. The Super Finance Company experiences a 7% default rate on one-year loans. If the Super Finance Company charges 16% on loans, what should the Happy Finance Company charge to obtain the same return?

6-21. Agatha pays 770 for a 1000 face value bond paying interest at 11% convertible semiannually, and redeemable at par in 20 years. If her desired yield was 12% convertible semiannually, what rate of default did she expect? Assume that once default occurs, no further payments are made.

6-22. Charles buys a 1000 face value 20-year bond redeemable at par with semiannual coupons at 12% convertible semiannually. He determines his purchase price to yield 14% convertible semi-annually, and to allow for a default probability of 1% per half-year. Exactly 7 years later, Charles sells the bond to Elizabeth, who determines her purchase price to yield 10% convertible semiannually, and to allow for a 2% half-yearly probability of default. Assume that the probability of default in any given year is independent of the probability of default in any other year. Find each of the following:
  (a)   Charles' purchase price.
  (b)   Elizabeth's purchase price.
  (c)   The yield rate to Charles, assuming no default occurred during the first seven years.

CHAPTER SEVEN
LIFE TABLES AND POPULATION PROBLEMS

7.1 INTRODUCTION

In Chapter 6 we saw how to combine the theory of interest with elementary probability theory to obtain the present value of contingent payments. In practical situations the following question is crucial: how do we determine the appropriate probabilities to be used in these calculations?

The answer is that we must have data to guide us. We must know what percentage of borrowers do not repay their loans, and we must be able to identify high-risk borrowers and either refuse to lend them money at all, or lend them money at higher rates of interest than we use for low-risk customers.

In almost all of the examples we study in the remainder of this text, the probabilities required are those of surviving to certain ages or of dying before certain ages. Data required to calculate these probabilities is collected empirically and is published in *life tables*. In this chapter we will introduce the basic notation underlying life tables, and see how to calculate required probabilities. Section 7.2 will consider the life tables as presenting survival data for a given fixed initial population. In Section 7.4 we will see how the same table can also be interpreted as giving information about a stationary population.

Historically, attempts were made by de Moivre, Gompertz, Makeham and others to find an analytic function $S(x)$ which would describe survival from age 0 to age x. In Section 7.3 we will examine some of these possibilities.

Finally, we briefly examine in Section 7.6 a few of the basic ideas of multiple decrement theory.

7.2 LIFE TABLES

TABLE 7.1

Age	ℓ_x	d_x	$1000q_x$
0	1,000,000	1580	1.58
1	998,420	680	68
2	997,740	485	.49
3	997,255	435	.44

In Table 7.1 we have presented an excerpt from a typical life table. In such a table the column ℓ_x denotes the number of lives which have survived to age x. For this to make sense, we have to assume a starting population ℓ_0. In our case $\ell_0 = 1,000,000$, but any value would have sufficed. As we shall see, it is the ratio of entries in the table, not the individual numbers, which is important. In particular, the ratio $\frac{\ell_x}{\ell_0}$ represents the probability of surviving from birth to age x. As a general function of x, it is called the *survival function* and is denoted $S(x)$.

Note that in Table 7.1, $\ell_1 = 998,420$. This means that 1580 lives have died in the first year of life, and this is the entry d_0. In general, d_x denotes the number of lives, out of those aged x, which do not survive to age $x + 1$. Thus

$$d_x = \ell_x - \ell_{x+1}. \tag{7.1}$$

q_x denotes the probability that a life aged x will not survive to age $x + 1$. Thus

$$q_x = \frac{d_x}{\ell_x}. \tag{7.2}$$

In our case, the final column tells us that $q_2 = \frac{.49}{1000} = .00049$, and $\frac{485}{997,740} = .00049$ as well.

Using a life table we can compute numerous probabilities concerning survival. In Example 7.1, we use Table 7.1 to assist us. In Examples 7.2 and 7.3 we will determine expressions which could be converted to numerical answers if we had access to a complete life table.

Example 7.1

Use Table 7.1 to find each of the following:
(a) The probability that a newborn will live to age 3.
(b) The probability that a newborn will die between age 1 and age 3.

Solution

(a) This equals $\frac{\ell_3}{\ell_0} = \frac{997,255}{1,000,000} = .997255$.

(b) The number of deaths between ages 1 and 3 is $\ell_1 - \ell_3$. Thus the probability is $\frac{\ell_1 - \ell_3}{\ell_0} = \frac{1165}{1,000,000} = .001165$. □

Example 7.2

Find an expression for each of the following:
(a) The probability that an 18-year-old lives to age 65.
(b) The probability that a 25-year-old dies between ages 40 and 45.
(c) The probability that a 25-year-old does *not* die between ages 40 and 45.
(d) The probability that a 30-year-old dies before age 60.

Solution

(a) This equals $\frac{\ell_{65}}{\ell_{18}}$.

(b) Since the number of people dying between age 40 and age 45 is $\ell_{40} - \ell_{45}$, this is $\frac{\ell_{40} - \ell_{45}}{\ell_{25}}$.

(c) This is the complement of (b), so the answer is given by $1 - \frac{\ell_{40} - \ell_{45}}{\ell_{25}}$. Alternatively, we could obtain this as the sum of $\frac{\ell_{25} - \ell_{40}}{\ell_{25}}$, the probability of dying before age 40, and $\frac{\ell_{45}}{\ell_{25}}$, the probability of dying after age 45.

(d) This is $\frac{\ell_{30} - \ell_{60}}{\ell_{30}}$. □

Example 7.3

There are four persons, now aged 40, 50, 60 and 70. Find an expression for the probability that both the 40-year-old and the 50-year-old will die within the five-year period starting ten years from now, but neither the 60-year-old nor the 70-year-old will die during that five-year period.

Solution

Working out each probability separately and multiplying the results, we obtain $\left(\frac{\ell_{50} - \ell_{55}}{\ell_{40}}\right)\left(\frac{\ell_{60} - \ell_{65}}{\ell_{50}}\right)\left(1 - \frac{\ell_{70} - \ell_{75}}{\ell_{60}}\right)\left(1 - \frac{\ell_{80} - \ell_{85}}{\ell_{70}}\right)$. □

This is all well and good, but how was such a life table constructed in the first place? The numbers ℓ_x and d_x do not represent actual numbers of real people, so where did they come from? The answer is that q_x was estimated from observations of mortality data from a suitable study sample, and these values of q_x, together with the arbitrary starting value ℓ_0, determine the whole table.

This is done as follows. Start with ℓ_0. We know that $q_0\ell_0 = d_0$. Now we can find $\ell_1 = \ell_0 - d_0$. Then $q_1\ell_1 = d_1$, $\ell_2 = \ell_1 - d_1$, and so on. In general, we continue with the basic identities

$$q_x\ell_x = d_x \tag{7.3}$$

and

$$\ell_{x+1} = \ell_x - d_x. \tag{7.4}$$

Example 7.4

A scientist studies the mortality patterns of Golden-Winged Warblers. She establishes the following probabilities of deaths: $q_0 = .40$, $q_1 = .20$, $q_2 = .30$, $q_3 = .70$ and $q_4 = 1$. Starting with $\ell_0 = 100$, construct a life table.

Solution

Age	ℓ_x	d_x	q_x
0	100	40	.40
1	60	12	.20
2	48	14	.30
3	34	24	.70
4	10	10	1.0

□

Before continuing let us introduce a bit more notation. We let p_x represent the probability that an individual just turning age x will survive to age $x + 1$. Hence

$$p_x = \frac{\ell_{x+1}}{\ell_x} = 1 - q_x. \tag{7.5}$$

More generally,

$_np_x =$ the probability that an individual just turning age x will survive to age $x + n$.

$_nq_x =$ the probability that an individual just turning age x will not survive to age $x + n$.

Thus

$$_np_x = \frac{\ell_{x+n}}{\ell_x} = 1 - {}_nq_x. \tag{7.6}$$

The reader should rewrite the answers to Examples 7.2 and 7.3 using this new notation. In the special case of $x = 0$, we have $_np_0 = S(n)$, the survival function defined on page 128.

| Example 7.5 |

Explain both mathematically and verbally why each of the following is true.

(a) $\ell_x - \ell_{x+n} = d_x + d_{x+1} + \cdots + d_{x+n-1}$.

(b) $_{m+n}p_x = {}_mp_x \cdot {}_np_{x+m}$.

| Solution |

(a) Mathematically,
$$d_x + d_{x+1} + \cdots + d_{x+n-1} = (\ell_x - \ell_{x+1}) + (\ell_{x+1} - \ell_{x+2})$$
$$+ \cdots + (\ell_{x+n-1} - \ell_{x+n}) = \ell_x - \ell_{x+n}.$$

Verbally, $\ell_x - \ell_{x+n}$ is the number of people alive at age x but dead at age $x + n$, (i.e., the number of people who die between age x and age $x + n$). But $d_x + \cdots + d_{x+n-1}$ is just the sum of the numbers of people dying at various ages between age x and age $x + n - 1$ (inclusive), which is the same as above.

(b) Mathematically,
$$_{m+n}p_x = \frac{\ell_{x+m+n}}{\ell_x} = \frac{\ell_{x+m}}{\ell_x} \cdot \frac{\ell_{x+m+n}}{\ell_{x+m}} = {}_mp_x \cdot {}_np_{x+m}.$$

Verbally, $_{m+n}p_x$ is the probability that a person aged x lives $m + n$ years. To do this, he has to first live m years and then, at age $x + m$, live n more years. Hence $_{m+n}p_x$ is the product of the probabilities of these two events, namely $_mp_x \cdot {}_np_{x+m}$. $\qquad\square$

Example 7.6

30% of those who die between ages 25 and 75 die before age 50. The probability of a person aged 25 dying before age 50 is 20%. Find $_{25}p_{50}$.

Solution

We want to find $_{25}p_{50} = \frac{\ell_{75}}{\ell_{50}}$. We are given $.30(\ell_{25} - \ell_{75}) = \ell_{25} - \ell_{50}$, and that $\frac{\ell_{25} - \ell_{50}}{\ell_{25}} = .20$. The second relation says that $.80\ell_{25} = \ell_{50}$, or $\ell_{25} = 1.25\ell_{50}$. When substituted in the first expression, this gives $.30(1.25\ell_{50} - \ell_{75}) = 1.25\ell_{50} - \ell_{50}$. Thus $.125\ell_{50} = .30\ell_{75}$, and finally $\frac{\ell_{75}}{\ell_{50}} = \frac{.125}{.3} = .4167$. $\qquad\square$

Finally, let us remark that the expressions $_np_x$ and $_nq_x$ have only been defined thus far for integral values of n. What should we do in other cases? Say, for example, we want to find $_{1/4}p_{20}$, the probability that a person aged 20 lives to age $20\frac{1}{4}$. This information is not obtainable directly from a life table, but we can obtain a good approximation by assuming that deaths occur uniformly over a given year. In that case we would expect that $\frac{1}{4} \cdot d_{20}$ individuals die during the first $\frac{1}{4}$ of the year, leaving $\ell_{20} - \frac{1}{4} \cdot d_{20}$ alive. Hence an approximate value for $_{1/4}p_{20}$ is

$$
\begin{aligned}
_{1/4}p_{20} &= \frac{\ell_{20} - \frac{1}{4} \cdot d_{20}}{\ell_{20}} \\
&= \frac{\ell_{20} - \frac{1}{4}(\ell_{20} - \ell_{21})}{\ell_{20}} \\
&= \frac{\frac{3}{4}\ell_{20} + \frac{1}{4}\ell_{21}}{\ell_{20}}.
\end{aligned}
$$

In other words, we have used linear interpolation between ℓ_{20} and ℓ_{21} in the life table. It is possible to use more sophisticated finite difference formulae, but linear interpolation seems to be sufficiently accurate for most purposes.

Example 7.7

Using Table 7.1 and assuming a uniform distribution of deaths over each year, find each of the following:
(a) $_{4/3}p_1$
(b)   The probability that a newborn will survive the first year, but die in the first two months thereafter.

Solution

(a)   By linear interpolation we obtain

$$_{4/3}p_1 = \frac{\ell_2 - \frac{1}{3} \cdot d_2}{\ell_1} = \frac{\ell_2 - \frac{1}{3}(\ell_2 - \ell_3)}{\ell_1} = \frac{\frac{2}{3}\ell_2 + \frac{1}{3}\ell_3}{\ell_1} = .999157.$$

(b)   The number dying in the period described is $\frac{1}{6} \cdot d_1$. Hence, the

answer is $\dfrac{\frac{1}{6} \cdot d_1}{\ell_0} = .00011333.$ □

7.3   ANALYTIC FORMULAE FOR ℓ_x

Calculations of the type described in the previous section are often straightforward if we assume a simple analytic formula for ℓ_x. Here is an example.

Example 7.8

Given $\ell_x = 1000\left(1 - \frac{x}{105}\right)$, determine each of the following:

(a) ℓ_0 (b) ℓ_{35} (c) q_{20} (d) $_{15}p_{35}$ (e) $_{15}q_{25}$
(f)   The probability that a 30-year-old dies between ages 55 and 60.
(g)   The probability that a 30-year-old dies after age 70.
(h)   The probability that a 15-year-old reaches age 110.
(i)   The probability that, given a 20-year-old and a 30-year-old, one but not both of these individuals reaches age 70.

Solution

(a) $\ell_0 = 1000\left(1 - \frac{0}{105}\right) = 1000.$

(b) $\ell_{35} = 1000\left(1 - \frac{35}{105}\right) = 667$

(note the answer must be an integer).

(c) $q_{20} = \dfrac{\ell_{20} - \ell_{21}}{\ell_{20}} = 1 - .98824 = .01176.$

(d) $_{15}p_{35} = \dfrac{\ell_{50}}{\ell_{35}} = .78571.$

(e) $_{15}q_{25} = 1 - {}_{15}p_{25} = 1 - \dfrac{\ell_{40}}{\ell_{25}} = .1875.$

(f) $\dfrac{\ell_{55} - \ell_{60}}{\ell_{30}} = .0667.$

(g)   This is equal to the probability that a 30-year-old reaches age 70, which is $_{40}p_{30} = \dfrac{\ell_{70}}{\ell_{30}} = .4667.$

(h) Observe that $\ell_{105} = 0$, so no one is left alive at age 105. Hence the required probability is 0. Note that our formula for ℓ_x can only be used for values of x satisfying $0 \le x \le 105$.

(i) We must consider separately the two possible cases and add the results. The probability that the 20-year-old reaches age 70 but the 30-year-old does not is ${}_{50}p_{20} \cdot (1 - {}_{40}p_{30})$, which is evaluated as $\frac{\ell_{70}}{\ell_{20}}\left(1 - \frac{\ell_{70}}{\ell_{30}}\right) = .2196$. The probability that the 20-year-old does not reach age 70 but the 30-year-old does is $(1 - {}_{50}p_{20}) \cdot {}_{40}p_{30}$, which is .2745. Hence the answer is $.2196 + .2745 = .4941$. □

Of course there is no reason to expect that there will be any totally reliable formula for ℓ_x, but it may well be true that some function will give a very good approximation to the observed values of ℓ_x, and this function could then be used in practice for making calculations and predictions about the future state of the population.

What properties should a formula for ℓ_x possess? First of all, it will certainly be decreasing. We would also expect ℓ_x to decrease more rapidly for very small x and for x around 65 or 70 than for middle values, since individuals in those age groups are subject to higher probabilities of dying. Figure 7.1 gives a typical curve for ℓ_x derived from empirical data.

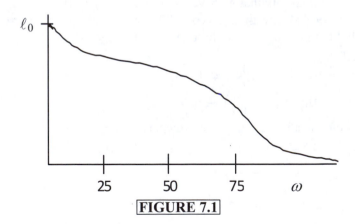

FIGURE 7.1

Note that there is some age ω at which no survivors remain. ω is called the *terminal age* of the population.

As a first approximation, Abraham de Moivre suggested in the early 1700's that ℓ_x be represented by a straight line. In Example 7.8, we saw a particular case of de Moivre's idea. The general formula in this type of setting will be

$$\ell_x = a\left(1 - \frac{x}{\omega}\right), \tag{7.7}$$

where $a = \ell_0$ is the starting population. Note that ℓ_x decreases steadily to a final value of $\ell_\omega = 0$, so ω is the terminal age for this group of lives. Although very rough, de Moivre's approximation is reasonable in the middle range of ages.

| Example 7.9 |

Let $\ell_x = \sqrt{100 - x}$.
(a)   Calculate $_{28}p_{36}$.
(b)   Henry and Henrietta are both 19 years old. Find the probability that Henry lives at least 17 years, Henrietta lives at most 45 years, and at least one of them survives for 32 years.

| Solution |

(a) $_{28}p_{36} = \frac{\ell_{64}}{\ell_{36}} = \frac{6}{8} = .75.$

(b)   We will work out several cases and then add the results. The probability that Henry lives for 32 years and Henrietta does not is $\left(\frac{\ell_{51}}{\ell_{19}}\right)\left(1 - \frac{\ell_{51}}{\ell_{19}}\right) = \left(\frac{7}{9}\right)\left(\frac{2}{9}\right) = \frac{14}{81}.$ Note that the additional conditions on the problem do not affect this case, but they do affect the case where Henrietta lives 32 years and Henry does not. This probability is $\left(\frac{\ell_{36} - \ell_{51}}{\ell_{19}}\right)\left(\frac{\ell_{51} - \ell_{64}}{\ell_{19}}\right) = \left(\frac{1}{9}\right)\left(\frac{1}{9}\right) = \frac{1}{81}.$ Finally we calculate the probability that both persons survive for 32 years. This is $\left(\frac{\ell_{51}}{\ell_{19}}\right)\left(\frac{\ell_{51} - \ell_{64}}{\ell_{19}}\right) = \left(\frac{7}{9}\right)\left(\frac{1}{9}\right) = \frac{7}{81}.$ Hence the answer is $\frac{14}{81} + \frac{1}{81} + \frac{7}{81} = \frac{22}{81}.$ □

In Section 1.6 we introduced the concept of force of interest. The corresponding notion here is called *force of mortality*. The force of mortality at age x is denoted by μ_x, and is defined by

$$\mu_x = -\frac{D(\ell_x)}{\ell_x}. \tag{7.8a}$$

Multiplying by ℓ_x we have $-D(\ell_x) = \ell_x \mu_x$, which is called the *expected density* of deaths.

Example 7.10

Find μ_x for the ℓ_x given in Example 7.8.

Solution

$$D(\ell_x) = -\frac{1000}{105}, \text{ so } \mu_x = -\frac{-\frac{1000}{105}}{1000\left(1-\frac{x}{105}\right)} = \frac{1}{105\left(1-\frac{x}{105}\right)} = \frac{1}{105-x}.$$

$\square$

Example 7.11

Find the force of mortality for the ℓ_x given in Example 7.9, and the expected density of deaths at age 36.

Solution

$$D(\ell_x) = \frac{1}{2}(100-x)^{-1/2}(-1) = -\frac{1}{2\sqrt{100-x}}, \text{ so the force of mortality}$$

is $\mu_x = -\dfrac{-\frac{1}{2\sqrt{100-x}}}{\sqrt{100-x}} = \dfrac{1}{2(100-x)}.$ The expected density of deaths at

age 36 is $\ell_{36}\mu_{36} = \dfrac{\sqrt{100-36}}{2(100-36)} = \dfrac{1}{16}.$

$\square$

We observe that, as with force of interest, force of mortality is an instantaneous measure of the rate at which death occurs. Note that in both examples μ_x becomes infinitely large as x approaches the terminal age of the population, reflecting the certainty of death as survivors approach that age. The minus sign in the definition of μ_x is simply a convenient way of guaranteeing that all answers will be positive. (Recall that ℓ_x is a decreasing function, so its derivative is negative.)

As with force of interest, we can express the formula for μ_x in terms of logarithms as

$$\mu_x = -D(\ln \ell_x). \tag{7.8b}$$

Then it follows that $\int_0^x \mu_r \, dr = -\ln \ell_x + \ln \ell_0$, which leads to the relationship

$$e^{-\int_0^x \mu_r \, dr} = \frac{\ell_x}{\ell_0} = {}_xp_0 = S(x). \tag{7.8c}$$

We will now briefly consider two other formulae for ℓ_x which have been used over the years. In the early 1800's, Benjamin Gompertz investigated the case where $D\left(\frac{1}{\mu_x}\right) = -h \cdot \frac{1}{\mu_x}$ for some constant h. By integrating, we see that this is the same as $ln\left(\frac{1}{\mu_x}\right) = -hx + A$ for some constant A or, in other words,

$$\mu_x = Bc^x \qquad (7.9)$$

for suitable constants B and c. Using this definition of μ_x and the relations given by (7.8c), we obtain Gompertz' formula

$$\ell_x = kg^{c^x}, \qquad (7.10)$$

where k, g, c are suitable constants. Note that $\ell_0 = kg$. By choosing the constants g and c appropriately, this formula can be made to approximate the ℓ_x curve very well, especially in the middle age range.

In the middle 1800's, W. M. Makeham took a more sophisticated approach, assuming that

$$\mu_x = A + Bc^x. \qquad (7.11)$$

After integration, we see that this gives

$$\ell_x = ks^x g^{c^x}, \qquad (7.12)$$

where k, s, g, c are suitable constants. Note that $\ell_0 = kg$. Makeham's formula is more accurate than Gompertz', but both approximations have been extremely useful in the historical construction of life tables.

7.4   THE STATIONARY POPULATION

The life table introduced in Section 7.2 traced the future survival of a particular group of ℓ_0 newborn individuals. The symbol ℓ_x represented the number of those individuals who survive to age x and d_x represented the number who die between age x and age $x + 1$. Other symbols were introduced as needed.

Imagine now a population in which births occur at even intervals throughout the year, and the level of mortality remains the same from year to year. Let us assume that there are ℓ_0 annual births. The symbols p_x and q_x will retain their original meanings. It may be shown under these conditions that, after a period of time, the total population will remain stationary and the age distribution will remain constant. Our life table can now be used to study this "stationary population", but some of the symbols introduced earlier take on a different meaning in this context.

As mentioned above, ℓ_0 will be the number of births occurring in any given one-year period. This period could be January 1 to December 31, but it is equally true that ℓ_0 births will occur between May 17 and May 16 of the following year. Because of the stationary population, the number of deaths must equal the number of births in any given year, so ℓ_0 is also the total number of deaths occurring in any twelve month period.

More generally, ℓ_x will represent the number of people who reach their x^{th} birthday during any given year. Since $d_x = q_x \ell_x$, d_x represents the number of those individuals who die before reaching age $x + 1$. But the assumption of constant mortality over time allows us to conclude that d_x is also equal to the number of people who die during any given year between ages x and $x + 1$. This latter interpretation is the important one for stationary population problems. Similar reasoning allows us to conclude that $\ell_x - \ell_{x+n}$ is the number of annual deaths that occur between age x and age $x + n$.

Now let us deal with an important kind of problem which arises in population study. If we take a census of the population at some fixed point in time, how many people aged x last birthday will we discover? We will denote this number by the symbol L_x.

In the year immediately preceding the census date, ℓ_x individuals will achieve age x. However, some of these will die before the census is taken. Assuming uniform distribution of births and deaths, we see that, we could expect $\frac{1}{2} \cdot d_x$ deaths to occur. Hence an approximate value for L_x is given by

$$L_x = \ell_x - \frac{1}{2} \cdot d_x = \frac{1}{2}(\ell_x + \ell_{x+1}). \qquad (7.13a)$$

The precise definition of L_x is

$$L_x = \int_0^1 \ell_{x+t}\, dt. \qquad (7.13b)$$

The number of individuals aged x and over at any fixed point in time is given by the symbol T_x, where

$$T_x = \sum_{i=0}^{\infty} L_{x+i}. \tag{7.14}$$

Under the uniform distribution assumption we have

$$T_x = \sum_{i=0}^{\infty} \tfrac{1}{2}(\ell_{x+i} + \ell_{x+i+1}) = \tfrac{1}{2} \cdot \ell_x + \sum_{i=1}^{\infty} \ell_{x+i}. \tag{7.15a}$$

The precise definition of T_x, using (7.14) and (7.13b), is

$$T_x = \int_0^{\infty} \ell_{x+t} \, dt. \tag{7.15b}$$

Before giving an example, let us review the basic difference between ℓ_x and d_x, on the one hand, and L_x and T_x on the other hand, in the stationary population model. L_x and T_x represent numbers of individuals at a fixed point in time; L_x, for example, is the number of people aged x last birthday at that instant. ℓ_x and d_x, however, represent numbers of individuals achieving their x^{th} birthday or dying at age x last birthday in a given calendar year.

Example 7.12

An organization has a constant total membership. Each year 500 new members join at exact age 20. Twenty per cent leave after 10 years, 10% of those remaining leave after 20 years, and the rest retire at age 65. Express each of the following in terms of life table functions:
(a)   The number who leave at age 40 each year.
(b)   The size of the membership.
(c)   The number of retired people alive at any given time.
(d)   The number of members who die each year.

Solution

(a)   If the number of new entrants were ℓ_{20}, we would argue as follows: At age 30, $.80\ell_{30}$ of the original entrants are still members. By age 40 this has become $.80\ell_{40}$, and the number who leave is $(.10)(.80\ell_{40}) = .08\ell_{40}$. Since the number of new entrants is 500, the correct answer is $\dfrac{500}{\ell_{20}}(.08\ell_{40}) = \dfrac{40\ell_{40}}{\ell_{20}}$.

(b)   This is given by the total number of individuals aged 20 and over, and would be simply T_{20} if ℓ_{20} individuals started and no one left except by death. Taking into account the various ways of leaving the population, we obtain $\frac{500}{\ell_{20}}\left(T_{20} - .20T_{30} - .08T_{40} - .72T_{65}\right)$. This expression says that, since 20% leave the population at age 30, $.20T_{30}$ of the expected individuals are not present (for each age over 30, 20% of those people have left). Similar reasoning applies to the other terms, and the remaining $.72T_{65}$ all retire at age 65.

(c)   This is just $\frac{500}{\ell_{20}}(.72T_{65}) = \frac{360T_{65}}{\ell_{20}}$, the number of people aged 65 and over in the total population who did not leave at an earlier age.

(d)   Since the population is stationary, this is given by the expression $\frac{500}{\ell_{20}}(\ell_{20} - .20\ell_{30} - .08\ell_{40} - .72\ell_{65})$. Note that the above is just the number of new entrants each year, minus the number of people who do not die but leave the membership for other reasons.   □

A measure of the risk of dying which is often useful in dealing with stationary populations is the *central death rate*. This is denoted by m_x and is defined as

$$m_x = \frac{d_x}{L_x}. \tag{7.16}$$

Numerous identities relating m_x to other symbols are available and easy to derive. The reader should verify the following, which assume a uniform distribution of deaths:

$$m_x = \frac{d_x}{\ell_x - \frac{1}{2} \cdot d_x} = \frac{q_x}{1 - \frac{1}{2} \cdot q_x}, \tag{7.17}$$

$$q_x = \frac{m_x}{1 + \frac{1}{2} \cdot m_x}, \tag{7.18}$$

and

$$p_x = \frac{1 - \frac{1}{2} \cdot m_x}{1 + \frac{1}{2} \cdot m_x}. \tag{7.19}$$

7.5 EXPECTATION OF LIFE

In this section we continue with our study of a population, as introduced in Section 7.4. The results presented here do not require that the population be stationary. We are interested first in obtaining an expression for the average future lifetime, denoted e_x, of a person at age x. This is just the expected value of the future lifetime, and our discussion in Chapter 6 indicates that the answer should be given by

$$e_x = \sum_{t=0}^{\infty} t\,({}_tp_x - {}_{t+1}p_x).\tag{7.20}$$

In other words, we are multiplying each possible number of years t by the probability that an individual will live that many full years but no more. The above expression is called the *curtate expectation* and can be simplified as follows:

$$
\begin{aligned}
e_x &= (1)(p_x - {}_2p_x) + (2)({}_2p_x - {}_3p_x) + \cdots \\
&= p_x + {}_2p_x + {}_3p_x + \cdots \\
&= \sum_{t=1}^{\infty} {}_tp_x.
\end{aligned}\tag{7.21}
$$

Curtate expectation counts only full years of future life, as shown by (7.20). A more accurate measure is the *complete expectation*, denoted by $\overset{\circ}{e}_x$, and defined by

$$\overset{\circ}{e}_x = \int_0^{\infty} {}_tp_x\,dt.\tag{7.22}$$

A special case of work done later in this text (see Section 8.3) shows that when a uniform distribution of deaths is assumed we obtain the useful approximation

$$\overset{\circ}{e}_x \approx e_x + \frac{1}{2}.\tag{7.23}$$

From Formulas (7.22) and (7.15b) we easily obtain

$$\overset{\circ}{e}_x = \frac{T_x}{\ell_x}. \tag{7.24}$$

If we cross-multiply this identity, we obtain $T_x = \ell_x \overset{\circ}{e}_x$. Since $\overset{\circ}{e}_x$ is the average number of future years of life for each of ℓ_x individuals, we see that T_x is the *total* number of years of future life for these individuals. This interpretation of T_x has meaning in any population, whether or not stationary, and will be extremely important in the exercises.

| Example 7.13 |

If $_t p_{35} = (.98)^t$ for all t, find e_{35} and $\overset{\circ}{e}_{35}$ without approximation. Compare the latter with the approximate value of $\overset{\circ}{e}_{35}$ given by (7.23).

| Solution |

$$e_{35} = \sum_{t=1}^{\infty} {}_t p_{35} = \sum_{t=1}^{\infty} .98^t = \frac{.98}{1 - .98} = 49.$$

$$\overset{\circ}{e}_{35} = \int_0^\infty {}_t p_{35}\, dt = \int_0^\infty .98^t dt = \frac{(.98)^t}{\ln .98}\bigg|_0^\infty = 49.498.$$

Approximately, $\overset{\circ}{e}_{35} = e_{35} + \frac{1}{2} = 49.50.$ $\qquad\qquad\square$

| Example 7.14 |

Interpret verbally the expression $T_x - T_{x+n} - n \cdot \ell_{x+n}$.

| Solution |

T_x is the total future lifetime for a group of ℓ_x individuals after they turn age x, and T_{x+n} is the total future lifetime for the same individuals after age $x + n$. Therefore $T_x - T_{x+n}$ represents the total future lifetime in the next n years for ℓ_x individuals after they turn age x. Now $n \cdot \ell_{x+n}$ is exactly the number of years between age x and age $x + n$ lived by the ℓ_{x+n} individuals who survive to age $x + n$. Hence $T_x - T_{x+n} - n \cdot \ell_{x+n}$ is the total number of years to be lived by those of the ℓ_x individuals who will die in the next n years. $\qquad\qquad\square$

The complete expectation $\overset{\circ}{e}_x$ is especially helpful when solving problems concerning the average age at death. In particular, since $\overset{\circ}{e}_x$ represents expected future lifetime, we see that the average age at death of a person currently aged x is given by

$$x + \overset{\circ}{e}_x = x + \frac{T_x}{\ell_x}. \qquad (7.25)$$

Putting $x = 0$ in this expression, we have $\overset{\circ}{e}_0 = \frac{T_0}{\ell_0}$, the average age at death for all deaths among the ℓ_0 individuals.

A more intricate problem involving average age at death is illustrated by the following example.

$\boxed{\text{Example 7.15}}$

Find the average age at death of those who die between age x and age $x + n$.

$\boxed{\text{Solution}}$

In Example 7.14 we saw that the total number of future years to be lived by this group of individuals is given by $T_x - T_{x+n} - n \cdot \ell_{x+n}$. Since there are $\ell_x - \ell_{x+n}$ individuals in the group, we see that the average future lifetime is given by $\dfrac{T_x - T_{x+n} - n \cdot \ell_{x+n}}{\ell_x - \ell_{x+n}}$. Hence the average age at death is equal to $x + \dfrac{T_x - T_{x+n} - n \cdot \ell_{x+n}}{\ell_x - \ell_{x+n}}$. $\square$

Examples 7.14 and 7.15 most commonly arise in a stationary population setting. In Example 7.15, for example, the result gives the average age at death for *all* those in the stationary population who die between ages x and $x+n$, not just those who are the survivors from one particular group of ℓ_0 newborns. Similarly, $\overset{\circ}{e}_0$ is the average age at death for all deaths in the stationary population.

7.6 MULTIPLE DECREMENTS

Up to now we have been assuming that, except for retirement at a certain age, death is the only cause of decrement acting on a body of lives. Consider the case of an employer, however, where disability or withdrawal would be other reasons for terminating employment. The insurance company covering claims for the employer would want to treat death and disability separately, since the amounts of the claims would be different. It might also be true that, in some situations, different causes of death should be analyzed separately.

Multiple decrement theory is the area of mathematics which deals with these kinds of problems; it allows us to study each kind of decrement individually, and to draw conclusions from the results. In this section we will examine very briefly some of the basic terminology and notation. Our goal is merely to introduce these ideas to the student, in case they are required later on.

Let us assume we have m causes of decrement acting independently on a body of lives. Our original ℓ_x will now be written $\ell_x^{(\tau)}$, the total number of lives attaining age x. Note that we have now returned to our original view of a life table as presenting the survivorship data for a fixed initial group of ℓ_0 individuals. Now if $(1), (2), \ldots, (m)$ are the m causes of decrement, we denote by $d_x^{(k)}$ the number of decrements from cause (k) between ages x and $x + 1$. Also, $d_x^{(\tau)}$ is the total number of decrements from all causes, so we have

$$d_x^{(\tau)} = \sum_{k=1}^{m} d_x^{(k)}, \tag{7.26}$$

and we also have

$$\ell_x^{(\tau)} - d_x^{(\tau)} = \ell_{x+1}^{(\tau)}. \tag{7.27}$$

$q_x^{(k)}$ is the probability that a life aged x will leave within one year because of cause (k), so we have

$$q_x^{(k)} = \frac{d_x^{(k)}}{\ell_x^{(\tau)}}. \tag{7.28}$$

$q_x^{(\tau)}$ and $p_x^{(\tau)}$ are analagous to our old q_x and p_x, so we have

$$q_x^{(\tau)} = \frac{d_x^{(\tau)}}{\ell_x^{(\tau)}} = \sum_{k=1}^{m} q_x^{(k)} \tag{7.29}$$

and

$$p_x^{(\tau)} = 1 - q_x^{(\tau)} = \frac{\ell_{x+1}^{(\tau)}}{\ell_x^{(\tau)}}. \tag{7.30}$$

Similarly,

$$_n p_x^{(\tau)} = \frac{\ell_{x+n}^{(\tau)}}{\ell_x^{(\tau)}} \tag{7.31}$$

and

$$_n q_x^{(\tau)} = 1 - _n p_x^{(\tau)}. \tag{7.32}$$

It is easy to see how a multiple-decrement table can be constructed from sample data. There will be a separate column for each $d_x^{(k)}$. Starting with $\ell_0^{(\tau)}$, we obtain $d_0^{(k)} = q_0^{(k)} \ell_0^{(\tau)}$ for each value of k, and then add to get $d_0^{(\tau)} = \sum_{k=1}^{m} d_0^{(k)}$. Next we obtain $\ell_1^{(\tau)} = \ell_0^{(\tau)} - d_0^{(\tau)}$ and proceed inductively as before.

We can also talk about a central rate of decrement for each cause, as was done for death alone in Section 7.4. The central rate of decrement from all causes at age x, assuming uniform distribution of decrements, is

$$m_x^{(\tau)} = \frac{d_x^{(\tau)}}{\ell_x^{(\tau)} - \frac{1}{2} \cdot d_x^{(\tau)}}. \tag{7.33}$$

The central rate of decrement from cause (k) is given by

$$m_x^{(k)} = \frac{d_x^{(k)}}{\ell_x^{(\tau)} - \frac{1}{2} \cdot d_x^{(\tau)}}. \tag{7.34}$$

As before, several identities follow immediately. We will do one example here and leave others to the exercises.

Example 7.16

Show that $q_x^{(k)} = \dfrac{m_x^{(k)}}{1 + \frac{1}{2} \cdot m_x^{(\tau)}}.$

Solution

$$\frac{m_x^{(k)}}{1 + \frac{1}{2} \cdot m_x^{(\tau)}} = \frac{\dfrac{d_x^{(k)}}{\ell_x^{(\tau)} - \frac{1}{2} \cdot d_x^{(\tau)}}}{1 + \frac{1}{2}\left(\dfrac{d_x^{(\tau)}}{\ell_x^{(\tau)} - \frac{1}{2} \cdot d_x^{(\tau)}}\right)} = \frac{d_x^{(k)}}{\ell_x^{(\tau)}} = q_x^{(k)}. \qquad \square$$

We may also define the force of decrement from all causes combined. Analogous to Formula (7.8a) we have

$$\mu_x^{(\tau)} = -\frac{D(\ell_x^{(\tau)})}{\ell_x^{(\tau)}}. \tag{7.35}$$

The force of decrement from cause k is defined by

$$\mu_x^{(k)} = -\frac{D(\ell_x^{(k)})}{\ell_x^{(\tau)}}, \tag{7.36}$$

where $\ell_x^{(k)} = d_x^{(k)} + d_{x+1}^{(k)} + \cdots$. Then it follows that $\ell_x^{(\tau)} = \sum_{k=1}^{m} \ell_x^{(k)}$, which

leads to

$$\mu_x^{(\tau)} = \sum_{k=1}^{m} \mu_x^{(k)}. \tag{7.37}$$

| Example 7.17 |

For a person age x, $\mu_{x+t}^{(1)} = .03$ and $\mu_{x+t}^{(2)} = .02$ for $t \geq 0$, where (1) indicates death due to illness and (2) indicates death due to all other causes. Find each of the following.

(a)   The probability that (x) will die within the next 8 years.
(b)   The probability that (x) will die within the next 8 years due to illness.

| Solution |

(a)   We know that $\mu_{x+t}^{(\tau)} = .03 + .02 = .05$, so

$$_tp_x^{(\tau)} = e^{-\int_x^{x+t} \mu_r^{(\tau)} dr} = e^{-.05t}. \text{ Then}$$

$$_8q_x^{(\tau)} = 1 - {}_8p_x^{(\tau)} = 1 - e^{-.40} = .3297.$$

(b)   Our approach this time uses the multiple-decrement analogue to the single-decrement formula derived in Exercise 7-26(b). We have

$$_8q_x^{(1)} = \int_0^8 {}_tp_x^{(\tau)} \mu_{x+t}^{(1)} dt$$

$$= .03 \int_0^8 e^{-.05t} dt$$

$$= -.03 \left(\frac{e^{-.05t}}{.05} \right) \Big|_0^8$$

$$= .1978. \qquad \qquad \square$$

Finally we remark that the *absolute annual rate of decrement*, $q_x^{\prime(k)}$, is a concept which the student may encounter. These rates arise from consideration of the family of single decrement tables associated with any multiple decrement table. The theory behind this is more advanced than we wish to go into, but there is a formula which allows us to approximate the absolute rates of decrement when the probabilities $q_x^{(k)}$ are given. This is

$$q_x'^{(k)} \approx q_x^{(k)}\left(1 + \frac{1}{2}\left(q_x^{(\tau)} - q_x^{(k)}\right)\right). \tag{7.38}$$

Another important relationship is

$$p_x^{(\tau)} = \prod_{k=1}^{m}(1 - q_x'^{(k)}), \tag{7.39}$$

which is derived from (7.37) and can be verified approximately by use of (7.38).

Some questions involving absolute rates of decrement can be tricky and require careful handling. Here is one example, and others appear in the exercises.

| Example 7.18 |

A company is affected by two preretirement decrements, mortality (*m*) and termination (*t*). Assume $\ell_{30} = 5000$ and $\ell_{31} = 4800$. If the absolute rate of death is .003, find $q_{30}^{(t)}$.

| Solution |

We are given that $.003 = q_{30}'^{(m)} = q_{30}^{(m)}\left[1 + \frac{1}{2}\left(q_{30}^{(\tau)} - q_{30}^{(m)}\right)\right]$. We are also given that $q_{30}^{(\tau)} = \frac{200}{5000} = .04$, so $.003 = q_{30}^{(m)}\left[1 + \frac{1}{2}\left(.04 - q_{30}^{(m)}\right)\right]$, or $[q_{30}^{(m)}]^2 - 2.04q_{30}^{(m)} + .006 = 0$. Using the quadratic formula, we obtain the two answers $\frac{2.04 \pm \sqrt{(2.04)^2 - 4(.006)}}{2}$. The feasible solution (between 0 and 1) is $q_{30}^{(m)} = \frac{2.04 - \sqrt{(2.04)^2 - .024}}{2} = .00295$. Finally, $q_{30}^{(t)} = q_{30}^{(\tau)} - q_{30}^{(m)} = .03705$. □

EXERCISES

7.1   Introduction;   7.2 Life Tables

7-1.   For a certain type of insect, we find that $q_0 = .70$, $q_1 = .30$, $q_2 = .40$ and $q_3 = 1.0$. Starting with $\ell_0 = 1000$, construct a life table.

7-2.   Write expressions for each of the following:
   (a)   The probability that a 20-year-old lives 25 years.
   (b)   The probability that a 20-year-old reaches age 25.
   (c)   The probability that a 20-year-old dies between ages 25 and 26.
   (d)   The probability that a 20-year-old lives for at least 40 years.
   (e)   The probability that a pair of 20-year-olds do not both survive to age 60.

7-3.   80% of people age 25 survive to age 60. 40% of people who die between age 25 and age 60 do so before age 45.   Find the probability that a 45-year-old will die before reaching age 60.

7-4.   Four persons are all aged 30.
   (a)   Find an expression for the probability that any three of them will survive to age 60, with the other dying between age 50 and age 55.
   (b)   Find an expression for the probability that at least 2 of the persons will survive for at most 30 years.

7-5.   Explain, both mathematically and verbally, why the following are true.
   (a) $\ell_x = d_x + d_{x+1} + d_{x+2} + \cdots$
   (b) $\ell_{x+n} = \ell_x \cdot p_x \cdot p_{x+1} \cdot \cdots \cdot p_{x+n-1}$
   (c) $_{m+n}p_x = {_n}p_x \cdot {_m}p_{x+n}$
   (d) $q_x + p_x \cdot q_{x+1} + {_2}p_x \cdot q_{x+2} + \cdots = 1$

7-6. Complete the missing entries in the following table.

x	ℓ_x	d_x	p_x	q_x
0	1000	100		
1				
2	750		.80	
3				
4	300			.60
5				
6	0			

7-7. If $p_x = .95$ for all x, find each of the following:
  (a) p_{20} (b) $_2q_{30}$
  (c) The probability that a 20-year-old dies at age 50 last birth-day.
  (d) The probability that a 20-year-old dies between age 50 and age 55.

7-8. Find an expression for the probability that a 30-year-old will die in the second half of the year following her 35th birthday.

7-9. Derive each of the following approximations, where $0 < t < 1$.
  (a) $\ell_{x+t} = \ell_x - t \cdot d_x$
  (b) $\ell_{x+t} = (1-t) \cdot \ell_x + t \cdot \ell_{x+1}$
  (c) $_tp_x = 1 - t \cdot q_x$

7-10. Let $_{n|m}q_x$ denote the probability that a person aged x will die between ages $x + n$ and $x + n + m$. (When $m = 1$ it is omitted in this notation.)
  (a) Show that $_{n|m}q_x = \dfrac{\ell_{x+n} - \ell_{x+n+m}}{\ell_x}$.
  (b) Show that $_{n|m}q_x = {}_np_x - {}_{n+m}p_x$. Explain this identity verbally.
  (c) Show that $_{n|m}q_x = {}_np_x(1 - {}_mp_{x+n})$. Explain this identity verbally.

7-11. You are given the following probabilities:
  (i)   That two persons age 35 and 45 will both live for 10 years
        equals .80.
  (ii) That a person age 60 will die within 5 years, whereas
        another person age 55 will live for 5 years is .05.
  (iii) That a person age 35 will live 30 years is .60.
  Find the probability that a person age 35 will die between ages 55
  and 60.

7-12. The probability that a person age 10 will survive to age 30 is .80.
  Sixty per cent of the deaths between ages 10 and 40 occur after age
  30. The probability that three lives aged 30, 50 and 70 will all
  survive for 20 years is .20. Find $_{50}p_{40}$.

7.3 Analytic Formulae for ℓ_x

7-13. Given $\ell_x = 1000\left(1 - \frac{x}{120}\right)$, determine each of the following:
  (a) ℓ_0 (b) ℓ_{120} (c) d_{33} (d) $_{20}p_{30}$ (e) $_{30}q_{20}$
  (f) The probability that a 25-year-old lives for at least 20 years
       and at most 25 years.
  (g) The probability that three 25-year-olds all survive to age 80.

7-14. For the ℓ_x given in Question 13, calculate general formulae for p_x,
  q_x and μ_x. Then sketch graphs of all four functions.

7-15. Prove that in the general case of de Moivre's formula, given by
  (7.7), we have $\mu_x = \frac{1}{\omega - x}$.

7-16. Obtain an expression for μ_x if $\ell_x = ks^x w^{x^2} g^{c^x}$. (This is called
  Makeham's second formula.)

7-17. Show that Gompertz' formula for ℓ_x implies $p_x = g^{c^x(c-1)}$.

7-18. Show that Makeham's formula for ℓ_x implies $p_x = sg^{c^x(c-1)}$.

7-19. (a)   Starting with Gompertz' formula $\ell_x = kg^{c^x}$, verify that the force of mortality is $\mu_x = Bc^x$ for suitable B.

(b)   Starting with Makeham's formula $\ell_x = ks^x g^{c^x}$, verify that $\mu_x = A + Bc^x$ for suitable A and B.

7-20. Show that, under de Moivre's formula, $_n|q_x$ is independent of n. (See Question 7-10 for the definition of this notation.)

7-21. If $\ell_x = 100,000 \left(\frac{c-x}{c+x} \right)$ and $\ell_{35} = 44,000$, find each of the following:

(a)   The value of c.

(b)   The terminal age in the life table.

(c)   The probability of surviving from birth to age 50.

(d)   The probability that a person aged 15 will die between age 40 and age 50.

7-22. If $\ell_x = 250 (64 - .80x)^{1/3}$, find each of the following:

(a) $_{70}p_0$

(b) μ_{70}

(c)   The terminal age of the population.

7-23. If $\mu_x = .0017$ for $20 \le x \le 30$, find each of the following:

(a) p_{20} (b) $_5p_{20}$ (c) q_{23} (d) $_5q_{23}$ (e) $_4|q_{23}$ (f) $_4|_3q_{23}$

7-24. Show that if uniform distribution of deaths over year of age x is assumed, then $_tp_x\mu_{x+t} = q_x$ for all $0 < t < 1$.

7-25. During the first 12 months of life, infants in a developing country are subject to a force of mortality given by $\mu_x = \frac{1}{3+x}$, where x is measured in months. Calculate the probability that a newborn will survive for 4 months but not for 7 months.

7-26. (a)   Show that $_np_x = e^{-\int_x^{x+n} \mu_r \, dr} = e^{-\int_0^n \mu_{x+t} \, dt}$.

(b)   Use (7.8a) to derive the formula $_nq_x = \int_0^n {_tp_x}\mu_{x+t} \, dt$.

7-27. If x is fixed and t is a variable, show that $\mu_{x+t} = \frac{-D_t(_tp_x)}{_tp_x}$.

7.4   The Stationary Population

7-28. A service club has a constant membership of 1,000. X new
      entrants are added each year at exact age 35.   Withdrawals are
      either by death or by retirement.   40% of those who reach age 50
      retire at that time and all others retire at age 65.   Express each of
      the following in terms of population functions:
      (a)   The number of annual entrants at age 35.
      (b)   The number of members who retire each year at age 50.
      (c)   The number of members who die each year.

7-29. Estimate m_x if $\ell_x = 5825$ and $\ell_{x+1} = 5713$.

7-30. Prove that $m_x \geq q_x$ for all ages x.   When does equality occur?

7-31. Verify that $m_x = \mu_{x+1/2}$ for the function $\ell_x = 1000\left(1 - \frac{x}{105}\right)$.

7-32. Before 1980, a stationary population of 500,000 was maintained by
      10,000 annual births.   40% of the population was under age 15.
      Beginning in 1980, annual births increased to 12,000.   Assuming
      mortality rates did not change at any age, what was the total
      population on January 1, 1995?

7.5   Expectation of Life

7-33. If $\ell_x = 1000\left(1 - \frac{x}{100}\right)$, calculate e_{90} and $\overset{\circ}{e}_{90}$ (both exactly and
      approximately).

7-34. Using integration by parts, show that $\overset{\circ}{e}_x = \displaystyle\int_0^\infty t \cdot {}_t p_x \mu_{x+t}\, dt$.

7-35. You are given the following values for a stationary population:

x	ℓ_x	$\overset{\circ}{e}_x$
0	10,000	69.0
55	8,250	19.5
70	5,380	10.3

      Find the average age at death for those who survive to age 55 but
      die before age 70.

7-36. We are given the values $\ell_{50} = 8200$, $\overset{\circ}{e}_{50} = 20$, $\ell_{70} = 5000$, and $\overset{\circ}{e}_{70} = 10$.
   (a)   Find the average age at death for those surviving to age 50.
   (b)   Find the average age at death for those surviving to age 70.
   (c)   Find the average age at death for those who survive to age 50 but die before age 70.
   (d)   If $\ell_0 = 10{,}000$ and the average age at death of the entire population (assumed to be stationary) is 65, find the average age at death for those who do not survive to age 50.

7-37. In a stationary population of 120,000 lives, the number of deaths is 2000 annually. The complete expectation of life for a 40-year-old is 30 years. 60% of the population is under age 40.
   (a)   What is the average age at death for an individual in this population?
   (b)   What is the average age at death for an individual who dies before age 40?

7-38. An army of mercenaries has a constant size of 1000. Each year all new entrants are at exact age 25, and any soldier reaching age 55 must retire. No one can leave the army except by death or retirement (at age 55). There are seventy deaths each year among soldiers, the average age at death being 35. (a) How many new soldiers enter each year? (b) How many soldiers retire each year?

7-39. Find an expression for the expected age at death of a person who survives to age 40 and either dies before age 50 or dies after age 75.

7-40. In a small country with a stationary population, a special system is used for supporting the elderly. On January 1, each person whose age is between 20 and 65 contributes 100 to a pool. On the same date, payments of K are made from the pool to all persons aged 65 and over, with the entire pool being allocated.
   (a)   Derive an expression for K.
   (b)   If $K = 500$, $\ell_{20} = 2 \cdot \ell_{65}$, and the complete expectation of life at age 65 is 15 years, what is the complete expectation of life at age 20?

7.6 Multiple Decrements

7-41. Consider a population in which three decrements are acting, namely (a), (b), (c).

    (i)   Write an expression for the probability that a 40-year-old will leave the population because of decrement (b) at age 47 last birthday.

    (ii)   Write an expression for the probability that a 40-year-old will leave the population because of decrement (b) or (c) between ages 44 and 48.

    (iii)   Write formulae for $q_{30}^{(a)}$ and $m_{30}^{(a)}$.

    (iv)   If it is discovered that $q_x^{(a)} + q_x^{(b)} = 1 - p_x^{(\tau)}$ for all $x \geq 50$, what can you conclude about decrement (c)?

7-42. Show that $p_x^{(\tau)} = \dfrac{1 - \frac{1}{2} \cdot m_x^{(\tau)}}{1 + \frac{1}{2} \cdot m_x^{(\tau)}}$, assuming uniform distribution of decrements.

7-43. In the first year following training for soldiers, the central death and withdrawal rates are $m_x^{(d)} = a$ and $m_x^{(w)} = b$, respectively. What is the probability that a soldier just finishing training will still be a soldier one year later?

7-44. A company is affected by two preretirement decrements, mortality (d) and disability (i). Assume $\ell_{50}^{(\tau)} = 10{,}000$ and $\ell_{51}^{(\tau)} = 9300$. If the absolute rate of disability at age 50 is .06, find $d_{50}^{(d)}$.

7-45. Under a multiple decrement table, at each age from 50 to 70 the absolute rate of death is 2% and the absolute rate of termination for all causes other than death is 4%. Find a good approximation to each of the following probabilities:

    (a)   That an employee, aged 55, will still be employed at age 60

    (b)   That an employee, aged 55, will work for at least 5 years and at most 10 years with the company.

    (c)   That an employee, aged 55, will die while employed between his 58th and 59th birthdays.

CHAPTER EIGHT
LIFE ANNUITIES

8.1 BASIC CONCEPTS

In Section 6.3 we saw how to calculate the present value of contingent payments, and in Chapter 7 we learned how probabilities concerning survival can be calculated from life tables (or, occasionally, from an analytic formula). In the next two chapters we will combine these ideas to solve problems involving payments which are contingent on either survival or death.

Example 8.1

Yuanlin is 38 years old. If he reaches age 65, he will receive a single payment of 50,000. If $i = .12$, find an expression for the value of this payment to Yuanlin today.

Solution

The probability of survival to age 65 is $_{27}p_{38}$. Hence the answer is $50{,}000(_{27}p_{38})(1.12)^{-27}$. □

To obtain a numerical answer to Example 8.1 we could consult life tables. If, for example, $\ell_{38} = 8327$ and $\ell_{65} = 5411$, then we would have $_{27}p_{38} = \frac{5411}{8327} = .64981$, so the value would be equal to $50{,}000(.64981)(1.12)^{-27} = 1523.60$. On the other hand, if we assumed in Example 8.1 that $\ell_x = \ell_0 \left[1 - \frac{x}{105} \right]$, then $_{27}p_{38} = \frac{\ell_{65}}{\ell_{38}} = \frac{40}{67}$, and the value would be $50{,}000 \left(\frac{40}{67} \right)(1.12)^{-27} = 1399.81$.

Example 8.1 is an illustration of what is called a *pure endowment*, and a formula for the general case is easy to find. Assume that a unit of money is to be paid t years from now to an individual currently aged x, if the individual survives to that time. The value of this payment at the present time is equal to

$$_{t}E_x = (_{t}p_x)(1+i)^{-t} = v^{t} \, _{t}p_x. \qquad (8.1)$$

This important expression will be used to move payment values from one time point to another in the rest of this text. The present value of a pure endowment is also called the *net single premium* for the pure endowment.

A more common type of situation is called a *life annuity*. Example 6.14 was one illustration of a life annuity, and here is another.

Example 8.2

Aretha is 27 years old. Beginning one year from today, she will receive 10,000 annually for as long as she is alive. Find an expression for the present value of this series of payments assuming $i = .09$.

Solution

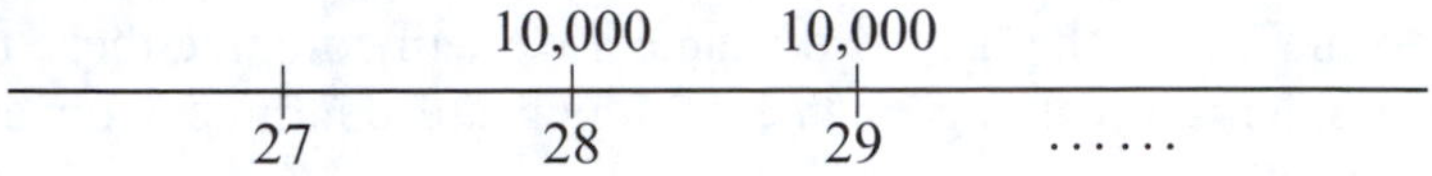

FIGURE 8.1

We can view this as a series of pure endowments of the type described in the previous example. Thus the answer is

$$10,000(p_{27})(1.09)^{-1} + 10,000(_2p_{27})(1.09)^{-2} + \cdots$$

$$= \sum_{k=1}^{\infty} (10,000)(_kp_{27})(1.09)^{-k}.$$

Although this appears to be an infinite sum, in practice it will be finite since $_kp_{27} = 0$ eventually. □

Now, however, we have a serious problem. If $_kp_{27}$ is obtained from a life table for each k, it appears that there is no nice way of calculating this sum. Unlike our examples in Chapter 3, where the terms formed a geometric sequence, we would here have to resort to adding terms one at a time.

To get around this difficulty life tables have columns in which these terms have already been added together. In other words, there are life tables constructed in conjunction with a number of commonly encountered rates of interest, and for various values of x and i it will be possible to look up such sums in the tables. The name given to these sums is *commutation functions*, and we will study them carefully in the next section.

A general formula for a life annuity is easily written down. As with interest-only annuities, we will assume constant payments of 1 per year for as long as the individual is alive, with the first payment due at the end if the year, as illustrated in Figure 8.2.

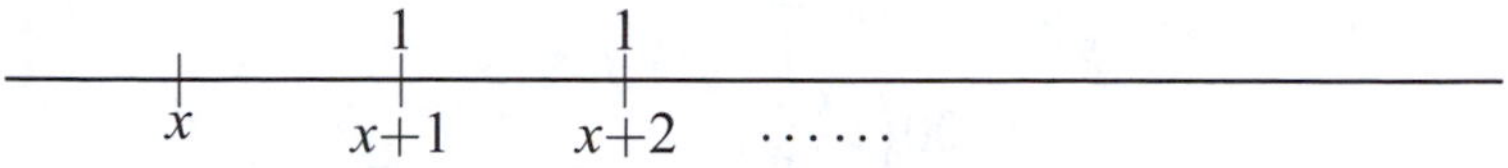

FIGURE 8.2

The symbol for the present value of these payments to a life aged x is a_x, and the formula is

$$a_x = (1+i)^{-1}p_x + (1+i)^{-2}\,_2p_x + \cdots$$

$$= \sum_{t=1}^{\infty} (1+i)^{-t}\,_tp_x$$

$$= \sum_{t=1}^{\infty} v^t\,_tp_x. \qquad (8.2)$$

Again we remark that the present value is also called the *net single premium* for the annuity. (In some texts the phrase *actuarial present value* is also used; in this text we will continue to use the simpler *present value*.)

If we have a formula for ℓ_x or p_x, we might be able to sum the above series algebraically.

Example 8.3

Consider Aretha's life annuity in Example 8.2. Find the net single premium for this annuity in each of the following cases:
(a) $p_x = .95$ for each x
(b) $\ell_x = \ell_0\left[1 - \dfrac{x}{105}\right]$

Solution

(a)   Since $_kp_x = (.95)^k$ for all k, the required value is

$$10,000a_{27} = \sum_{k=1}^{\infty} (10,000)(.95)^k(1.09)^{-k}$$

$$= \sum_{k=1}^{\infty} (10,000)\left[\frac{.95}{1.09}\right]^k$$

$$= \frac{10,000\left(\frac{.95}{1.09}\right)}{1 - \frac{.95}{1.09}} = 67,857.14.$$

(b)   In this case, $_kp_x = \frac{\ell_{x+k}}{\ell_x} = \frac{105 - x - k}{105 - x}$ for all k, so we have

$$10,000\left[\left(\frac{77}{78}\right)(1.09)^{-1} + \left(\frac{76}{78}\right)(1.09)^{-2} + \cdots\right] = \frac{10,000}{78}(Da)_{\overline{77}|.09},$$

since payments will be 0 after 77 years. From Formula (3.29), we

have $\frac{10,000}{78}\left[\frac{77 - a_{\overline{77}|}}{.09}\right] = 93,879.59.$ ☐

Now let us introduce a bit more notation. Perhaps a life annuity has payments which will end after a certain period.

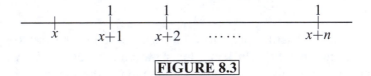

FIGURE 8.3

A *temporary* life annuity which will only continue for a maximum of n years is denoted $a_{x:\overline{n}|}$, and the formula is

$$a_{x:\overline{n}|} = \sum_{t=1}^{n} (1 + i)^{-t} {}_tp_x$$

$$= \sum_{t=1}^{n} v^t {}_tp_x. \qquad (8.3)$$

An n-year *deferred* life annuity is one in which the first payment to a person now aged x does not occur until age $x + n + 1$.

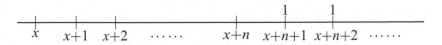

FIGURE 8.4

This is denoted by $_n|a_x$, and we have

$$_n|a_x = \sum_{t=1}^{\infty} (1+i)^{-n-t} {}_{n+t}p_x$$

$$= \sum_{t=n+1}^{\infty} v^t {}_t p_x. \tag{8.4}$$

We note that $_n|a_x$ can be thought of as omitting the first n payments from a_x, so we have

$$_n|a_x = a_x - a_{x:\overline{n}|}. \tag{8.5}$$

As with interest-only annuities in Chapter 3, there are *annuities-due* in life contingencies as well as annuities-immediate. The notation is analogous: $\ddot{a}_x$ denotes a life annuity whose first payment occurs immediately.

Time diagrams for $\ddot{a}_x$, $\ddot{a}_{x:\overline{n}|}$, and $_n|\ddot{a}_x$ are shown below.

FIGURE 8.4a

FIGURE 8.4b

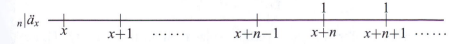

FIGURE 8.4c

Hence we have

$$\ddot{a}_x = 1 + a_x, \qquad (8.6)$$

$$\ddot{a}_{x:\overline{n}|} = 1 + a_{x:\overline{n-1}|}, \qquad (8.7)$$

and

$$_n|\ddot{a}_x = {}_{n-1}|a_x. \qquad (8.8)$$

However, the reader should be careful! Because of the uncertainty of payments in life annuities, other formulae do not carry over directly. For instance, the identity $\ddot{a}_{\overline{n}|} = (1 + i) a_{\overline{n}|}$ does *not* extend to life annuities $\ddot{a}_{x:\overline{n}|} = (1 + i) a_{x:\overline{n}|}$. To obtain the correct analogue, we note that

$$\ddot{a}_{x:\overline{n}|} = 1 + \sum_{t=1}^{n-1} (1 + i)^{-t} {}_t p_x$$

$$= (1 + i) \left[(1 + i)^{-1} + \sum_{t=1}^{n-1} (1 + i)^{-t-1} {}_t p_x \right].$$

Therefore

$$p_{x-1} \ddot{a}_{x:\overline{n}|} = (1 + i) \left[(1 + i)^{-1} p_{x-1} + \sum_{t=1}^{n-1} (1 + i)^{-t-1} {}_t p_x \, p_{x-1} \right]$$

$$= (1 + i) \left[(1 + i)^{-1} p_{x-1} + \sum_{t=1}^{n-1} (1 + i)^{-t-1} {}_{t+1} p_{x-1} \right]$$

$$= (1 + i) \left[\sum_{t=1}^{n} (1 + i)^{-t} {}_t p_{x-1} \right]$$

$$= (1 + i) a_{x-1:\overline{n}|}.$$

This is usually written as

$$a_{x-1:\overline{n}|} = v \, p_{x-1} \, \ddot{a}_{x:\overline{n}|}. \qquad (8.9)$$

The reader should try to give a verbal explanation for this identity. Other relationships similar to (8.9) are presented in the exercises.

8.2 COMMUTATION FUNCTIONS

In this section we will introduce those commutation functions which are important when dealing with life annuities. After learning how to manipulate these functions, we will see some further examples of life annuity problems.

Recall first from Section 8.1 that a pure endowment of 1 to be paid n years hence to a life currently age x has present value $v^n \, {}_np_x$. The symbol ${}_nE_x$ is used to denote such an endowment, so

$$_nE_x = v^n \left[\frac{\ell_{x+n}}{\ell_x} \right] = \frac{v^{x+n} \, \ell_{x+n}}{v^x \, \ell_x}. \tag{8.10}$$

The important expression $v^x \ell_x$ which appears in both numerator and denominator is given the symbol D_x. That is

$$D_x = v^x \, \ell_x, \tag{8.11}$$

so we have

$$_nE_x = \frac{D_{x+n}}{D_x}. \tag{8.12}$$

Now we recall the formula for a life annuity,

$$a_x = \sum_{t=1}^{\infty} v^t \, {}_tp_x = \sum_{t=1}^{\infty} {}_tE_x. \tag{8.13}$$

We can also write this as $a_x = \sum_{t=1}^{\infty} \frac{D_{x+t}}{D_x} = \frac{1}{D_x}(D_{x+1} + D_{x+2} + \cdots)$.

We define a new commutation function

$$N_x = \sum_{t=0}^{\infty} D_{x+t}. \tag{8.14}$$

Then we have the formula

$$a_x = \frac{N_{x+1}}{D_x}. \tag{8.15}$$

Clearly if we have values of N_x tabulated, then we can easily calculate a_x. It is here that commutation functions are very useful in life contingencies.

| Example 8.4 |

Marvin, aged 38, purchases a life annuity of 1000 per year. From tables, we learn that $N_{38} = 5600$ and $N_{39} = 5350$. Find the net single premium Marvin should pay for this annuity (a) if the first 1000 payment occurs in one year; (b) if the first 1000 payment occurs now.

| Solution |

$$\begin{array}{ccc} & 1000 & 1000 \\ \hline 38 & 38 & 40 \quad \cdots\cdots \end{array}$$

| FIGURE 8.5 |

(a)   The net single premium is $1000\left(\dfrac{N_{39}}{D_{38}}\right)$, from Formula (8.15). Observe that $D_{38} = N_{38} - N_{39} = 250$, so the price is given by $1000\left(\dfrac{5350}{250}\right) = 21{,}400$.

(b)   Since $\ddot{a}_x = 1 + a_x$, the price is 22,400.   □

Example 8.4(b) could also be obtained using the general formula

$$\ddot{a}_x = \frac{N_x}{D_x}. \tag{8.16}$$

Here are some other basic identities, all of which can be obtained by suitable substitution of commutation functions into formulae derived in Section 8.1. The student should verify that all of these identities are correct.

$$a_{x:\overline{n}|} = \sum_{t=1}^{n} \frac{D_{x+t}}{D_x} = \frac{N_{x+1} - N_{x+n+1}}{D_x} \tag{8.17}$$

$$_{n|}a_x = \frac{N_{x+n+1}}{D_x} \tag{8.18}$$

$$\ddot{a}_{x:\overline{n}|} = \frac{N_x - N_{x+n}}{D_x} \tag{8.19}$$

Analogous to the interest-only annuity symbols $s_{\overline{n}|}$ and $\ddot{s}_{\overline{n}|}$ for accumulated values of annuities, we have the life contingent symbols $s_{x:\overline{n}|}$ and $\ddot{s}_{x:\overline{n}|}$ for the accumulated values of life annuities. Recall the meaning of $_nE_x$ defined by (8.1). Then we have

$$a_{x:\overline{n}|} = {}_nE_x \cdot s_{x:\overline{n}|} \qquad (8.20a)$$

and

$$\ddot{a}_{x:\overline{n}|} = {}_nE_x \cdot \ddot{s}_{x:\overline{n}|}. \qquad (8.21a)$$

Using (8.12), (8.17), and (8.19) for $_nE_x$, $a_{x:\overline{n}|}$, and $\ddot{a}_{x:\overline{n}|}$, respectively, we have the commutation function expressions

$$s_{x:\overline{n}|} = \frac{N_{x+1} - N_{x+n+1}}{D_{x+n}} \qquad (8.20b)$$

and

$$\ddot{s}_{x:\overline{n}|} = \frac{N_x - N_{x+n}}{D_{x+n}}. \qquad (8.21b)$$

Other commutation function expressions can be written down and given verbal interpretation, such as the one in the following example.

| Example 8.5 |
State verbally the meaning of $\dfrac{N_{35} - N_{55}}{D_{20}}$.
| Solution |
This is the present value, or net single premium, for a life annuity bought by a 20-year-old, with first payment at age 35 and a maximum of 20 payments in total, as illustrated by Figure 8.6.

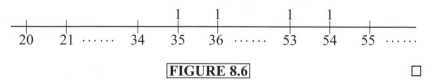

FIGURE 8.6 ☐

Here are further examples involving commutation functions. More can be found in the exercises.

| Example 8.6 |
Given $N_x = 5000$, $N_{x+1} = 4900$, $N_{x+2} = 4810$ and $q_x = .005$, find i.

Solution

We have $D_x = N_x - N_{x+1} = 100$, and $D_{x+1} = N_{x+1} - N_{x+2} = 90$, so
$\frac{90}{100} = \frac{D_{x+1}}{D_x} = \frac{v^{x+1}\ell_{x+1}}{v^x\ell_x} = vp_x$. But $p_x = 1 - .005 = .995$. Hence
$i = \frac{.995}{.90} - 1 = .1056$.   □

Example 8.7

Margaret, aged 65, purchases a life annuity which will provide annual payments of 1000 commencing at age 66. For the next year only, Margaret's probability of survival is higher than that predicted by the life tables and, in fact, is equal to $p_{65}+.05$, where p_{65} is taken from the standard life table. Based on that standard table, we have the values $D_{65} = 300$, $D_{66} = 260$ and $N_{67} = 1450$. If $i = .09$, find the net single premium for this annuity.

Solution

We will attack this from first principles. The general formula for the price of a 1000 life annuity is $1000a_{65} = \sum_{t=1}^{\infty} 1000(_tp_{65})v^t$, where $_tp_{65}$ is the probability that the *individual involved* survives t years. Now, in Margaret's case, these probabilities will not be the standard ones. To avoid confusion of symbols, let us write $_t\tilde{p}_{65}$ for the probability that Margaret survives t years. Hence our net single premium is equal to $\sum_{t=1}^{\infty}(1000)(_t\tilde{p}_{65})v^t$. Now $\tilde{p}_{65} = p_{65}+.05$, but the two-year probability $_2\tilde{p}_{65}$ is $\tilde{p}_{65} \cdot \tilde{p}_{66} = (p_{65}+.05)p_{66}$, since it is only in the first year that Margaret's probability of survival is unusual. In general, we see that $_t\tilde{p}_{65} = (p_{65}+.05)_{t-1}p_{66}$, for $t \geq 2$. Hence the net single premium is

$$1000\tilde{a}_{65} = 1000(p_{65}+.05)v + \sum_{t=2}^{\infty}(1000)(p_{65}+.05)_{t-1}p_{66}\,v^t$$

$$= 1000p_{65}v + \sum_{t=2}^{\infty}(1000)p_{65}\,_{t-1}p_{66}v^t + 50v + \sum_{t=2}^{\infty}50\,_{t-1}p_{66}\,v^t$$

$$= 1000p_{65}v + \sum_{t=2}^{\infty}(1000)\,_tp_{65}\,v^t + 50v + 50v\sum_{t=1}^{\infty}\,_tp_{66}\,v^t$$

$$= 1000a_{65} + 50v + 50v\,a_{66}$$

$$= 1000\left(\frac{N_{66}}{D_{65}}\right) + \frac{50}{1.09}\left(1 + \frac{N_{67}}{D_{66}}\right).$$

Now $N_{66} = N_{67} + D_{66} = 1710$. Hence our price is

$$1000\left(\frac{1710}{300}\right) + \frac{50}{1.09}\left(1+\frac{1450}{260}\right) = 6001.69.\qquad\square$$

The previous example could be a special case of a more general situation where a "select" group of the population has a different mortality experience from that given in the life tables. Sometimes, as in the last example, a group of people will have a higher than average probability of survival, perhaps because they are in excellent health. In other cases, the select group might have a higher than usual mortality rate, perhaps because of employment in dangerous surroundings.

The notation $p_{[x]}$ and $q_{[x]}$ is often used to denote these differing probabilities if a person age x is in the first year of being in the select group. Probabilities in subsequent years of being in the select group are denoted $p_{[x]+1}, p_{[x]+2}$, and so on.

Other notation involving select groups follows naturally. For example, $a_{[30]}$ would be the net single premium for a life annuity of 1, first payment in one year, to a person aged 30 in his first year as a member of the select group.

A life table which involves a select group is often called a *select-and-ultimate* table.

Example 8.8

A select-and-ultimate table has a select period of two years. Select probabilities are related to ultimate probabilities by the relationships $p_{[x]} = \left(\frac{11}{10}\right)p_x$ and $p_{[x]+1} = \left(\frac{21}{20}\right)p_{x+1}$. An ultimate table shows $D_{60} = 1900$, $D_{61} = 1500$, and $\ddot{a}_{60:\overline{20|}} = 11$, when $i = .08$. Find the select temporary annuity $\ddot{a}_{[60]:\overline{20|}}$.

Solution

We will proceed from first principles. We have $\ddot{a}_{[60]:\overline{20|}} = 1 + \sum_{t=1}^{19} v^t\, {}_t\tilde{p}_{60}$,

where ${}_t\tilde{p}_{60}$ is the probability of survival for t years of a person entering the select period at age 60. Now we know $\tilde{p}_{60} = p_{[60]} = \left(\frac{11}{10}\right)p_{60}$ and ${}_2\tilde{p}_{60} = p_{[60]}p_{[60]+1} = \left(\frac{231}{200}\right){}_2p_{60}$. In general, ${}_t\tilde{p}_{60} = \left(\frac{231}{200}\right){}_tp_{60}$, $t \geq 2$, since the select period is only 2 years. Therefore the annuity value is

$$\ddot{a}_{[60]:\overline{20}|} = 1 + \left(\frac{11}{10}\right) vp_{60} + \left(\frac{231}{200}\right) v^2 \,_2p_{60} + \cdots + \left(\frac{231}{200}\right) v^{19} \,_{19}p_{60}$$

$$= \left(\frac{231}{200}\right) \ddot{a}_{60:\overline{20}|} - \frac{31}{200} - \frac{11}{200} \cdot vp_{60}.$$

We are given that $\ddot{a}_{60:\overline{20}|} = 11$. Also $vp_{60} = \dfrac{v^{61} \ell_{61}}{v^{60} \ell_{60}} = \dfrac{D_{61}}{D_{60}} = \dfrac{15}{19}$. Thus

$$\ddot{a}_{[60]:\overline{20}|} = \left(\frac{231}{200}\right)(11) - \frac{31}{200} - \left(\frac{11}{200}\right)\left(\frac{15}{19}\right) = 12.51. \qquad \square$$

Another variation on the idea of changing life tables is illustrated by the following example.

| Example 8.9 |

The following values are based on a unisex life table:

$$N_{38} = 5600, \; N_{39} = 5350, \; N_{40} = 5105, \; N_{41} = 4865, \; N_{42} = 4625$$

It is assumed that this table needs to be set forward one year for males and set back two years for females. If Michael and Brenda are both age 40, find the net single premium that each should pay for a life annuity of 1000 per year, if the first payment occurs immediately.

| Solution |

Michael should be treated as if he were age 41, so his premium will be
$$\frac{1000 N_{41}}{D_{41}} = \frac{1000(4865)}{240} = 20{,}270.83.$$
Brenda should be treated as if she were age 38, so her premium will be
$$\frac{1000 N_{38}}{D_{38}} = \frac{1000(5600)}{250} = 22{,}400.00. \qquad \square$$

8.3 ANNUITIES PAYABLE m^{thly}

In practice life annuities are often payable more frequently than once a year, with monthly being a very common frequency. Exactly the same situation arose with interest-only annuities in Chapter 3, as with mortgages, for example, where the payments were usually monthly. We encountered no difficulty in dealing with this in Chapter 3, where we simply converted the given interest rate to an equivalent rate for the payment period and proceeded as usual.

However life annuities do present a problem. We are totally dependent on commutation functions for calculating values of a_x, and commutation functions are only tabulated for standard rates of interest, and for *yearly* probabilities of survival. To apply commutation functions to life annuities payable monthly, for example, we would need tables which don't exist. Another method must be found.

We denote by $a_x^{(m)}$ the present value of an immediate life annuity to a life aged x where each yearly payment of 1 is divided into m evenly-spaced payments of $\frac{1}{m}$ each, the first due at age $x + \frac{1}{m}$. Recall that a similar notation was introduced for interest-only annuities in Exercise 30 of Chapter 3. The difference between a_x and $a_x^{(m)}$ is illustrated in Figure 8.7.

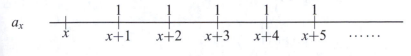

FIGURE 8.7a

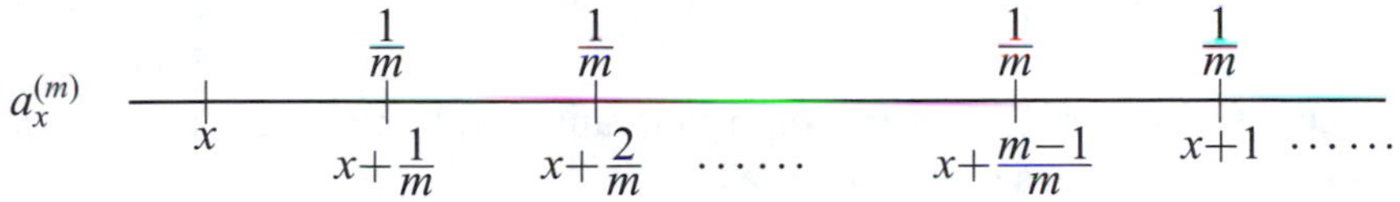

FIGURE 8.7b

We now proceed to derive a good approximate formula for $a_x^{(m)}$. If, for the moment, we allow ourselves to use D_y for non-integral values of y, then we have

$$a_x^{(m)} = \frac{1}{mD_x}[D_{x+1/m} + D_{x+2/m} + \cdots]$$

$$= \frac{1}{mD_x}\left[\sum_{i=0}^{\infty}\sum_{j=1}^{m} D_{x+i+j/m}\right]. \tag{8.22}$$

Using linear interpolation between successive D_y for integer y, we obtain

$$D_{x+i+j/m} \approx D_{x+i} + \frac{j}{m}(D_{x+i+1} - D_{x+i}). \tag{8.23}$$

Substitution of (8.23) into (8.22) yields

$$a_x^{(m)} \approx \frac{1}{mD_x}\left[\sum_{i=0}^{\infty}\sum_{j=1}^{m}\left(D_{x+i}+\frac{j}{m}(D_{x+i+1}-D_{x+i})\right)\right]$$

$$= \frac{1}{mD_x}\left[mD_x-\sum_{j=1}^{m}\frac{j}{m}\cdot D_x\right]+\frac{1}{mD_x}\left[\sum_{i=1}^{\infty}m\cdot D_{x+i}\right]$$

$$= 1+a_x-\frac{1}{m^2}\sum_{j=1}^{m}j$$

$$= a_x+1-\frac{m(m+1)}{2m^2}$$

$$= a_x+\frac{m-1}{2m}. \tag{8.24}$$

Formula (8.24) for $a_x^{(m)}$ is very important, and will be required numerous times in this and subsequent sections.

| Example 8.10 |

Linda, aged 47, purchases a life annuity consisting of monthly payments of 1000 each, the first payment due in one month. Find the net single premium for this annuity if $D_{47}=850$ and $N_{48}=6000$.

| Solution |

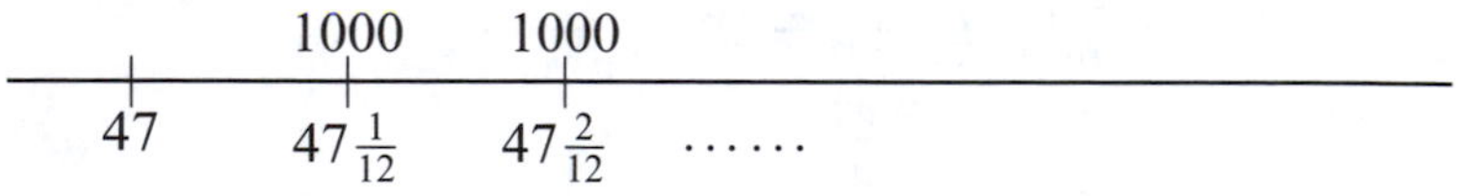

FIGURE 8.8

Since the total yearly payment is 12,000, the answer is $12{,}000a_{47}^{(12)}$. Our approximation (8.24) gives us $a_{47}^{(12)}=a_{47}+\frac{11}{24}$. Hence the answer is

$$12{,}000\left(\frac{N_{48}}{D_{47}}+\frac{11}{24}\right)=12{,}000\left(\frac{6000}{850}+\frac{11}{24}\right)=90{,}205.88\,. \qquad \square$$

What if our m^{thly} life annuity is deferred for n years, with the first payment to be made at age $x + n + \frac{1}{m}$? We then have

$$_n|\, a_x^{(m)} = \left(\frac{D_{x+n}}{D_x}\right) a_{x+n}^{(m)}$$

$$\approx \left(\frac{D_{x+n}}{D_x}\right)\left(a_{x+n} + \frac{m-1}{2m}\right)$$

$$= \,_n|\, a_x + \left(\frac{m-1}{2m}\right)\left(\frac{D_{x+n}}{D_x}\right). \tag{8.25}$$

Using (8.24) and (8.25) together, it is easy to obtain a formula for a temporary life annuity payable m times a year for n years. We have

$$a_{x:\overline{n}|}^{(m)} = a_x^{(m)} - \,_n|\, a_x^{(m)}$$

$$\approx a_x + \frac{m-1}{2m} - \left[\,_n|\, a_x + \left(\frac{m-1}{2m}\right)\left(\frac{D_{x+n}}{D_x}\right)\right]$$

$$= a_x - \,_n|\, a_x + \frac{m-1}{2m}\left(1 - \frac{D_{x+n}}{D_x}\right)$$

$$= a_{x:\overline{n}|} + \frac{m-1}{2m}\left(1 - \,_nE_x\right). \tag{8.26}$$

Example 8.11

Find Linda's premium in Example 8.10 if the annuity is to last only 20 years. Assume $N_{68} = 1400$ and $D_{67} = 310$.

Solution

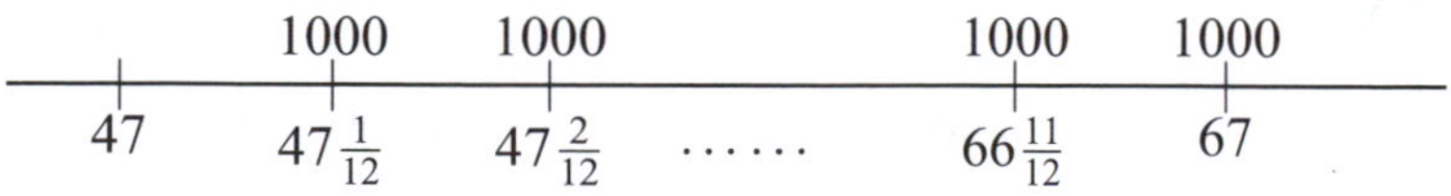

FIGURE 8.9

The answer is

$$12{,}000a_{47:\overline{20}|}^{(12)} = 12{,}000\left[a_{47:\overline{20}|} + \tfrac{11}{24}\left(1-\tfrac{D_{67}}{D_{47}}\right)\right]$$

$$= 12{,}000\left[\tfrac{N_{48}-N_{68}}{D_{47}} + \tfrac{11}{24}\left(1-\tfrac{310}{850}\right)\right]$$

$$= 12{,}000\left[\tfrac{6000-1400}{850} + \tfrac{11}{24}\left(\tfrac{540}{850}\right)\right]$$

$$= 68{,}435.29. \qquad\qquad \square$$

Similarly, we can define $\ddot{a}_x^{(m)}$ as being just like $a_x^{(m)}$, but with the first payment of $\tfrac{1}{m}$ occurring immediately. Hence we have

$$\ddot{a}_x^{(m)} = a_x^{(m)} + \tfrac{1}{m}. \qquad\qquad (8.27)$$

It follows from (8.24) and (8.27) that

$$\ddot{a}_x^{(m)} \approx a_x + \tfrac{m-1}{2m} + \tfrac{1}{m}$$

$$= \ddot{a}_x - 1 + \tfrac{m-1}{2m} + \tfrac{1}{m}$$

$$= \ddot{a}_x - \tfrac{m-1}{2m}. \qquad\qquad (8.28)$$

Next we wish to define a corresponding m^{thly} commutation function, $N_x^{(m)}$, for $\ddot{a}_x^{(m)}$. Analogous to $\ddot{a}_x = \tfrac{N_x}{D_x}$, we would like to have $\ddot{a}_x^{(m)} = \tfrac{N_x^{(m)}}{D_x}$. However, we know from (8.28) that $\ddot{a}_x^{(m)} \approx \tfrac{N_x}{D_x} - \tfrac{m-1}{2m}$, or $\ddot{a}_x^{(m)} = \tfrac{N_x - \tfrac{m-1}{2m}D_x}{D_x}$. We conclude that the appropriate definition is

$$N_x^{(m)} = N_x - \tfrac{m-1}{2m}D_x. \qquad\qquad (8.29)$$

Corresponding annuities $_n|\ddot{a}_x^{(m)}$ and $\ddot{a}_{x:\overline{n}|}^{(m)}$ are defined as expected, and identities for these are given in the exercises. We will give one example here showing how formulae for these related annuities can be expressed in terms of commutation functions.

Example 8.12

Show that $_n|a_x^{(m)} \approx \dfrac{N_{x+n+1} + \frac{m-1}{2m} \cdot D_{x+n}}{D_x} = \dfrac{N_{x+n}^{(m)} - \frac{1}{m} \cdot D_{x+n}}{D_x}.$

Solution

From (8.25) we have

$$_n|a_x^{(m)} \approx {}_n|a_x + \left(\frac{m-1}{2m}\right)\left(\frac{D_{x+n}}{D_x}\right)$$

$$= \frac{N_{x+n+1}}{D_x} + \frac{\left(\frac{m-1}{2m}\right)D_{x+n}}{D_x}$$

$$= \frac{N_{x+n} - D_{x+n} + \left(\frac{m-1}{2m}\right)D_{x+n}}{D_x}$$

$$= \frac{N_{x+n} - \left(\frac{m+1}{2m}\right)D_{x+n}}{D_x}$$

$$= \frac{N_{x+n}^{(m)} - \frac{1}{m} \cdot D_{x+n}}{D_x}. \qquad \square$$

Just as we did in Section 3.5, we can now define a *continuous* life annuity $\bar{a}_x$ as

$$\bar{a}_x = \lim_{m \to \infty} a_x^{(m)}. \qquad (8.30)$$

An integral representation for $\bar{a}_x$ can be obtained by changing the summation sign in (8.2) to an integral, obtaining

$$\bar{a}_x = \int_0^\infty v^t \, {}_tp_x \, dt. \qquad (8.31)$$

This expression is useful if we have an analytic formula for $_tp_x$. In any case, an approximate value for $\bar{a}_x$ can be found by taking the limit of the approximate Formula (8.24) for $a_x^{(m)}$ derived earlier. We obtain

$$\bar{a}_x = \lim_{m \to \infty} a_x^{(m)} \approx \lim_{m \to \infty} \left[a_x + \frac{m-1}{2m}\right] = a_x + \frac{1}{2}. \qquad (8.32)$$

In terms of commutation functions, we obtain the approximate formula

$$\bar{a}_x \approx \frac{N_{x+1}}{D_x} + \frac{1}{2} = \frac{N_x - D_x + \frac{1}{2} \cdot D_x}{D_x} = \frac{N_x - \frac{1}{2} \cdot D_x}{D_x}. \qquad (8.33)$$

If we define a continuous commutation function $\bar{N}_x$ to be

$$\bar{N}_x = N_x - \frac{1}{2} \cdot D_x, \qquad (8.34)$$

then it follows from (8.33) that we can write

$$\bar{a}_x = \frac{\bar{N}_x}{D_x}. \qquad (8.35)$$

The reader will be asked to derive formulae for the continuous life annuities $\bar{a}_{x:\overline{n}|}$ and $_{n|}\bar{a}_x$ in the exercises.

| Example 8.13 |

Find the value of a continuous life annuity of 2000 per year for a 50-year-old if we assume that $\delta = .08$ and $\mu_x = .05$ for all x.

| Solution |

From Section 7.3, we know that $_t p_{50} = \frac{_{50+t} p_0}{_{50} p_0} = \frac{e^{-\int_0^{50+t} .05 dx}}{e^{-\int_0^{50} .05 dx}} = e^{-.05t}$.

From Section 1.6, we know that $v = e^{-.08}$. Hence the answer is

$$2000 \bar{a}_{50} = 2000 \int_0^\infty e^{-.08t} e^{-.05t} \, dt$$

$$= 2000 \int_0^\infty e^{-.13t} \, dt$$

$$= 2000 \left(\frac{1}{.13} \right)$$

$$= 15{,}384.62. \qquad \square$$

Note that the above example is rather unrealistic, because the age of the individual involved had no effect on the final answer!

8.4 VARYING LIFE ANNUITIES

Up to now we have assumed that all payments in a life annuity are the same size. As with interest-only annuities, however, this may not be the case, and the methods of handling varying payments are exactly the same here as they were in Section 3.6. We will develop formulae for the special cases where payments are increasing or decreasing in arithmetic progression. In other situations an argument from first principles will be appropriate.

Example 8.14

Ernest, aged 50, purchases a life annuity which offers him annual payments of 5000 for 5 years, 3000 for the five subsequent years, and 8000 each year after that. If the first payment occurs in exactly one year, find an expression for the net single premium that Ernest should pay for this annuity.

Solution

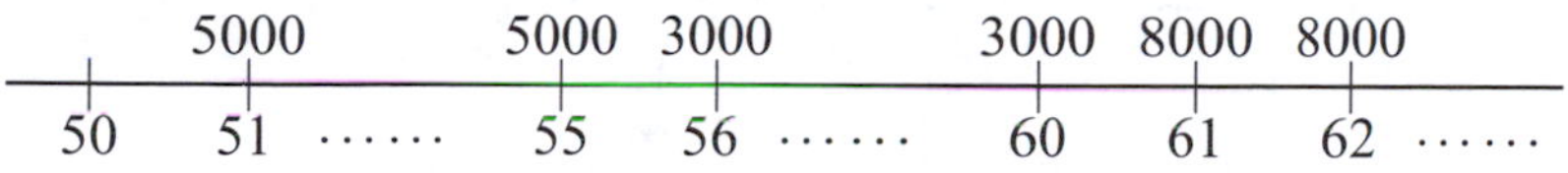

```
         5000              5000  3000        3000  8000  8000
  ───┼────┼──────────┼─────┼───────────┼─────┼─────┼───────
    50    51 ······   55    56  ······  60    61    62 ······
```

FIGURE 8.10

There are several ways to solve this problem. We could, for example, view this as the sum of a 3000 life annuity, a 2000 temporary life annuity with a term of 5 years, and a 5000 life annuity deferred for 10 years. Hence the premium is equal to

$$\frac{3000N_{51} + 2000(N_{51}-N_{56}) + 5000N_{61}}{D_{50}} = \frac{5000N_{51} + 5000N_{61} - 2000N_{56}}{D_{50}}.$$

We note that there are other correct ways of analyzing the above payments. We could view this as an 8000 life annuity, with 5000 subtracted for each of the next 10 years and 2000 added back on for each of the next 5 years. This gives

$$\frac{8000N_{51} - 5000(N_{51} - N_{61}) + 2000(N_{51} - N_{56})}{D_{50}}$$

$$= \frac{5000N_{51} + 5000N_{61} - 2000N_{56}}{D_{50}}, \text{ as before.} \qquad \square$$

Let us now consider the case of annuities increasing in arithmetical sequence. Let $(Ia)_x$ denote the present value at age x of a life annuity, first payment in one year, having payments of 1, 2, 3, $\ldots$.

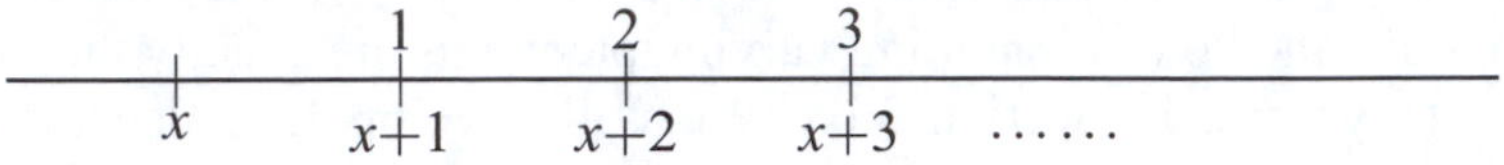

FIGURE 8.11

The general formula for $(Ia)_x$ is

$$(Ia)_x = \sum_{t=1}^{\infty} t v^t {}_t p_x. \tag{8.36}$$

Note that we can write the above as

$$(Ia)_x = \sum_{t=1}^{\infty} v^t {}_t p_x + \sum_{t=2}^{\infty} v^t {}_t p_x + \sum_{t=3}^{\infty} v^t {}_t p_x + \cdots$$

$$= a_x + {}_{1|}a_x + {}_{2|}a_x + \cdots$$

$$= \sum_{t=0}^{\infty} {}_{t|}a_x. \tag{8.37}$$

In terms of commutation functions, we have

$$(Ia)_x = \sum_{t=0}^{\infty} \frac{N_{x+t+1}}{D_x}. \tag{8.38}$$

Defining the new commutation function

$$S_x = \sum_{t=0}^{\infty} N_{x+t}, \tag{8.39}$$

we then have the formula

$$(Ia)_x = \frac{S_{x+1}}{D_x}. \tag{8.40}$$

An increasing life annuity with a term of n years is denoted by $(Ia)_{x:\overline{n}|}$.

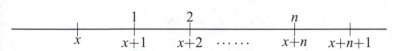

FIGURE 8.12

We clearly have

$$(Ia)_{x:\overline{n}|} = \sum_{t=1}^{n} t v^t {}_t p_x. \tag{8.41}$$

A good way of thinking about this is to observe that

$$
\begin{aligned}
(Ia)_{x:\overline{n}|} &= (Ia)_x - \sum_{t=n+1}^{\infty} t v^t {}_t p_x \\
&= (Ia)_x - v^n {}_n p_x \sum_{k=1}^{\infty} (n+k) v^k {}_k p_{x+n} \\
&= (Ia)_x - v^n {}_n p_x \cdot n \sum_{k=1}^{\infty} v^k {}_k p_{x+n} - v^n {}_n p_x \sum_{k=1}^{\infty} k v^k {}_k p_{x+n} \\
&= (Ia)_x - v^n {}_n p_x \cdot n \cdot a_{x+n} - v^n {}_n p_x (Ia)_{x+n} \\
&= \frac{S_{x+1}}{D_x} - n \cdot \frac{D_{x+n}}{D_x} \cdot \frac{N_{x+n+1}}{D_{x+n}} - \frac{D_{x+n}}{D_x} \cdot \frac{S_{x+n+1}}{D_{x+n}} \\
&= \frac{S_{x+1} - S_{x+n+1} - n \cdot N_{x+n+1}}{D_x}. \tag{8.42}
\end{aligned}
$$

Example 8.15

Georgina, aged 50, purchases a life annuity which will pay her 5000 in one year, 5500 in two years, continuing to increase by 500 per year thereafter. Find the price if $S_{51} = 5000$, $N_{51} = 450$, and $D_{50} = 60$.

Solution

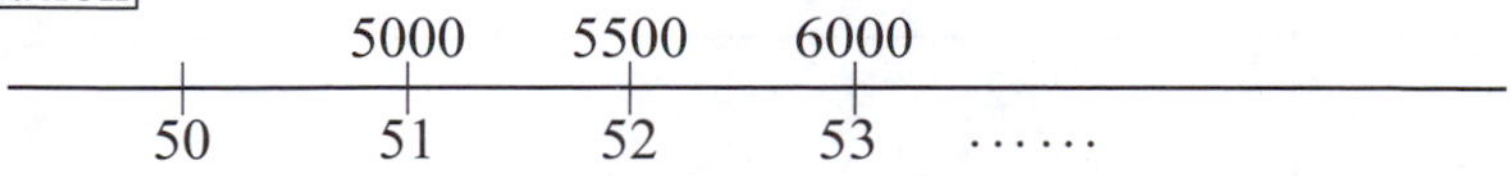

$$
\begin{array}{ccccc}
& 5000 & 5500 & 6000 & \\
\hline
50 & 51 & 52 & 53 & \cdots\cdots
\end{array}
$$

FIGURE 8.13

To make this fit the pattern, we must view the annuity as the sum of a level life annuity of 4500 and an increasing life annuity which starts at 500. We have

$$4500a_{50} + 500(Ia)_{50} = 4500\left(\frac{N_{51}}{D_{50}}\right) + 500\left(\frac{S_{51}}{D_{50}}\right)$$

$$= 4500\left(\frac{450}{60}\right) + 500\left(\frac{5000}{60}\right) = 75{,}416.67. \quad \square$$

Example 8.16

Repeat Example 8.15 if the payments reach a maximum level of 8000, and then remain constant for life. Assume $S_{58} = 2100$.

Solution

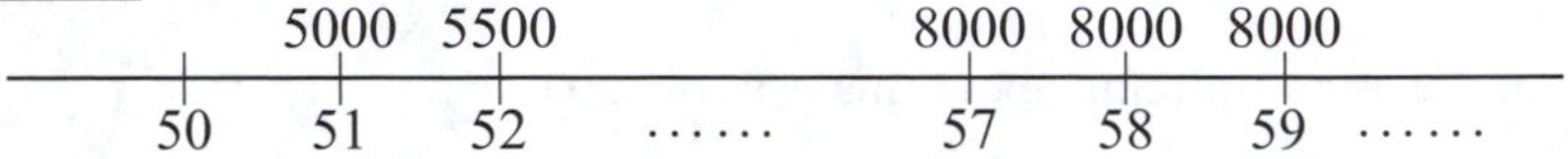

FIGURE 8.14

There are several correct ways to solve this problem; here is one approach, but the reader is encouraged to find others. Instead of the payments increasing to 8500, 9000, 9500, and so on, they stay constant at 8000. So we can imagine subtracting an increasing life annuity of 500, 1000, ... from the original to obtain our answer. Since the 8500 payment occurs when Georgina is 58, the subtracted annuity should start with that payment. Hence the price is

$$4500a_{50} + 500(Ia)_{50} - 500(Ia)_{57} \cdot \frac{D_{57}}{D_{50}} = 75{,}416.67 - 500\left(\frac{S_{58}}{D_{50}}\right)$$

$$= 75{,}416.67 - 500\left(\frac{2100}{60}\right)$$

$$= 57{,}916.67. \quad \square$$

We can also talk about $(Da)_{x:\overline{n}|}$, a decreasing life annuity with n annual payments of n, $n-1$, $n-2$, ..., 3, 2, 1, the first payment in one year.

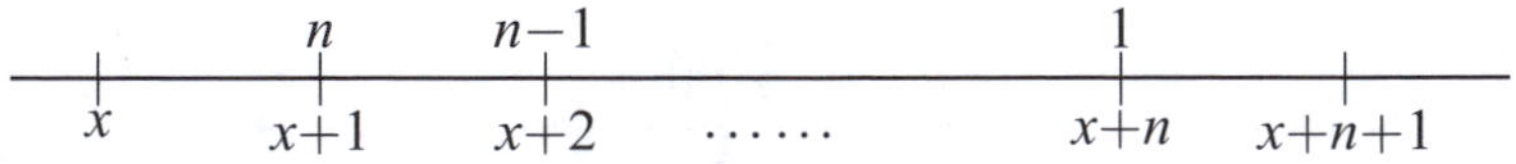

FIGURE 8.15

The reader will be asked to derive a formula for $(Da)_{x:\overline{n}|}$ in terms of commutation functions in the exercises. Here we simply note the important identity

$$(Da)_{x:\overline{n}|} + (Ia)_{x:\overline{n}|} = (n+1)\,a_{x:\overline{n}|}. \tag{8.43}$$

The reader will not be surprised to learn of the existence of symbols such as $(I\ddot{a})_x$, $(D\ddot{a})_{x:\overline{n}|}$, and so on. Fortunately, these symbols mean exactly what we would expect from our earlier work, so we will leave them for the exercises.

Example 8.17

Two annuities are of equal value to Jim, aged 25. The first is guaranteed and pays him 4000 per year for 10 years, with the first payment in 6 years. The second is a life annuity with the first payment of X in one year. Subsequent payments are annual, increasing by .0187% each year. We are given that $i = .09$. We are also told that $N_{26} = 930$ and $D_{25} = 30$ in the 7% interest tables. Find X.

Solution

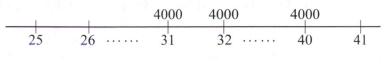

4000   4000   4000

25   26 ······ 31   32 ······ 40   41

FIGURE 8.16a

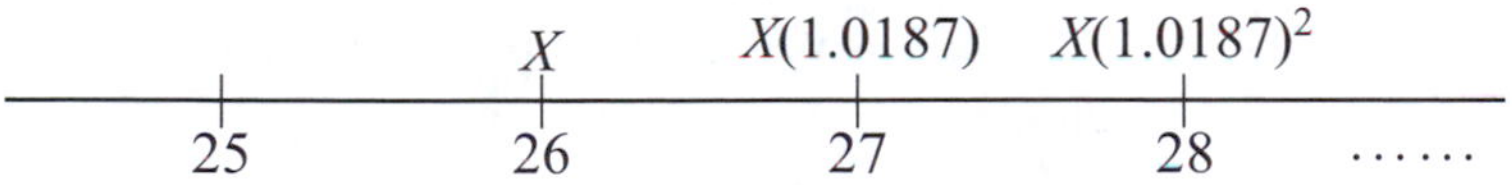

X $X(1.0187)$ $X(1.0187)^2$

25   26   27   28   ······

FIGURE 8.16b

Since the first annuity is guaranteed, its present value is equal to $v^5(4000)a_{\overline{10}|.09} = 16{,}684.15$. The second annuity has present value

$$p_{25}(1.09)^{-1}X + {}_2p_{25}(1.09)^{-2}X(1.0187)$$
$$+ \cdots + {}_tp_{25}(1.09)^{-t}X(1.0187)^{t-1} + \cdots$$

$$= X\left(\frac{1}{1.0187}\right)\left[p_{25}\left(\frac{1.0187}{1.09}\right) + {}_2p_{25}\left(\frac{1.0187}{1.09}\right)^2 + \cdots\right]$$

$$= X\left(\frac{1}{1.0187}\right)[p_{25}(1.07)^{-1} + {}_2p_{25}(1.07)^{-2} + \cdots]$$

$$= X\left(\frac{1}{1.0187}\right)a_{25} \text{ at } 7\%$$

$$= X\left(\frac{1}{1.0187}\right)\left(\frac{930}{30}\right).$$

But the two annuities are of equal value, so

$$X = \frac{(16,684.15)(30)(1.0187)}{930} = 548.26. \qquad \square$$

8.5 ANNUAL PREMIUMS AND PREMIUM RESERVES

One possible way to pay for a deferred life annuity would be with a *series* of premium payments rather than a net single premium. Most commonly the premium payments would continue for the length of the deferred period, but other situations are possible. Problems of this type should be treated in the same way as equations of value earlier in the text: the present values of the two annuities (premiums and benefits) should be set equal to each other.

| Example 8.18 |

Arabella, aged 25, purchases a deferred life annuity of 500 per month, with the first benefit coming in exactly 20 years. She intends to pay for this annuity with a series of annual premiums paid at the beginning of each year for the next 20 years, dependent on survival. Find her net annual premium if $D_{25} = 9000$, $D_{45} = 5000$, $\ddot{a}_{25} = 15$ and $\ddot{a}_{45} = 11.5$.

Solution
Let P be the net annual premium.

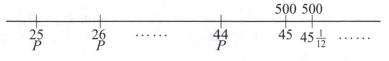

FIGURE 8.17

The present value of her future premiums is $P\ddot{a}_{25:\overline{20}|}$, and the present value of future benefits is $6000_{20|}\ddot{a}_{25}^{(12)}$. Hence we have

$$P = \frac{6000\left(\ddot{a}_{45} - \frac{11}{24}\right)\frac{D_{45}}{D_{25}}}{\ddot{a}_{25} - \ddot{a}_{45} \cdot \frac{D_{45}}{D_{25}}} = 4{,}274.19. \qquad \square$$

A general formula for problems of the above type is easily obtained, but the reader should be cautioned against memorizing too many formulae. Most of these problems are more easily handled from first principles. However, if we let $_tP(_n|\ddot{a}_x)$ be the annual premium, payable at the beginning of each year for t years, for an n-year deferred life annuity-due, then the equation of value is clearly

$$_tP(_n|\ddot{a}_x) \cdot \ddot{a}_{x:\overline{t}|} = _n|\ddot{a}_x,$$

so

$$_tP(_n|\ddot{a}_x) = \frac{_n|\ddot{a}_x}{\ddot{a}_{x:\overline{t}|}} = \frac{N_{x+n}}{N_x - N_{x+t}}. \tag{8.44}$$

If we compare this notation with Example 8.18, we see that Arabella's net premium is denoted by the symbol $_{20}P\left(_{20}|\ddot{a}_{25}^{(12)}\right)$.

Next we consider the concept of reserves. This is analogous to the concept of "outstanding principal" discussed in Chapter 4, so the reserve is just the present value of all future benefits minus the present value of all future premiums. In this section we are specifically concerned with the reserve after t years of an n-year deferred life annuity of 1 which is being paid for by annual premiums for n years, of size $_nP(_n|\ddot{a}_x)$ each.

The symbol for the reserve after t years is $_t^nV(_n|\ddot{a}_x)$. Two cases must be considered.

If $t \geq n$, then all premiums have been paid. In this case, the reserve will just equal the value at age $x + t$ of all future benefits, which is $\ddot{a}_{x+t}$. Therefore

$$\,_t^nV(_n|\ddot{a}_x) = \ddot{a}_{x+t} = \frac{N_{x+t}}{D_{x+t}}, \quad \text{if } t \geq n. \tag{8.45a}$$

If $t < n$, then the present value of all future benefits is $_{n-t|}\ddot{a}_{x+t}$, and the present value of future premiums is equal to $P\ddot{a}_{x+t:\overline{n-t|}}$, where $P = \,_nP(_n|\ddot{a}_x)$. Hence

$$\,_t^nV(_n|\ddot{a}_x) = \,_{n-t|}\ddot{a}_{x+t} - P\ddot{a}_{x+t:\overline{n-t|}}$$

$$= \frac{N_{x+n} - P(N_{x+t} - N_{x+n})}{D_{x+t}}, \quad \text{if } t < n. \tag{8.45b}$$

Finally, let us realize that when calculating premiums for deferred annuities, there are practical aspects which we have not yet considered. For example, there may be expenses involved to the insurer in underwriting the risk, in issuing the contract, and in the continuing administration of the account. The premium which is actually charged in a business transaction, including expenses and other costs, is called the *gross premium*, and the amount by which the gross premium exceeds the net premium is called *loading*.

Problems involving loading should be solved from first principles. We present one example here; others can be found in the final section of the next chapter.

```
Example 8.19
```

Let us return to Arabella's annuity in Example 8.18. Assume that 50% of her first premium is required for initial underwriting expenses, and 10% of all subsequent premiums are needed for administration. In addition, 100 must be paid for issue expenses. Find Arabella's gross premium.

```
Solution
```

Let G be the gross premium. We again set up an equation of value, noting that the portions needed for expenses do not contribute to paying for the annuity, so we have $(\frac{1}{2}G) + (\frac{9}{10}G)a_{25:\overline{19|}} - 100 = 6000_{20|}\ddot{a}_{25}^{(12)}$. Thus

$$G = \frac{6000\,_{20|}\ddot{a}_{25}^{(12)} + 100}{.5 + .9a_{25:\overline{19|}}} = 5{,}021.16. \qquad \square$$

EXERCISES

8.1 Basic Concepts

8-1. Find the net single premium for a 28-year pure endowment of 20,000 sold to a male aged 36, in each of the following cases. Assume $i = .12$.

   (a) $\ell_{36} = 9618, \ell_{64} = 7100$
   (b) $p_x = .96$ for all x
   (c) $p_x = .98$ if $0 \le x < 40, p_x = .95$ if $40 \le x < 70$
   (d) $\ell_x = \ell_0 \left[1 - \frac{x}{110}\right]$
   (e) $\ell_x = \sqrt{100 - x}$

8-2. Henri, 11 years old, wins first prize in the Parisian Lottery. He can have 1,000,000 francs if alive at age 21, or X francs today. Find X if $i = .13$ and $_{10}p_{11} = .975$.

8-3. Elaine, aged 30, purchases a contract which provides for three payments of 2000 each at ages 40, 50 and 55, if she is alive. Given $\ell_x = 110 - x$ and $i = .09$, find the net single premium for this contract.

8-4. Find the net single premium for a life annuity of 5000 per year, with the first payment due in one year, sold to a 30-year-old in each of the following cases.

   (a) $p_x = .96$ for each x, and $i = .09$.
   (b) $\ell_x = 1000\left[1 - \frac{x}{115}\right]$, and $i = .13$.

8-5. Do Question 4 if the first payment is deferred until age 40.

8-6. Do Question 4 if the maximum number of payments will be 40.

8-7. Find an expression for the present value of a life annuity which will pay 500 at the end of every two years if $i = .13$ and the annuity is sold to a person aged 45.

8-8. Do Question 7 if $p_x = .96$ for all x.

8-9. Do Question 7 if $\ell_x = \ell_0 \left[1 - \frac{x}{115}\right]$.

8-10. For a given population, $\ell_x = 120 - x$. Given that $i = .07$, find the net single premium at age 60 for a deferred life annuity with annual payments of 1000 commencing at age 70 if at most twenty payments will be made.

8-11. Derive each of the following identities.

    (a) $a_x = v p_x \ddot{a}_{x+1}$

    (b) $\ddot{a}_x = 1 + v p_x \ddot{a}_{x+1}$

    (c) $\ddot{a}_{x:\overline{n}|} = a_{x:\overline{n}|} + 1 - v^n \, {}_n p_x$

    (d) ${}_n|a_x = v^n \, {}_n p_x \, a_{x+n}$

    (e) $a_{x:\overline{n+m}|} = a_{x:\overline{m}|} + v^m \, {}_m p_x \, a_{x+m:\overline{n}|}$

    (f) $p_{x-1} \cdot \ddot{a}_x = (1 + i) a_{x-1}$

8-12. Give verbal explanations for each of the identities in Question 11.

8-13. Julio's mortality for $1 \leq t \leq 4$ is governed by ${}_t p_x = .3(4 - t)$, and Harold's mortality for $1 \leq t \leq 5$ is governed by ${}_t p_x = .25(5 - t)$. If $i = .07$, find the value at time 0 of an annuity which pays 1000 at the end of each year as long as *both* Julio and Harold are alive.

8-14. Repeat Question 13 if the annuity is paid as long as *either* Julio or Harold is still alive.

8-15. Assume in Question 13 that Noreen's mortality is also governed by ${}_t p_x = .3(4 - t)$.

    (a)   Find the value at $t = 0$ of a life annuity paying 1000 at the end of each year as long as *at least two* of Julio, Harold and Noreen survive.

    (b)   Do part (a) if the annuity is paid only if *at most two* of Julio, Harold and Noreen survive.

8.2 Commutation Functions

8-16. Andrea, aged 25, purchases a life annuity of 2000 per year. From tables, we find $N_{25} = 2450$, $N_{27} = 2290$ and $D_{26} = 75$.
  (a) Find the net single premium Andrea should pay for this annuity if the first payment occurs in one year.
  (b) Find the net single premium Andrea should pay for this annuity if the first payment occurs in two years.
  (c) Find the net single premium Andrea should pay for this annuity if the first payment occurs immediately.
  (d) Find i if $p_{25} = .9353$.

8-17. Brenda, aged 38, purchases a 20,000 life annuity with the first payment in 10 years.
  (a) Find Brenda's net single premium in terms of commutation functions.
  (b) Find Brenda's net single premium in terms of commutation functions, if payments 15 through 24 inclusive are to be omitted.
  (c) Find Brenda's net single premium in terms of commutation functions if the first 5 payments are guaranteed to Brenda or her estate, but all subsequent payments are contingent upon survival.

8-18. State verbally the meaning of each of the following.
  (a) $\dfrac{N_{50} - N_{70}}{D_{30}} + 10 \cdot {}_{40}E_{30}$
  (b) $\dfrac{N_{x+1} + N_{x+2} + \cdots}{D_x}$

8-19. Given $N_x = 2000$, $N_{x+1} = 1900$, $N_{x+2} = 1820$ and $i = .11$, find q_x.

8-20. Determine which of the following expressions are equal to each other.
  (a) $a_{x:\overline{n}|} - \ddot{a}_{x:\overline{n}|} + 1$
  (b) $\dfrac{N_{x+n} - N_{x+n+1}}{D_x}$
  (c) $v^n p_{x+n}$
  (d) ${}_nE_x$

8-21. Harold, aged 60, purchases a life annuity which will provide annual payments of 1000 commencing at age 61. For the year beginning at age 60 only, Harold is subject to a higher risk of death, namely $q_{60} + .10$, where q_{60} is from the standard life table. Given $N_{60} = 4650$, $N_{61} = 3950$, $N_{62} = 3350$ and $i = .07$, find the net single premium for this annuity.

8-22. A select-and-ultimate disabled life table has a select period of two years. Select probabilities are related to ultimate probabilities by the rules $p_{[x]} = \frac{1}{3} \cdot p_x$ and $p_{[x]+1} = \frac{1}{2} \cdot p_{x+1}$. Given $\ddot{a}_{25} = 17$, $D_{25} = 2000$, and $D_{26} = 1800$, find $a_{[25]}$.

8-23. Assume $i = .08$ and that we are dealing with a four-year select period. We know that $q_{[30]} = .40$, $p_{[30]+1} = .80$, $q_{[30]+2} = .10$ and $q_{[30]+3} = .10$. Also $D_{34} = 1000$ and $D_{35} = 920$. Find the probability that a person entering the select group at age 30 (a) will remain in the population for 5 years; (b) will remain in the population for at most 3 years.

8.3 Annuities Payable m^{thly}

8-24. (a) How much money must be invested to provide John, aged 50, with monthly payments of 400 for life if $a_{50} = 16.5$? The first payment will occur in exactly one month.

  (b) Repeat part (a) if the payment is 1200 every three months, the first payment occurring in exactly three months.

  (c) Repeat part (a) if the first 400 payment occurs immediately.

  (d) Can you solve part (a) if the first payment occurs in exactly 13 months? If not, what additional information is required?

8-25. Derive each of the following approximate formulae:

  (a) $_n|\ddot{a}_x^{(m)} = {}_n|\ddot{a}_x - \left(\frac{m-1}{2m}\right){}_nE_x$

  (b) $\ddot{a}_{x:\overline{n}|}^{(m)} = \ddot{a}_{x:\overline{n}|} - \left(\frac{m-1}{2m}\right)(1 - {}_nE_x)$

8-26. Explain verbally why the formula $\ddot{a}_{x:\overline{n}|}^{(m)} = \frac{1}{m} + \ddot{a}_{x:\overline{n}|}$ is incorrect.

8-27. Derive each of the following:

(a) $a_x^{(m)} = \dfrac{N_{x+1} + \left(\frac{m-1}{2m}\right)D_x}{D_x} = \dfrac{N_x^{(m)}}{D_x} - \dfrac{1}{m}.$

(b) $_n|\ddot{a}_x^{(m)} = \dfrac{N_{x+n}^{(m)}}{D_x}$

8-28. Express $\ddot{a}_{x:\overline{n}|}^{(m)}$ in terms of commutation functions. Give two answers, one involving $N_y^{(m)}$ terms, and one using regular N_y terms.

8-29. Marvin, aged 50, purchases an annuity of k per month, the first payment to be made immediately. For the first 60 months, payments will be guaranteed (i.e., will be made independent of Marvin's survival). After that, payments will continue for as long as Marvin is alive. Marvin pays 50,000 for the entire package. Let $i = .07$, $D_{50} = 5200$, $D_{55} = 4100$, and $N_{55} = 60,000$. Find k.

8-30. Repeat Question 29 if no payments are guaranteed. Assume, in addition, that $N_{50} = 83,500$.

8-31. Jeannette, aged 65, is about to retire. Her salary is 70,000 per year and, because of her long service and senior position, she will receive a pension of 50% of her final salary at the end of each year as long as she survives. Find the present value of these benefits if $N_{65} = 700$ and $D_{65} = 82$.

8-32. Repeat Question 31 if the yearly payment is to be divided into twelve equal monthly payments, the first occurring in one month.

8-33. Marilyn, aged 45, works for the same company as Jeannette (Question 31) and will have the same retirement benefit, beginning at age 65. Marilyn's current salary is 25,000 per year and her salary will increase at 7% each year for the next 20 years. If $i = .08$, and it is assumed that Marilyn will not die before age 65, find the present value to Marilyn of her future retirement benefits.

8-34. Repeat Question 33 if the yearly pension payment is to be divided into twelve equal monthly payments, the first occurring one month after retirement.

8-35. Repeat Questions 33 and 34 if death is possible before retirement, and we assume that $_{20}p_{45} = .84$.

8-36. Edgar was entitled to a monthly life annuity of 400 at age 65, but died on the day before the first payment was due. A death benefit, equal in value to half the value of the annuity, was payable to his beneficiary. Edgar's beneficiary is his girlfriend Linda, aged 22. The benefit is a 48-month temporary life annuity, commencing immediately, of X per month. Find X if $D_{65} = 100$, $N_{65} = 900$, $D_{22} = 2500$, $N_{22} = 53,000$, $D_{26} = 1950$, and $N_{26} = 43,500$.

8-37. Derive each of the following approximate formulae:

(a) $\overline{a}_{x:\overline{n}|} \approx a_{x:\overline{n}|} + \frac{1}{2}(1 - {}_nE_x)$

(b) $\overline{a}_{x:\overline{n}|} \approx \frac{1}{2}(a_{x:\overline{n}|} + \ddot{a}_{x:\overline{n}|})$

(c) ${}_n|\overline{a}_x \approx {}_n|a_x + \frac{1}{2} \cdot {}_nE_x$

8-38. Express $\overline{a}_{x:\overline{n}|}$ and ${}_n|\overline{a}_x$ in terms of commutation functions.

8-39. (a) Find the present value of a continuous life annuity of 1000 per year for a 40-year-old if we assume that $\delta = .06$ and $\mu_x = .04$ for all x.

(b) Redo part (a) if the annuity is temporary, lasting for only 30 years.

(c) Redo part (b) if the force of mortality changes to $\mu_x = .05$ for all $x \geq 50$.

8-40. A man is offered the choice of a continuous life annuity paying 20,000 per year or a continuous 5-year annuity with certain payments at X per year, followed by a continuous life annuity paying X per year. Assuming $\delta = .05$ and $\mu_x = .06$ for all x, find X such that the two annuities are equivalent.

8.4 Varying Life Annuities

8-41. Pauline purchases a life annuity which will pay 2000 in one year's time, with annual payments that will increase by 400 per year thereafter. Find the present value of this annuity if Pauline is aged 36, given $N_{37} = 24,000$, $S_{37} = 300,000$ and $D_{36} = 1500$.

8-42. Repeat Question 41 if a maximum of 10 payments is to be made. Assume $S_{47} = 160,000$ and $N_{47} = 9,500$.

8-43. Repeat Question 41 if payments increase to a maximum of 5600 and then remain constant thereafter. Make the same assumptions as in Question 42.

8-44. Repeat Question 41 if, instead of increasing, the payments decrease by 400 per year until reaching zero. Assume $S_{42} = 185,000$ and $N_{42} = 15,000$.

8-45. Prove each of the following identities.

(a) $\quad (Da)_{x:\overline{n}|} = \sum_{t=1}^{n} a_{x:\overline{t}|}$

(b) $\quad (Da)_{x:\overline{n}|} = \dfrac{n \cdot N_{x+1} - (S_{x+2} - S_{x+n+2})}{D_x}$

(c) $\quad (I\ddot{a})_x = \dfrac{S_x}{D_x}$

8-46. Express in commutation symbols the present value at age x of a life annuity which commences with a payment of 10 at age x, increases annually by 1 for 5 years to a maximum of 15, and then decreases annually by 1 until it reaches zero.

8-47. Find formulae for $_n|(I\ddot{a})_x$ and $(D\ddot{a})_{x:\overline{n}|}$ in terms of commutation symbols.

8-48. As with level life annuities, $(Ia)_x^{(m)}$ represents an increasing annuity where each yearly payment is divided into m equal payments paid at intervals of length $\frac{1}{m}$. Derive the following approximate formulae:

(a) $\quad (Ia)_x^{(m)} = (Ia)_x + \dfrac{m-1}{2m}\, \ddot{a}_x$ \hfill (8.46a)

(b) $\quad (I\ddot{a})_x^{(m)} = (I\ddot{a})_x - \dfrac{m-1}{2m}\, \ddot{a}_x$ \hfill (8.46b)

8-49. A 40-year-old purchases a life annuity with annual payments which will commence in exactly 10 years. The first payment is 1000 and payments will increase by 8% per year. If $i = .08$, show that the net single premium for this annuity is

$$\left(\dfrac{1000}{(1.08)^{10}}\right)(_{10}p_{40})(1 + e_{50}).$$

8-50. Let $(I\bar{a})_x$ denote the present value of a continuous life annuity (to a person age x) which pays at the rate of 1 per year during the first year, at the rate of 2 per year during the second year, and so on. Explain verbally why $(I\bar{a})_x$ is approximately equal to $(Ia)_x + \frac{1}{2}\ddot{a}_x$.

8-51. Let $(\bar{I}\bar{a})_x$ denote the net single premium for a continuous life annuity (to a person age x) which pays at the rate of t per year at the moment of attaining age $x+t$.

(a)   Explain why $(\bar{I}\bar{a})_x = \int_0^\infty t\, v^t \,{}_t p_x \, dt$.

(b)   Show that $(\bar{I}\bar{a})_x$ is approximately equal to $(Ia)_x + \frac{1}{12}$.

8.5   Annual Premiums and Premium Reserves

8-52. Repeat Example 8.18 if Arabella is paying for the annuity with semiannual instead of annual premiums.

8-53. Eric, aged 40, purchases a deferred life annuity which will provide monthly payments of 300 at the beginning of each month commencing at age 60. Eric pays a premium at the beginning of each year for the next 20 years. His first premium is 4000, and the remainder are each equal to X. Find X if $D_{40} = 500$, $N_{40} = 8600$, $D_{60} = 120$, and $N_{60} = 1000$.

8-54. Again consider Eric's purchase of the deferred life annuity in Question 53. This time, if Eric dies before reaching age 60, net premiums paid prior to death are refunded with interest. Using the same data as in Question 53, and assuming $i = .08$, find X.

8-55. Repeat Question 53 if 1000 out of the first premium is required for issue expenses, and 20% of each subsequent premium of X is required for administrative upkeep.

8-56. If 30% of each gross premium is required for loading (when paying for a deferred annuity), what is the ratio of the gross premium to the net premium?

CHAPTER NINE
LIFE INSURANCE

9.1 BASIC CONCEPTS

In the previous chapter we saw how techniques from the theory of interest can be combined with elementary probability theory to study life annuities, which are annuities contingent upon survival. Now we will see how the same ideas can be used to study life insurance, where the contingency of interest is that of dying at certain times in the future. We saw one example of this type of problem in Section 6.3. Here is another.

Example 9.1

Rose is 38 years old. She wishes to purchase a life insurance policy which will pay her estate 50,000 at the end of the year of her death. If $i = .12$, find an expression for the (actuarial) present value of this benefit.

Solution

FIGURE 9.1

The expected value of this benefit payable $t + 1$ years hence is the probability that Rose dies at age last birthday $38 + t$ multiplied by 50,000, which is $({}_tp_{38})(q_{38+t})(50,000)$. The present value of the entire policy is the sum of the present values of these terms, which is $50,000\sum_{t=0}^{\infty}({}_tp_{38})(q_{38+t})(1.12)^{-t-1}$. Note that v^{t+1} is required since payment is at the end of the tth year. $\qquad\square$

To obtain a numerical answer to Example 9.1, we could consult life tables but, as with life annuities, it would be laborious to add all the terms together. We will see in Section 9.2 that commutation functions can be used to aid in the calculation. On the other hand, if a simple formula for p_x is assumed, it may be that this sum can be calculated. For example, if $p_x = .94$ for all x, then $_tp_{38} = (.94)^t$ from which we find $q_{38+t} = 1 - p_{38+t} = .06$, so our present value is

$$50,000 \sum_{t=0}^{\infty} (.94)^t (.06)(1.12)^{-t-1} = 50,000 \left(\frac{.06}{1.12} \right) \sum_{t=0}^{\infty} \left(\frac{.94}{1.12} \right)^t$$

$$= 50,000 \left(\frac{.06}{1.12} \right) \left(\frac{1}{1 - \frac{.94}{1.12}} \right)$$

$$= 16,666.67.$$

Example 9.1 is an illustration of a *whole life policy*, a policy where a fixed amount, the *face value*, is paid to the insured's beneficiary at the end of the year of death, whenever that may be. The price of such a policy with face value of 1, to an insured aged x, is given by the symbol A_x. The formula is

$$A_x = \sum_{t=0}^{\infty} {}_tp_x \, q_{x+t} v^{t+1}. \tag{9.1}$$

Note that eventually $_tp_x = 0$, so this sum is actually finite. It will be assumed for the rest of Sections 9.1 and 9.2, as well as in the exercises for these sections, that insurances are payable at the end of the year of death.

$\boxed{\text{Example 9.2}}$

Michael is 50 years old and purchases a whole life policy with face value 100,000. If $\ell_x = 1000 \left(1 - \frac{x}{105} \right)$ and $i = .08$, find the price of this policy.

$\boxed{\text{Solution}}$

The required price is $100,000 A_{50} = 100,000 \sum_{t=0}^{54} {}_tp_{50} \, q_{50+t} \, (1.08)^{-t-1}$.

Note that our sum terminates at $t = 54$ because $_tp_{50} = 0$ for all larger values. We have $_tp_{50} = \frac{\ell_{50+t}}{\ell_{50}} = \frac{105 - 50 - t}{105 - 50} = \frac{55 - t}{55}$, and $q_{50+t} = 1 - p_{50+t} = 1 - \frac{105-51-t}{105-50-t}$. Hence the premium is

$$100,000 \sum_{t=0}^{54} \left(\frac{55 - t}{55} \right) \left(\frac{1}{55 - t} \right) (1.08)^{-t-1}$$

$$= \left(\frac{100,000}{55} \right) \left(\frac{1}{1.08} \right) \left(\frac{1 - \left(\frac{1}{1.08} \right)^{55}}{1 - \left(\frac{1}{1.08} \right)} \right) = 22,397.48. \quad \square$$

In some cases a company will sell *term insurance*, which means that the face value is paid only if death occurs within a prescribed period. If the period is n years and the insured is aged x, then the price is denoted $A^1_{x:\overline{n}|}$ (for a payment of 1), and the formula is

$$A^1_{x:\overline{n}|} = \sum_{t=0}^{n-1} {}_tp_x q_{x+t}\, v^{t+1}. \tag{9.2}$$

Example 9.3

Calculate the price of Rose's insurance in Example 9.1 and Michael's insurance in Example 9.2 if both policies are in force for a term of only 30 years. For Rose, assume $p_x = .94$ for all x.

Solution

In Rose's case, the price is

$$50,000 \sum_{t=0}^{29} {}_tp_{38}\, q_{38+t}\, (1.12)^{-t-1} = 50,000 \sum_{t=0}^{29} (.94)^t (.06)(1.12)^{-t-1}$$

$$= 50,000 \left(\frac{.06}{1.12}\right) \left(\frac{1 - \left(\frac{.94}{1.12}\right)^{30}}{1 - \frac{.94}{1.12}}\right)$$

$$= 16,579.74.$$

In Michael's case, we obtain

$$100,000 \sum_{t=0}^{29} {}_tp_{50}\, q_{50+t}\, (1.08)^{-t-1}$$

$$= 100,000 \sum_{t=0}^{29} \left(\frac{55-t}{55}\right) \left(\frac{1}{55-t}\right)(1.08)^{-t-1}$$

$$= \left(\frac{100,000}{55}\right) \left(\frac{1}{1.08}\right) \left(\frac{1 - \left(\frac{1}{1.08}\right)^{30}}{1 - \left(\frac{1}{1.08}\right)}\right)$$

$$= 20,468.70. \qquad \square$$

We could also talk about ${}_n|A_x$, the price for *deferred insurance*, where the policy of face amount 1 is purchased at age x but does not come into force until age $x + n$. This is not as important as the other two cases, so we will not stress it here, but it should be noted that

$$A_x = A^1_{x:\overline{n}|} + {}_n|A_x. \qquad (9.3)$$

Finally, there is *n*-year *endowment insurance*. In this case the face value is paid if death occurs within a prescribed *n*-year period or, if the policyholder is still alive at the end of *n* years, he receives the face value at that time. The price for this benefit, with face value 1, is denoted $A_{x:\overline{n}|}$, and is the sum of *n*-year term insurance and a pure endowment (see Section 8.1) at age $x + n$. Hence we have

$$A_{x:\overline{n}|} = A^1_{x:\overline{n}|} + {}_nE_x. \qquad (9.4)$$

In this context the symbol $A_{x:\overline{n}|}^{1}$ is sometimes used in place of ${}_nE_x$.

| Example 9.4 |

Calculate the price of Rose's insurance in Example 9.1 and Michael's insurance in Example 9.2 if both policies are to be 30-year endowment insurance. For Rose, assume $p_x = .94$ for all x.

| Solution |

We will use the results of Example 9.3 and simply add a 30-year pure endowment in each case. For Rose, $16,579.74 + 50,000({}_{30}p_{38})(1.12)^{-30}$, which is $16,579.74 + 50,000(.94)^{30}(1.12)^{-30} = 16,840.52$. For Michael, we obtain $20,468.70 + (100,000)({}_{30}p_{50})(1.08)^{-30}$, which is
$20,468.70 + (100,000)(\frac{25}{55})(1.08)^{-30} = 24,985.85$.   □

The reader will show in the exercises that

$$A^1_{x:\overline{n}|} < A_x < A_{x:\overline{n}|}. \qquad (9.5)$$

Note that the examples given in this section support these inequalities.

9.2 COMMUTATION FUNCTIONS AND BASIC IDENTITIES

We begin this section by introducing two new commutation functions, which will be helpful in solving problems involving insurance. We will also develop some nice relationships between the insurance symbols A_x, $A^1_{x:\overline{n}|}$, and $A_{x:\overline{n}|}$, and the annuity symbols discussed in Chapter 8. Using these identities life insurance problems can sometimes be solved by using the commutation functions defined in Chapter 8.

Note first that all of our insurance formulae involve sums of terms like $({}_t p_x) q_{x+t} v^{t+1}$, which can be expressed as

$$\left(\frac{\ell_{x+t}}{\ell_x}\right)\left(\frac{d_{x+t}}{\ell_{x+t}}\right) v^{t+1} = \left(\frac{d_{x+t}}{\ell_x}\right) v^{t+1} = \frac{d_{x+t}\, v^{x+t+1}}{\ell_x\, v^x}. \tag{9.6}$$

The denominator in (9.6) is our familiar D_x. The numerator is denoted by C_{x+t}, so we have the new commutation function

$$C_x = v^{x+1}\, d_x. \tag{9.7}$$

Analogous to N_x, we define

$$M_x = \sum_{t=0}^{\infty} C_{x+t}. \tag{9.8}$$

In terms of these symbols we then obtain

$$\begin{aligned} A_x &= \sum_{t=0}^{\infty} {}_t p_x\, q_{x+t}\, v^{t+1} \\ &= \sum_{t=0}^{\infty} \frac{C_{x+t}}{D_x} \\ &= \frac{M_x}{D_x}. \end{aligned} \tag{9.9}$$

For term insurance we have

$$\begin{aligned} A^1_{x:\overline{n|}} &= \sum_{t=0}^{n-1} \frac{C_{x+t}}{D_x} \\ &= \frac{M_x - M_{x+n}}{D_x}. \end{aligned} \tag{9.10}$$

Since $A_{x:\overline{n|}} = A^1_{x:\overline{n|}} + {}_n E_x$, we have

$$A_{x:\overline{n|}} = \frac{M_x - M_{x+n} + D_{x+n}}{D_x}. \tag{9.11}$$

Example 9.5

Find the net single premium for Rose's insurance in Example 9.1 if $M_{38} = 2500$ and $D_{38} = 7200$.

Solution

The premium is $50{,}000 \left(\frac{2500}{7200} \right) = 17{,}361.11$.   □

The student should try to obtain a "feeling" for how these commutation formulae work. After some practice it should be possible to write down the price for complicated benefits directly in terms of commutation functions. The following example also shows that this can be done in more than one way.

Example 9.6

Juan, aged 40, purchases an insurance policy paying 50,000 if death occurs within the next 20 years, 100,000 if death occurs between ages 60 and 70, and 30,000 if death occurs after that. Find the net single premium for this policy in terms of commutation functions.

Solution

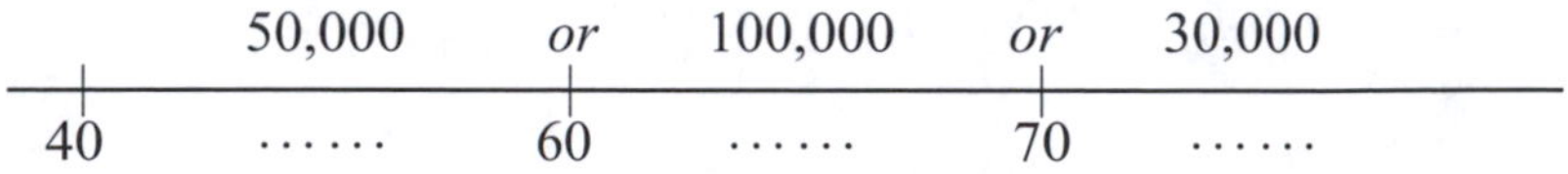

$$
\begin{array}{ccccccc}
& 50{,}000 & or & 100{,}000 & or & 30{,}000 & \\
\hline
40 & \cdots\cdots & 60 & \cdots\cdots & 70 & \cdots\cdots &
\end{array}
$$

FIGURE 9.2

The answer is $\dfrac{50{,}000(M_{40} - M_{60}) + 100{,}000(M_{60} - M_{70}) + 30{,}000 M_{70}}{D_{40}}$.

The reader can see how the above is obtained as a sum of 3 different benefits. Simplifying, we obtain $\dfrac{50{,}000 M_{40} + 50{,}000 M_{60} - 70{,}000 M_{70}}{D_{40}}$.

Can you give a verbal explanation as to why this second expression is correct?

Another approach would be to consider the policy as a whole life policy of 30,000, plus a 30-year term policy of 20,000, plus a 10-year term policy, deferred for 20 years, of 50,000. This gives $\dfrac{30{,}000 M_{40} + 20{,}000(M_{40} - M_{70}) + 50{,}000(M_{60} - M_{70})}{D_{40}}$. We easily see that this expression is equivalent to the other two.   □

Example 9.7

Describe the benefit whose net single premium is $\dfrac{M_{50} - M_{70} + D_{80}}{D_{40}}$.

Solution

$\dfrac{M_{50} - M_{70}}{D_{40}}$ represents a 20-year term insurance deferred for 10 years to a person aged 40. $\dfrac{D_{80}}{D_{40}}$ is a pure endowment to be paid at age 80. Therefore this 40-year-old is insured for the 20-year period between age 50 and age 70. If she survives that period, and then 10 more years to reach age 80, she will receive a pure endowment at that time. $\square$

There are a number of important identities relating insurance and annuity symbols. Two of the most useful are derived as follows:

$$A_x = \sum_{t=0}^{\infty} {}_tp_x\, q_{x+t}\, v^{t+1}$$

$$= \sum_{t=0}^{\infty} {}_tp_x(1 - p_{x+t})v^{t+1}$$

$$= v\sum_{t=0}^{\infty} {}_tp_x\, v^{t} - \sum_{t=0}^{\infty} {}_tp_x\, p_{x+t}\, v^{t+1}$$

$$= v\ddot{a}_x - \sum_{t=0}^{\infty} {}_{t+1}p_x\, v^{t+1}$$

$$= v\ddot{a}_x - \sum_{t=1}^{\infty} {}_tp_x\, v^{t}$$

$$= v\ddot{a}_x - a_x \tag{9.12a}$$

$$= v\ddot{a}_x - (\ddot{a}_x - 1)$$

$$= 1 - d\ddot{a}_x \tag{9.12b}$$

These identities can be very helpful. If we are given appropriate values of N_x and D_x, together with the value of i, we can now compute A_x. We see therefore that the commutation symbols M_x and C_x are aids to calculation rather than absolute necessities.

Example 9.8

Phyllis, aged 40, purchases a whole life policy of 50,000.   If $N_{40} = 5000$, $N_{41} = 4500$ and $i = .08$, find the price of this policy.

Solution

We have

$$A_{40} = 1 - d\ddot{a}_{40} = 1 - \left(\frac{.08}{1.08}\right)\left(\frac{N_{40}}{D_{40}}\right)$$

$$= 1 - \left(\frac{08}{1.08}\right)\left(\frac{5000}{500}\right).$$

Thus the net single premium is $50,000 A_{40} = 12,962.96$. $\square$

There are many other identities which can be similarly derived, and we will leave these for the exercises.

9.3   INSURANCE PAYABLE AT THE MOMENT OF DEATH

Until now, we have always assumed that insurance is payable at the end of the year following death. In practice, however, this is often not the case and it is more common for insurance to be payable at the moment of death. We will now see how to deal with problems of this type.

In a similar manner to Section 8.3, we first consider the case where a payment of 1 is due at the end of the $\frac{1}{m}^{th}$ part of a year in which death occurs. The net single premium for this insurance to a life aged x is given by

$$A_x^{(m)} = v^{\frac{1}{m}}\left(\frac{\ell_x - \ell_{x+\frac{1}{m}}}{\ell_x}\right) + v^{\frac{2}{m}}\left(\frac{\ell_{x+\frac{1}{m}} - \ell_{x+\frac{2}{m}}}{\ell_x}\right) + \cdots. \qquad (9.13)$$

Taking the limit of this expression as m approaches infinity, we obtain the net single premium for insurance payable at the moment of death. Denoting this by $\overline{A}_x$, we have

$$\overline{A}_x = \lim_{m \to \infty} A_x^{(m)} = -\int_0^\infty v^t \cdot \frac{d(\ell_{x+t})}{\ell_x} = -\int_0^\infty v^t \cdot \frac{\ell_{x+t}}{\ell_x} \cdot \frac{d(\ell_{x+t})}{\ell_{x+t}}.$$

This gives us the important formula

$$\bar{A}_x = \int_0^\infty v^t \, {}_t p_x \mu_{x+t} \, dt. \tag{9.14}$$

Expressions like $\bar{A}^1_{x:\overline{n}|}$, $\bar{A}_{x:\overline{n}|}$, and so on, all exist and have the expected meanings. We immediately obtain

$$\bar{A}^1_{x:\overline{n}|} = \int_0^n v^t \, {}_t p_x \mu_{x+t} \, dt \tag{9.15}$$

and

$$\bar{A}_{x:\overline{n}|} = \int_0^n v^t \, {}_t p_x \mu_{x+t} \, dt + v^n \, {}_n p_x. \tag{9.16}$$

Example 9.9

Find the net single premium for a 100,000 life insurance policy, payable at the moment of death, purchased by a life aged 30 if it is assumed that $i = .06$ and ${}_t p_{30} = (.98)^t$ for all t.

Solution

We have $\bar{A}_{30} = \displaystyle\int_0^\infty v^t \, {}_t p_{30} \mu_{30+t} \, dt.$

Since $\mu_{30+t} = -\dfrac{D({}_t p_{30})}{{}_t p_{30}} = -ln(.98)$, the answer is

$$-100,000 \int_0^\infty \left(\frac{.98}{1.06}\right)^t ln(.98) \, dt = -100,000 ln(.98) \left[\frac{\left(\frac{.98}{1.06}\right)^t}{ln\left(\frac{.98}{1.06}\right)}\right]_0^\infty$$

$$= \frac{100,000 ln(.98)}{ln\left(\frac{.98}{1.06}\right)} = 25,745.24. \qquad \square$$

Example 9.10

Repeat Example 9.9 if the 30-year-old is purchasing 20-year endowment insurance instead of whole life insurance.

Solution

Now we want

$$100{,}000\overline{A}_{\,30:\overline{20}|} = 100{,}000(\overline{A}_{\,30:\overline{20}|}^{\,\,1} + v^{20}\,_{20}p_{30})$$

$$= 100{,}000\int_0^{20} v^t\,_tp_{30}\mu_{30+t}\,dt + 100{,}000v^{20}\,_{20}p_{30}$$

$$= -100{,}000ln(.98)\left[\frac{\left(\frac{.98}{1.06}\right)^t}{ln\left(\frac{.98}{1.06}\right)}\right]_0^{20} + 100{,}000\left(\frac{.98}{1.06}\right)^{20}$$

$$= \frac{100{,}000ln(.98)}{ln\left(\frac{.98}{1.06}\right)}\left[1 - \left(\frac{.98}{1.06}\right)^{20}\right] + 100{,}000\left(\frac{.98}{1.06}\right)^{20}$$

$$= 41{,}202.36. \qquad \square$$

Example 9.11

Repeat Examples 9.9 and 9.10 if we now assume $\delta = .06$ and $\ell_x = 105 - x,\ 0 \le x \le 105$.

Solution

We now have $_tp_{30} = \frac{75 - t}{75}$ and $\mu_{30+t} = \frac{1}{75 - t}$ for $0 \le t \le 75$. Then

$$100{,}000\overline{A}_{\,30} = 100{,}000\int_0^{75} e^{-.06t}\left(\frac{1}{75}\right)dt$$

$$= \frac{100{,}000}{75}\left[\frac{e^{-.06t}}{-.06}\right]_0^{75}$$

$$= 21{,}975.36.$$

For the endowment insurance,

$$100{,}000\overline{A}_{\,30:\overline{20}|} = 100{,}000\int_0^{20} e^{-.06t}\left(\frac{1}{75}\right)dt + 100{,}000e^{-.06(20)}\left(\frac{55}{75}\right)$$

$$= \frac{100{,}000}{75}\left[\frac{1 - e^{-1.2}}{.06}\right] + 100{,}000e^{-1.2}\left(\frac{55}{75}\right)$$

$$= 37{,}616.59. \qquad \square$$

In Section 8.3, the approximate formula $\bar{a}_x = a_x + \frac{1}{2}$ was derived, along with the corresponding formula for commutation functions $\bar{N}_x = N_x - \frac{1}{2}D_x$. In the case of insurance payable at the moment of death, the relationships are the very different looking $\bar{A}_x = \frac{i}{\delta}A_x$ and $\bar{M}_x = \frac{i}{\delta}M_x$. (See Exercise 9-39.)

Using integration by parts on the expression for $\bar{A}_x$ given by (9.14), we obtain the important identity

$$\bar{A}_x = 1 - \delta\bar{a}_x. \tag{9.17}$$

The reader should note the similarity of this to the formula $A_x = 1 - d\ddot{a}_x$ given by Formula (9.12b).

9.4   VARYING INSURANCE

In Section 3.6 we studied interest-only varying annuities such as $(Ia)_{\overline{n}|}$ and $(Da)_{\overline{n}|}$, and in Section 8.4 the corresponding life annuities, such as $(Ia)_x$, were introduced. Now we consider the analogous situation for life insurance.

We will denote *increasing whole life insurance* by $(IA)_x$. This is a policy which provides a death benefit of 1 in the first year, 2 in the second year, and so on, increasing by 1 per year, payable at the end of the year of death. We note that

$$
\begin{aligned}
(IA)_x &= \sum_{t=0}^{\infty} (t+1)\,_tp_x\, q_{x+t}\, v^{t+1} \\
&= \sum_{t=0}^{\infty} (t+1)\frac{C_{x+t}}{D_x} \\
&= \frac{1}{D_x}(C_x + 2C_{x+1} + 3C_{x+2} + \cdots) \\
&= \frac{1}{D_x}\Big((C_x + C_{x+1} + \cdots) + (C_{x+1} + C_{x+2} + \cdots) + \cdots\Big) \\
&= \frac{1}{D_x}(M_x + M_{x+1} + M_{x+2} + \cdots), \tag{9.18}
\end{aligned}
$$

using the commutation functions from Section 9.2. If we define a new commutation function

$$R_x = M_x + M_{x+1} + \cdots ,$$ (9.19)

we obtain

$$(IA)_x = \frac{R_x}{D_x}.$$ (9.20)

Example 9.12

Roger, aged 45, purchases a whole life policy which will pay 2000 for each year of his age at the end of the year of his death. Find the net single premium for this policy given $R_{45} = 500$, $M_{45} = 45$ and $D_{45} = 110$.

Solution

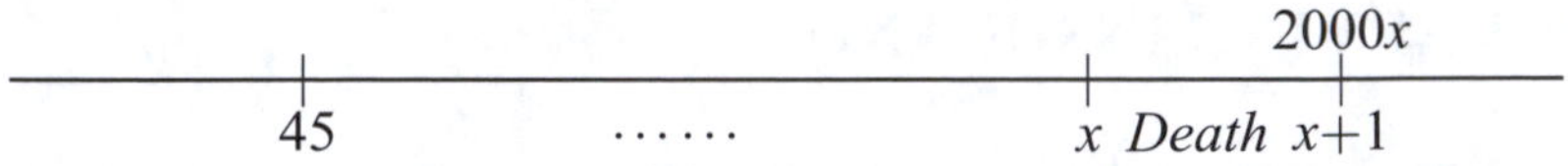

```
                                               2000x
 |——————————|————————————————————|————————————|——
    45              . . . . . .      x  Death  x+1
```

FIGURE 9.3

The insurance benefit is 90,000 in the first year, 92,000 in the second year, and so on. We can view this as the sum of an 88,000 level whole life policy and a 2,000 increasing whole life policy, so the premium is given by

$$88,000A_{45} + 2,000(IA)_{45} = 88,000\left(\frac{45}{110}\right) + 2,000\left(\frac{500}{110}\right) = 45,090.90.$$

□

Increasing term insurance, $(IA)^1_{x:\overline{n}|}$, refers to an increasing policy with a final benefit of n in the nth year. This can be viewed as a whole life increasing policy, $(IA)_x$, with the later benefits of $n+1$, $n+2$, ... deleted. These later benefits can, as in Example 9.12, be considered the sum of a constant benefit of n and an increasing benefit of 1, 2, 3, ... They must be evaluated at age $x + n$, and then brought back to age x. Thus we have

$$(IA)^1_{x:\overline{n}|} = (IA)_x - n \cdot A_{x+n}\left(\frac{D_{x+n}}{D_x}\right) - (IA)_{x+n}\left(\frac{D_{x+n}}{D_x}\right)$$

$$= \frac{R_x}{D_x} - n\left(\frac{M_{x+n}}{D_{x+n}}\right)\left(\frac{D_{x+n}}{D_x}\right) - \left(\frac{R_{x+n}}{D_{x+n}}\right)\left(\frac{D_{x+n}}{D_x}\right)$$

$$= \frac{R_x - R_{x+n} - n \cdot M_{x+n}}{D_x}. \tag{9.21}$$

Finally, we will derive a formula for decreasing term insurance, $(DA)^1_{x:\overline{n}|}$, where the first payment is n and payments decrease annually to a final benefit of 1 in the nth year. Noting that

$$(DA)^1_{x:\overline{n}|} + (IA)^1_{x:\overline{n}|} = (n+1)A^1_{x:\overline{n}|}, \tag{9.22}$$

we obtain

$$(DA)^1_{x:\overline{n}|} = (n+1)\left(\frac{M_x - M_{x+n}}{D_x}\right) - \frac{R_x - R_{x+n} - n \cdot M_{x+n}}{D_x}$$

$$= \frac{(n+1)M_x - R_x - M_{x+n} + R_{x+n}}{D_x}$$

$$= \frac{n \cdot M_x - R_{x+1} + R_{x+n+1}}{D_x}. \tag{9.23}$$

| Example 9.13 |

Again consider Roger, aged 45, of Example 9.12. Let us assume that his policy is as stated up to and including age 65, but after that the benefit will decrease by 13,000 per year until it reaches zero. Find the net single premium for this policy if, in addition to earlier information, we know that $M_{65} = 10$, $R_{65} = 210$ and $R_{76} = 110$.

| Solution |

The policy benefit reaches a maximum of 130,000 in the 21st year. It then decreases by 13,000 per year for 10 years. Hence the net single premium is $88,000A^1_{45:\overline{20}|} + 2,000(IA)^1_{45:\overline{20}|} + 13,000(DA)^1_{65:\overline{10}|}\left(\frac{D_{65}}{D_{45}}\right)$.

Note that we must be careful to count the 130,000 benefit only once in the above sum; it is counted in the $(DA)^1_{65:\overline{10}|}$ term. Our premium is

$$88{,}000\left(\frac{M_{45}-M_{65}}{D_{45}}\right) + 2{,}000\left(\frac{R_{45}-R_{65}-20M_{65}}{D_{45}}\right)$$

$$+\ 13{,}000\left(\frac{10M_{65}-R_{66}+R_{76}}{D_{65}}\right)\left(\frac{D_{65}}{D_{45}}\right)$$

$$= 88{,}000\left(\tfrac{35}{110}\right) + 2{,}000\left(\tfrac{90}{110}\right) + 13{,}000\left(\tfrac{10}{110}\right) = 30{,}818.18.\ \square$$

9.5 ANNUAL PREMIUMS AND RESERVES

In Section 8.5 we saw how a deferred life annuity might sometimes be paid for by a series of annual premiums rather than a single premium. This method of payment is extremely common with life insurance, and we will investigate it in this section.

  Clearly there are many different situations which can arise with this kind of problem. The cardinal rule of this book is that the student should think through problems rather than memorize formulae, and this rule certainly applies to the current section. The basic idea is that the present value of all future premium payments should equal the present value of all future benefits. Since the first payment will almost always occur at the time the policy is taken out, our basic equation of value will have the general form

$$P\ddot{a} = A. \tag{9.24}$$

Here A denotes some insurance symbol (whole life, term, varying, etc.), and $\ddot{a}$ denotes some annuity symbol (life, temporary, etc.). Here is an example.

$\boxed{\text{Example 9.14}}$

Marie, aged 30, wishes to purchase a whole life policy of 10,000, payable at the end of the year of death, with a series of premiums at the beginning of each year for as long as she survives. Find the amount of the premium in each of the following cases:
(a) $M_{30} = 2250$ and $N_{30} = 120{,}000$
(b) $N_{30} = 120{,}000$, $i = .07$ and $D_{30} = 10{,}000$

Solution

Let P be the amount of each premium. From Formula (9.24) we have
$P\ddot{a}_{30} = 10{,}000A_{30}$.

FIGURE 9.4

(a) In this case, $P = \dfrac{10{,}000M_{30}}{N_{30}} = 187.50$.

(b) Using the identity $A_x = 1 - d\ddot{a}_x$, derived in Section 9.2,

$$P = \frac{10{,}000(1 - d\ddot{a}_{30})}{\ddot{a}_{30}}$$

$$= \frac{10{,}000(D_{30} - d \cdot N_{30})}{N_{30}}$$

$$= \frac{10{,}000[10{,}000 - \left(\frac{.07}{1.07}\right)(120{,}000)]}{120{,}000} = 179.13. \qquad \square$$

We will present a few basic formulae for this type of question, but in general problems should be solved from first principles. Occasionally we will include subscripts with the premium P to indicate the type of insurance purchased. For example, if a whole life policy is to be paid for by a life annuity, the symbol is P_x and we have

$$P_x = \frac{A_x}{\ddot{a}_x} = \frac{M_x}{N_x}. \tag{9.25a}$$

If n-year term insurance is being purchased with n annual payments contingent on survival, we have

$$P^1_{x:\overline{n|}} = \frac{A^1_{x:\overline{n|}}}{\ddot{a}_{x:\overline{n|}}} = \frac{M_x - M_{x+n}}{N_x - N_{x+n}}. \tag{9.26}$$

If the number of premiums is limited to at most t, the symbol $_tP$ is employed. For n-year term insurance we have

$$_tP^1_{x:\overline{n|}} = \frac{M_x - M_{x+n}}{N_x - N_{x+t}}. \tag{9.27}$$

A bar over the P in any of these cases means that the premiums are paid continuously. For example

$$\overline{P}_x = \frac{A_x}{\overline{a}_x} = \frac{M_x}{\overline{N}_x}. \qquad (9.25b)$$

If insurance payments are made at the moment of death, then the net single premium symbol for the insurance is written in parentheses after the P. For example,

$$P(\overline{A}_x) = \frac{\overline{A}_x}{\ddot{a}_x} = \frac{\overline{M}_x}{N_x} \qquad (9.25c)$$

denotes the annual premium for a whole life insurance paid at the moment of death. If the premiums are paid continuously as well, then a bar is also used over the P, as in

$$\overline{P}(\overline{A}_x) = \frac{\overline{A}_x}{\overline{a}_x} = \frac{\overline{M}_x}{\overline{N}_x}. \qquad (9.25d)$$

An n-year term insurance, with benefit paid at the moment of death and premiums paid continuously for at most t years, $t < n$, is denoted by

$$_t\overline{P}(\overline{A}^1_{x:\overline{n}|}) = \frac{\overline{A}^1_{x:\overline{n}|}}{\overline{a}_{x:\overline{t}|}} = \frac{\overline{M}_x - \overline{M}_{x+n}}{\overline{N}_x - \overline{N}_{x+t}}. \qquad (9.28)$$

Other similar identities are given in the exercises. However the reader should be alert to problems which do not fit easily into any given formula. Here are two more examples. (Again, and for the rest of this section, we assume death benefits paid at the end of the year of death, unless specified otherwise.)

| Example 9.15 |

Matilda, aged 40, purchases an insurance policy which pays 1000 in the first year, increases by 1000 per year to a maximum of 10,000, and then remains constant. She wishes to pay for this policy with an initial payment of X and subsequent annual payments of $2X$ contingent on survival. Find X given $D_{40} = 390$, $N_{40} = 7500$, $R_{40} = 5000$ and $R_{50} = 3500$.

Solution

The value at age 40 of all future benefits is given by the expression $1000(IA)^1_{40:\overline{10}|} + 10,000A_{50}\left(\dfrac{D_{50}}{D_{40}}\right)$. Similarly, the value at age 40 of all future payments is given by $X\ddot{a}_{40} + X\ddot{a}_{41}\left(\dfrac{D_{41}}{D_{40}}\right)$. Equating, we obtain

$$X = \frac{1000(IA)^1_{40:\overline{10}|} + 10,000A_{50}\left(\dfrac{D_{50}}{D_{40}}\right)}{\ddot{a}_{40} + \ddot{a}_{41}\dfrac{D_{41}}{D_{40}}}$$

$$= \frac{(1000)(R_{40} - R_{50} - 10M_{50}) + 10,000M_{50}}{N_{40} + N_{41}}$$

$$= \frac{1000(1500)}{7500 + 7110} = 102.67. \qquad \square$$

Example 9.16

Garth, aged 45, purchases a life insurance policy by means of annual payments contingent on survival. The death benefit at any age is the sum of the net premiums paid to that time plus an additional 1000. Find the premium if $M_{45} = 1700$, $N_{45} = 45{,}000$ and $R_{45} = 27{,}000$.

Solution

If P is the annual premium, then the benefits are $P + 1000$, $2P + 1000$, $\cdots$. The present value of all future benefits is $1000A_{45} + P \cdot (IA)_{45}$. The present value of all future premiums is $P\ddot{a}_{45}$. Thus we have $P\ddot{a}_{45} = 1000A_{45} + P \cdot (IA)_{45}$, so $P = \dfrac{1000M_{45}}{N_{45} - R_{45}} = \dfrac{1000(1700)}{18{,}000} = 94.44$.

$\qquad \square$

It is also possible that payments for an insurance policy could be made at intervals other than yearly. If payments are to be made m times yearly on a whole life policy, the total annual premium is denoted by $P_x^{(m)}$ and we have

$$P_x^{(m)} = \frac{A_x}{\ddot{a}_x^{(m)}}. \qquad (9.29)$$

Using Formula (8.28) gives the approximate formula

$$P_x^{(m)} = \frac{A_x}{\ddot{a}_x - \frac{m-1}{2m}}$$

$$= \frac{M_x}{N_x - \left(\frac{m-1}{2m}\right)D_x}. \tag{9.30}$$

Example 9.17

Repeat Example 9.14(a) if the payments are to be made monthly. In addition to the given information, assume $D_{30} = 10,000$.

Solution

$$P_{30}^{(12)} = \frac{10,000M_{30}}{N_{30} - \frac{11}{24} \cdot D_{30}} = 194.95.$$ Note that this means each *monthly*

payment will be equal to $\frac{1}{12}(194.95) = 16.25$. □

The concept of loading, discussed in the final section of the last chapter, also applies in this setting. We will present two examples here and several more in the exercises.

Example 9.18

Kim purchases a 50,000 whole life policy at age 30. Premiums are payable at the beginning of each year for life. Expense provisions include (i) 20% of the first year gross premium for issuing expenses; (ii) 50% of the first year gross premium and 10% of each gross premium thereafter for administrative expenses; (iii) 100 for additional start-up expenses. Find the gross annual premium given $M_{30} = 1200$, $N_{30} = 100,000$ and $D_{30} = 4350$.

Solution

Let G be the gross annual premium. In every year except the first, $.9G$ contributes to the purchase of coverage. In the first year only $.3G - 100$ contributes to the insurance. Then $(.9G)\ddot{a}_{30} - .6G - 100 = 50,000A_{30}$, so

$$G = \frac{50,000A_{30} + 100}{(.9)\ddot{a}_{30} - .6} = \frac{50,000M_{30} + 100D_{30}}{.9N_{30} - .6D_{30}} = 691.56. \quad □$$

| Example 9.19 |

A whole life insurance policy is issued at age 35. The death benefit is 1000 in the first year and increases by 1000 per year thereafter. The gross annual premium is payable at the beginning of each year for the next 30 years. The following expense provisions apply:
(i)   40% of the first year's gross annual premium.
(ii) 10% of the gross annual premium after the first year.
(iii) 100 at issue.
(iv) 2 at the beginning of each year of the policy.
Find the gross annual premium given $D_{35} = 3000$, $N_{35} = 70{,}000$, $R_{35} = 20{,}000$ and $N_{65} = 28{,}000$.

| Solution |

The present value of all future death benefits is $1000(IA)_{35}$.   Letting G be the gross annual premium, we have the equation of value $1000(IA)_{35} = (.9G)\ddot{a}_{35:\overline{30}|} - .3G - 100 - 2\ddot{a}_{35}$.   The yearly expense of 2 is not restricted to 30 years, but continues for the life of the policy. Hence $2\ddot{a}_{35}$ is the appropriate present value of this expense. We obtain

$$G = \frac{1000(IA)_{35} + 100 + 2\ddot{a}_{35}}{(.9)\ddot{a}_{35:\overline{30}|} - .3} = \frac{1000R_{35} + 100D_{35} + 2N_{35}}{.9(N_{35}-N_{65}) - .3D_{35}} = 553.93.$$

□

In Section 8.5 we briefly encountered the concept of premium reserves. This idea takes on its main importance now in connection with insurance rather than annuities. The *reserve* is defined to be the excess of the present value of future benefits over the present value of future premiums. For a whole life policy of 1, issued to a person aged x and payable by net premiums at the beginning of each year, the net level premium reserve t years later is denoted $_tV_x$, and is given by

$$_tV_x = A_{x+t} - P_x \cdot \ddot{a}_{x+t}. \tag{9.31}$$

The reserve given by (9.31) is called the policy year *terminal reserve*, which means that t is assumed to be an integer, so that $_tV_x$ exists at the end of a policy year.

Many variations of Formula (9.31) are encountered, depending on the duration of the premium payments and the type of insurance. For example, if premiums are only paid for n years, then for $t \geq n$ the second term in (9.31) disappears, and we find that the reserve is simply equal to A_{x+t}.

Here are a few examples. Other situations arise in the exercises.

Example 9.20

Ralph purchases a 10,000 whole life policy at age 40. He pays for the policy with a series of premiums at the beginning of each year for the next twenty years. If $M_{40} = 1100$, $N_{40} = 57,000$ and $N_{60} = 28,000$, find the terminal reserve for this policy at each of the following ages:

(a)   Age 50, if $M_{50} = 820$, $N_{50} = 41,000$ and $D_{50} = 2010$.

(b)   Age 70, if $M_{70} = 290$ and $D_{70} = 750$.

(c)   Age 40, just *before* the premium is paid.

(d)   Age 40, just *after* the premium is paid.

Solution

(a)   We must first calculate the amount, P, of the premium. We have
$P\ddot{a}_{40:\overline{20|}} = 10,000A_{40}$, so $P = \dfrac{10,000M_{40}}{N_{40} - N_{60}} = 379.31$. At age 50 the
present value of future benefits is $10,000A_{50}$, and the present value of future premiums is $379.31\ddot{a}_{50:\overline{10|}}$. Thus the reserve is
$\dfrac{(10,000)(820) - (379.31)(13,000)}{2010} = 1,626.35$.

(b)   Since no further premiums are to be paid, the reserve is just
$10,000A_{70} = 10,000\left(\dfrac{290}{750}\right) = 3,866.67$.

(c)   The reserve is $10,000A_{40} - P\ddot{a}_{40:\overline{20|}} = 0$.

(d)   Since one premium payment has been made, the reserve is now
$10,000A_{40} - Pa_{40:\overline{19|}} = 10,000A_{40} - P\ddot{a}_{40:\overline{20|}} + P$. The first two
terms together are 0, from part (c), so the reserve is simply
$P = 379.31$.   □

Example 9.21

Annette, aged 50, purchases a whole life policy paying 50,000 for death in the first year, 55,000 the second year, and increasing by 5000 annually to a maximum of 100,000, at which point it remains constant. She will pay for this with an increasing series of annual payments of P immediately and then $2P$, $3P$, and so on, for as long as she survives. Find an expression, in terms of commutation functions, for her terminal reserve at age 55.

Solution

At age 55 the benefit is 75,000, so the present value of Annette's future benefits is $70,000A_{55} + 5000(IA)^1_{55:\overline{5}|} + 30,000A_{60}\dfrac{D_{60}}{D_{55}}$. The present value of future premiums is $(5P)\ddot{a}_{55} + P(I\ddot{a})_{55}$. The premium itself is found from $P(I\ddot{a})_{50} = 45,000A_{50} + 5000(IA)^1_{50:\overline{10}|} + 55,000A_{60}\left(\dfrac{D_{60}}{D_{50}}\right)$, so that $P = \dfrac{45,000M_{50} + 5000(R_{50}-R_{60}-10M_{60}) + 55,000M_{60}}{S_{50}}$. The terminal reserve at age 55 is therefore

$$\dfrac{1}{D_{55}}(70,000M_{55} + 5000R_{55} - 5000R_{60} + 5000M_{60})$$

$$- \left(\dfrac{5N_{55}+S_{55}}{D_{55}}\right)\left(\dfrac{45,000M_{50}+5000R_{50}-5000R_{60}+5000M_{60}}{S_{50}}\right).$$

$\square$

There are a number of useful formulae which can be developed for reserves. For example, using $A_{x+t} = 1 - d\ddot{a}_{x+t}$ (see Formula (9.12b)), we obtain

$$_tV_x = A_{x+t} - P_x\ddot{a}_{x+t}$$

$$= 1 - (P_x + d)\ddot{a}_{x+t}. \qquad (9.32)$$

Using $P_x = \dfrac{A_x}{\ddot{a}_x} = \dfrac{1 - d\ddot{a}_x}{\ddot{a}_x} = \dfrac{1}{\ddot{a}_x} - d$, we have the very useful formula

$$_tV_x = 1 - \dfrac{\ddot{a}_{x+t}}{\ddot{a}_x}. \qquad (9.33)$$

We also have

$$_tV_x = A_{x+t} - P_x \cdot \ddot{a}_{x+t}$$

$$= A_{x+t}\left(1 - \dfrac{P_x \cdot \ddot{a}_{x+t}}{A_{x+t}}\right)$$

$$= A_{x+t}\left(1 - \dfrac{P_x}{P_{x+t}}\right), \qquad (9.34)$$

since $P_{x+t} = \dfrac{A_{x+t}}{\ddot{a}_{x+t}}$. Substituting $A_{x+t} = P_{x+t} \cdot \ddot{a}_{x+t}$ into (9.34) gives

$$_tV_x = (P_{x+t} - P_x) \cdot \ddot{a}_{x+t}, \qquad (9.35)$$

which leads to

$$_tV_x = \frac{P_{x+t} - P_x}{P_{x+t} + d},\qquad(9.36)$$

since $\frac{1}{\ddot{a}_{x+t}} = P_{x+t} + d.$

Sometimes it is important to know the connection between the terminal reserves of two successive policy years. Problems of this type can either be worked out from first principles or by using the formula we will now derive. Again recall that $_tV_x = A_{x+t} - P_x \cdot \ddot{a}_{x+t}$. We note that A_{x+t} can be thought of as the value of the first year's benefit, vq_{x+t}, plus the present value of the remaining benefits, which is given by $vp_{x+t} \cdot A_{x+t+1}$. Similarly, $\ddot{a}_{x+t} = 1 + vp_{x+t} \cdot \ddot{a}_{x+t+1}$. Thus we have

$$_tV_x = vq_{x+t} + vp_{x+t} \cdot A_{x+t+1} - P_x(1 + vp_{x+t} \cdot \ddot{a}_{x+t+1})$$

$$= vp_{x+t}(A_{x+t+1} - P_x \cdot \ddot{a}_{x+t+1}) + vq_{x+t} - P_x$$

$$= (vp_{x+t}) \cdot {}_{t+1}V_x + vq_{x+t} - P_x.\qquad(9.37)$$

This formula can be used either to obtain $_tV_x$ given $_{t+1}V_x$, or to go in the other direction. A nicer symmetrical form is obtained by transposing P_x and multiplying by $1 + i$, obtaining

$$(1 + i)(_tV_x + P_x) = q_{x+t} + p_{x+t}(_{t+1}V_x).\qquad(9.38)$$

EXERCISES

9.1   Basic Concepts

9-1.   Find the price of whole life insurance with a face value of 100,000 sold to a person aged 40 in each of the following cases.
(a) $p_x = .96$ for all x and $i = .09$.
(b) $\ell_x = 1000\left(1 - \frac{x}{115}\right)$ and $i = .13$.

9-2.   Repeat Question 1 if the payment of 100,000 is to be made at the end of the 5-year period in which death occurs.

9-3.   Repeat Question 1 if the insurance is a term policy for 30 years.

9-4. Repeat Question 1 for 30-year endowment insurance.

9-5. Repeat Question 1 if the policy has a face value of 100,000 for the first 30 years only. If the insured survives to age 70, he is paid 70,000 and the remaining 30,000 is retained as a whole life benefit.

9-6. Repeat Question 1, if in each case, $i^{(12)} = .12$, but the benefits are still paid yearly.

9-7. Prove that the identity $A^1_{x:\overline{n}|} < A_x < A_{x:\overline{n}|}$ is true for all x and for all n.

9-8. Prove that $_n|A_x < A_x$ if $n \geq 1$. Give a verbal explanation for this inequality.

9-9. Julio's mortality for $1 \leq t \leq 4$ is assumed to be governed by the law $_tp_x = .3(4 - t)$. Harold's mortality for $1 \leq t \leq 5$ is governed by $_tp_x = .25(5 - t)$. If $i = .07$, find the price at time 0 of an insurance policy which will pay 100,000 at the end of the year in which the *second* of Julio or Harold dies.

9-10. Repeat Question 9 if the insurance is paid at the end of the year in which the *first* of the two men dies.

9-11. Repeat Question 9 if the policy is for 2-year endowment insurance.

9-12. Prove the identity $A_x = v(q_x + p_x A_{x+1})$.

9-13. Give a verbal argument for the identity in Question 12.

9-14. Prove that $A_x = (1-A_{x+n})A^1_{x:\overline{n}|} + A_{x:\overline{n}|} \cdot A_{x+n}$.

9-15. Obtain a formula for the net single premium at age x for an insurance policy which pays 1 at the end of 10 years if death occurs within that period, or at the end of the year of death if death occurs after 10 years.

9-16. Assume that a single rate of mortality, q_{x+n}, is increased to $q_{x+n} + k$ for some constant k. All other values of q_y remain unchanged. Show that A_x will be increased by the amount $kv^{n+1} {}_np_x(1 - A_{x+n+1})$.

9-17. The net single premium for a pure endowment of 10,000 issued at age x for n years is 8000 if the premium is to be returned in the event of death before age $x + n$. If the premium is not returned, the net single premium is 7000. Find the net single premium for a pure endowment of 10,000 issued at the same age and for the same period if half of the net premium is to be returned in the event of death.

9.2 Commutation Functions and Basic Identities

9-18. Herman, aged 45, purchases a whole life policy of 100,000. Find the net single premium if (a) $M_{45} = 250$ and $D_{45} = 520$; (b) $N_{45} = 8000$, $D_{45} = 520$ and $i = .04$.

9-19. Repeat Question 18(a) for a 20-year term insurance policy given $M_{65} = 35$.

9-20. Express the net single premium for the following policy, issued to a person aged 30, in terms of commutation functions: 50,000 if death occurs in the next 20 years, 100,000 if death occurs in the 20-year period after that, and 10-year endowment insurance of 50,000 after that.

9-21. Prove each of the following identities:

(a) $A_x = v - da_x$

(b) $A^1_{x:\overline{n}|} = v\ddot{a}_{x:\overline{n}|} - a_{x:\overline{n}|}$

(c) $A_{x:\overline{n}|} = v\ddot{a}_{x:\overline{n}|} - a_{x:\overline{n-1}|}$

(d) $A_{x:\overline{n}|} = 1 - d\ddot{a}_{x:\overline{n}|}$

(e) $a_{x:\overline{n}|} = \dfrac{v - A_{x:\overline{n+1}|}}{d}$

(f) $M_x = D_x - dN_x$

(g) $\dfrac{1 - ia_{x:\overline{t-1}|}}{1 + i} = \dfrac{M_x - M_{x+t} + D_{x+t}}{D_x}$

9-22. (a) Find the rate of interest if $a_x = 15.5$ and $A_x = .25$.

(b) Given $M_x = 3000$, $M_{x+1} = 2800$ and $q_x = .01$, find D_{x+1}.

9-23. Ronald, aged 40, purchases a whole life policy paying 10,000 during the next 10 years and 20,000 during the ten years after that. If Ronald is still alive at age 60, he will receive 200 at the end of each month for the rest of his life. Given $M_{40} = 750$, $M_{50} = 600$, $M_{60} = 420$, $D_{40} = 4500$, $D_{60} = 1100$ and $N_{60} = 10,000$, find the net single premium for this policy.

9-24. Angela, aged 55, purchases a deferred life annuity of 4000 per year commencing at age 65. Before age 65 there is a 10,000 death benefit payable at the end of the year of death. Find the net single premium for this package given $N_{55} = 250$, $N_{56} = 230$, $N_{65} = 110$, $N_{66} = 95$ and $i = .03$.

9-25. Repeat Question 24 if the life annuity is guaranteed, payable to either Angela or her estate, for 50 years.

9.3 Insurance Payable at the Moment of Death

9-26. (a) Find the net single premium for a 50,000 life insurance policy, payable at the moment of death, to a life aged 40 if it is assumed that $i = .06$ and $_t p_{40} = (.97)^t$ for all t.

(b) Do part (a) if the 40-year-old is purchasing 30-year term insurance instead of whole life insurance.

(c) Do part (a) if the 40-year-old is purchasing 30-year endowment insurance instead of whole life insurance.

9-27. (a) Find the price of a 100,000 life insurance policy, payable at the moment of death, bought by a life aged 40 if it is assumed that $\delta = .05$ and $\mu_x = .04$ for all x.

(b) Do part (a) if the 40-year-old is purchasing 30-year term insurance instead of whole life insurance.

(c) Do part (a) if the 40-year-old is purchasing 30-year endowment insurance instead of whole life insurance.

9-28. Repeat Question 27 if we continue to use $\delta = .05$ but now assume that the life is subject to a de Moivre's survival function with terminal age 110.

9-29. Do Question 28(a) if we assume the insurance is to be deferred for 20 years.

9-30. George is informed that the net single premium for a 200,000 whole life insurance policy, payable at the moment of death, is 70,000. If George is subject to a constant force of mortality $\mu_x = .03$, and if δ is also constant, find the net single premium for a 5-year deferred life policy of 200,000.

9-31. Helen is informed that the net single premium for 100,000 of whole life insurance, payable at the moment of death, is 65,000. If Helen is subject to a constant force of mortality $\mu_x = .0275$, and if δ is also constant, find the actuarial present value of a whole life annuity of 5000 per year payable continuously to Helen.

9-32. Brenda purchases life insurance which will pay 100,000 if she dies during the next 5 years and 200,000 if she dies after that. The benefits are payable at the moment of death. It is known that $\delta = .08$, and $\mu_x = .04$ for the next 8 years and $\mu_x = .05$ thereafter. Find the net single premium for this insurance.

9-33. (a)   If the force of interest is increased, but the force of mortality stays the same, does $\bar{A}_x$ increase or decrease? Explain your answer.

(b)   If the force of mortality is increased, but the force of interest stays the same, does $\bar{A}_x$ increase or decrease? Explain your answer.

9-34. Using integration by parts, derive the formula $\bar{A}_x = 1 - \delta \bar{a}_x$.

9-35. (a)   Derive the formula $\bar{A}^1_{x:\overline{n}|} = 1 - \delta \bar{a}_{x:\overline{n}|} - v^n\, {}_np_x$.

(b)   Derive the formula $\bar{A}_{x:\overline{n}|} = 1 - \delta \bar{a}_{x:\overline{n}|}$.

9-36. Assuming a constant force of mortality μ_x and a constant force of interest δ, find n such that $\bar{A}_{x:\overline{n}|} = 2\bar{A}^1_{x:\overline{n}|}$.

9-37. Herb purchase a 100,000 whole life insurance policy, with the benefit payable at the moment of death. The policy pays an additional 50,000 if death occurs during the first 5 years due to specified cause (a). Assuming $\delta = .07$, the force of decrement due to cause (a) is .005, and the force of decrement due to causes other than (a) is .045, find the net single premium for Herb's insurance.

9-38. A 20-year-old purchases a 100,000 whole life policy with benefit payable at the moment of death. Given $\delta = .05$ and $\mu_x = .02$ for all x, find each of the following:
   (a) The net single premium for this policy.
   (b) A number X such that the insurance company is 80% certain that the value at time of purchase of their eventual payout will be less than or equal to X. (Such a number X is sometimes called the 80th percentile of the present value of the benefit.)

9-39 (a) Assuming uniform distribution of deaths throughout the year of age x, show that $\overline{A}{}^{1}_{x:\overline{1}|} = \frac{i}{\delta} \cdot A^{1}_{x:\overline{1}|}$.
   (b) Extend the result of part (a) to show that $\overline{A}_x = \frac{i}{\delta} \cdot A_x$.

9.4 Varying Insurance

(Note: Unless stated otherwise, all exercises in Sections 9.4 and 9.5 assume death benefits payable at the end of the year of death.)

9-40. Tim, aged 50, purchases a whole life policy. In the first year his benefit is 20,000, and benefits increase by 5000 per year thereafter. Find the net single premium given $D_{50} = 500$, $R_{50} = 2300$ and $M_{50} = 220$.

9-41. Repeat Question 40 if Tim's policy is only to last for 20 years. In addition to the above data, assume $M_{70} = 60$ and $R_{70} = 400$.

9-42. Repeat Question 40 if Tim's policy is to increase as stated up to and including age 70, and then remain constant at 120,000 per year thereafter. Use the data given in Questions 40 and 41.

9-43. Do Question 40 if the insurance policy begins with an initial benefit at 120,000, and then decreases by 6000 annually until it reaches zero. Assume the data given in Questions 40 and 41.

9-44. Derive each of the following identities:
   (a) $(IA)_x = v(I\ddot{a})_x - (Ia)_x$
   (b) $(IA)_x = \ddot{a}_x - d(I\ddot{a})_x$

9-45. A whole life insurance policy is sold to the family of a newborn child. The policy pays 1000 if death occurs in the first year, 2000 in the second year, and so on up to 10,000 in the tenth year. The policy continues to provide coverage of 10,000 up to age 51. At age 51 and over it provides 50,000. Write the net single premium for this policy in terms of commutation functions.

9-46. Douglas is hired by XYZ Publishing Company at age 50, and will retire when he turns 65. On his 62nd birthday he becomes eligible for a death benefit paying 1000 for each year of service with XYZ. The benefit will terminate when he retires. Find the present value of this policy on his 62nd birthday, given $M_{62} = 800$, $M_{63} = 765$, $M_{64} = 728$, $M_{65} = 690$, $N_{62} = 22,000$, $N_{63} = 19,800$, $N_{64} = 17,700$ and $N_{65} = 15,700$.

9-47. Ellen, aged 60, purchases a life insurance policy paying 50,000 until age 65, 25,000 at age 65 and decreasing by 2500 per year thereafter until it reaches 5000, at which point it remains constant. Find the present value at age 60 of Ellen's future benefits given $M_{60} = 500$, $M_{65} = 350$, $D_{60} = 1200$, $R_{65} = 4000$, $R_{74} = 1600$ and $M_{74} = 150$.

9-48 Let $(I\overline{A})_x$ denote the net single premium for whole life insurance which pays 1 in the first year, 2 in the second year, and so on, increasing by 1 per year, payable at the moment of death. Similarly, let $(\overline{I}\,\overline{A})_x$ denote the net single premium for whole life insurance which pays t at the moment of death if death occurs at age $x+t$.
   (a)   Show that $(I\overline{A})_x = \ddot{a}_x - \delta(I\overline{a})_x$.
   (b)   Explain why $(\overline{I}\,\overline{A})_x = \int_0^\infty t\, v^t\, {}_tp_x\mu_{x+t}\, dt$.
   (c)   Show that $(\overline{I}\,\overline{A})_x = \overline{a}_x - \delta(\overline{I}\,\overline{a})_x$.
   (d)   Justify verbally the approximation $(\overline{I}\,\overline{A})_x = (I\overline{A})_x - \frac{1}{2}\overline{A}_x$.

9.5 Annual Premiums and Reserves

9-49. Roy, aged 50, purchases a whole life policy of 10,000 with a series of annual payments contingent on survival. Find the amount of each payment in each of the following cases:
   - (a) $M_{50} = 150$ and $N_{50} = 2200$
   - (b) $M_{50} = 150$, $i = .04$ and $D_{50} = 220$
   - (c) $M_{50} = 150$, $N_{50} = 2200$, $D_{50} = 220$ and the payments are made monthly

9-50. A 10,000 term insurance policy for 20 years is issued at age 45. The net annual premium for the first year is X and for each year thereafter is $2X$. Find X in each of the following cases:
   - (a) $M_{45} = 800$, $M_{65} = 520$, $N_{45} = 25,000$, $D_{45} = 1200$ and $N_{65} = 5500$.
   - (b) $N_{45} = 25,000$, $D_{45} = 1200$, $i = .03$, $N_{65} = 5500$ and $D_{65} = 400$.

9-51. Derive each of the following formulae:
   - (a) $P_{x:\overline{n}|} = \dfrac{A_{x:\overline{n}|}}{\ddot{a}_{x:\overline{n}|}} = \dfrac{M_x - M_{x+n} + D_{x+n}}{N_x - N_{x+n}}$
   - (b) $P_x = \dfrac{1}{\ddot{a}_x} - d$
   - (c) $P_{x:\overline{n}|} = \dfrac{1}{\ddot{a}_{x:\overline{n}|}} - d$
   - (d) $_tP_x = \dfrac{A_x}{\ddot{a}_{x:\overline{t}|}} = \dfrac{M_x}{N_x - N_{x+t}}$

9-52. A life insurance policy is issued at age 30. The initial death benefit is 10,000. At age 40 and each year thereafter, the death benefit increases by 5000 per year for ten years. No death benefit is payable after age 50. Annual premiums X are payable at the beginning of each year for 10 years. Find X given $M_{30} = 1200$, $M_{50} = 800$, $R_{40} = 33,000$, $R_{50} = 20,000$ $N_{30} = 90,000$, and $N_{40} = 68,000$.

9-53. Repeat Question 52 if the death benefits do not stop after 20 years, but increase indefinitely by 5000 per year, and if the premiums are payable for as long as the purchaser survives.

9-54. Aloysius, aged 40, purchases a life policy. Before age 60, the death benefit is the sum of the net premiums paid. At age 60 and later, the death benefit is 20,000. Find the net annual premium, payable at the beginning of each year for 20 years, given $i = .05$, $N_{60} = 13,000$, $N_{61} = 12,010$, $N_{40} = 61,000$, $R_{40} = 31,000$ and $R_{60} = 11,500$.

9-55. Repeat Question 54 if the death benefit before age 60 is the sum of the net premiums paid plus interest.

9-56. A 100,000 whole life policy is issued at age 25. Premiums are payable at the beginning of each year for life, and death benefits are payable at the end of the year of death. The following are required for expenses: 60% of the first year's gross premium, 20% of the gross premium in years two through five inclusive, and 10% of the gross premium in each subsequent year. Find the gross annual premium if $N_{25} = 120,000$, $N_{26} = 112,000$, $N_{30} = 96,000$ and $i = .06$.

9-57. Repeat Question 56 if an extra expense of 3 is required at the beginning of every year throughout the policy.

9-58. A whole life insurance policy is issued at age 30. The gross annual premium is 120 payable at the beginning of each year for life. Expense provisions include 50% of the first year's gross annual premium, 10% of each subsequent gross annual premium, and 200 at issue. Given $A_{30} = .068$ and $\ddot{a}_{30} = 15$, find the face amount of the policy.

9-59. A deferred life annuity, issued at age 35, will provide monthly payments of 1000 commencing at age 65. Annual premiums are payable at the beginning of each year for 20 years. During the deferred period, the death benefit is equal to the sum of the gross premiums paid. Gross premiums are equal to 110% of net premiums. Find the gross annual premium given $N_{65} = 5000$, $D_{65} = 500$, $N_{55} = 12,500$, $N_{35} = 38,000$, $R_{35} = 20,000$, $R_{55} = 7500$ and $M_{65} = 300$.

9-60. A life insurance policy issued at age 50 provides a death benefit of 10,000, less the sum of the gross annual premiums which would otherwise be paid after the date of death. Premiums are paid at the beginning of each year for 30 years. The loading is 10% of each net level annual premium. Find an expression for the gross annual premium.

9-61. Derive a formula in terms of commutation functions for the gross annual premium at age x, payable for n years, for a whole life insurance policy of 1, if the expenses consist of a flat amount of h per year, as long as payments continue, plus an additional amount of k in the first year, plus j percent of each premium paid, plus an extra expense of r in the year the claim is made.

9-62. Morgan, aged 40, purchases a whole life policy paying 50,000 in case of death within the next 10 years and 100,000 thereafter. Assume $M_{40} = 740$, $M_{50} = 580$ and $N_{40} = 59,000$.
   (a)   Find the net annual premium for this policy.
   (b)   Find the terminal reserve at age 45, assuming $M_{45} = 675$, $N_{45} = 42,000$ and $D_{45} = 1700$.
   (c)   Find the terminal reserve at age 55, assuming $M_{55} = 475$, $D_{55} = 1150$ and $N_{55} = 27,000$.
   (d)   In part (c), find the portion of Morgan's future benefits that are funded by his future premiums.

9-63. Rosalita, aged 20, purchases a whole life policy paying 5000 the first year and increasing by 5000 per year thereafter. She pays annual premiums at the beginning of each year of X for the first 10 years and $3X$ thereafter. Express in commutation functions each of the following:
   (a)   The value of X.
   (b)   The reserve just after the first premium payment.
   (c)   The terminal reserve at age 25.
   (d)   The terminal reserve at age 50.

9-64. Show that $_{\omega-x-1}V_x = v - P_x$, where ω is the terminal age of the population.

9-65. Benjamin, aged 35, purchases a 30-year term insurance policy with a face value of 50,000. Level premiums are payable at the beginning of each year for the next 20 years. Assume $i = .03$, $N_{35} = 7300$, $N_{36} = 7000$, $N_{55} = 2400$, $N_{56} = 2265$, $N_{65} = 1050$ and $N_{66} = 960$.

(a) Find the amount of each premium.

(b) Find the 10th year terminal reserve for this policy, assuming $N_{45} = 4200$ and $N_{46} = 4000$.

(c) Find the 20th year terminal reserve for this policy.

(d) Find the 30th year terminal reserve for this policy.

9-66. Repeat Question 65 if the death benefit, instead of having a face value of 50,000, is a 20-year interest-only annuity of 5000 per year with the first payment at the end of the year of death.

9-67. Betty, aged 40, purchases a 100,000 whole life policy with a single premium of 36,000. At the same time, Betty also purchases a 100,000 whole life policy with a net annual premium of 2200 payable at the beginning of each year for life. Assume i is the same for both policies. The *net amount at risk* (the excess of the face amount over the terminal reserve) for the tenth year on the first policy is equal to K, and the net amount at risk for the tenth year on the second policy is L. The net single premium at age 50 for a 100,000 whole life policy is 48,600. Find $\frac{K}{L}$.

9-68. Prove each of the following identities:

(a) $_tV_x = \dfrac{P_x(N_x - N_{x+t})}{D_{x+t}} - \dfrac{M_x - M_{x+t}}{D_{x+t}}.$

(b) $_tV_x = \dfrac{A_{x+t} - A_x}{1 - A_x}.$

9-69. Find $_{t+1}V_x$ given $P_x = .013$, $_tV_x = .13$, $q_{x+t} = .004$ and $i = .03$.

9-70. Show that $_tV_x = A_{x+t}\left(1 + \dfrac{1+i}{i} \cdot P_x\right) - \dfrac{1+i}{i} \cdot P_x.$

9-71. Show that $_tV_x = 1 - (1-_1V_x)(1-_1V_{x+1}) \cdots (1-_1V_{x+t-1}).$

9-72. Assuming $\delta = .07$ and $\mu_x = .04$ for all x, find each of the following:

(a) $P(\bar{A}_x)$ (b) $\bar{P}_x$ (c) $\bar{P}(\bar{A}_x)$ (d) $\bar{P}(\bar{A}_{x:\overline{5}|}^{1})$

9-73. As with premiums, reserves where the payments are made continuously are denoted by placing a bar over the V, and reserves where the insurance is payable at the moment of death are denoted by including the net single premium for the insurance in parantheses after the V.

(a)   Given $\bar{a}_x = 23$, $\bar{a}_{x+5} = 19$ and $\delta = .03$, find $_5\bar{V}(\bar{A}_x)$.

(b)   Given $\bar{a}_{x:\overline{n}|} = 16$, $\bar{a}_{x+10:\overline{n-10}|} = 13$ and $\delta = .03$,   find $_{10}\bar{V}(\bar{A}_{x:\overline{n}|})$.

9-74. Under "normal" circumstances, we would expect $_tV_x > 0$. Why?

CHAPTER TEN
STATISTICAL CONSIDERATIONS

10.1 MEAN AND VARIANCE

The concept of expected value was introduced in Section 6.2, and that idea was then applied in almost all of the calculations in subsequent chapters. For example, $A_x = \sum_{t=0}^{\infty} {}_tp_x q_{x+t} v^{t+1}$ is a sum of terms, each one of which is the product of the present value of one dollar paid at the end of a given year (v^{t+1}), times the probability of death occurring during that year (${}_tp_x q_{x+t}$). Such an expected value is called the *mean* of a random variable Z (in this case $Z = v^{t+1}$), and is denoted $E[Z]$.

Two important general properties of the mean, to be referred to later, are

$$E[Z_1 + Z_2] = E[Z_1] + E[Z_2] \tag{10.1}$$

and

$$E[rZ] = r \cdot E[Z], \tag{10.2}$$

for any number r.

Before proceeding, we should acknowledge that we are being less than rigorous in our presentation of concepts in this chapter. We hope, however, that this somewhat informal approach will be helpful to students whose background in statistics is not particularly strong.

One measure of the dispersion of a random variable Z is the concept of *variance*, denoted $Var(Z)$, which is defined to be equal to $E[(Z - E[Z])^2]$. In practice, we will always use the formula

$$Var(Z) = E[Z^2] - (E[Z])^2, \tag{10.3}$$

which can be derived using Properties (10.1) and (10.2). Here is an example.

Example 10.1

Let Z denote the present value random variable, at policy issue, for a whole life policy with a death benefit of 1 payable at the end of the year of death, purchased by a 20-year-old. Find $E[Z]$ and $Var(Z)$ if $i = .07$ and $_tp_{20} = (.97)^t$ for all t.

Solution

$E[Z]$ is the same as A_{20}, which is

$$\sum_{t=0}^{\infty}(.97)^t(.03)\left(\frac{1}{1.07}\right)^{t+1} = \frac{.03}{1.07}\left(\frac{1}{1 - \frac{.97}{1.07}}\right) = .30.$$

To calculate $Var(Z)$, we first find $E[Z^2]$. We see that Z^2 has the same probabilities as Z, but the present value of the death benefit is now

$$\left[\left(\frac{1}{1.07}\right)^{t+1}\right]^2 = \left(\frac{1}{1.07}\right)^{2t+2}. \text{ Hence}$$

$$E[Z^2] = \sum_{t=0}^{\infty}(.97)^t(.03)\left(\frac{1}{1.07}\right)^{2t+2}$$

$$= \frac{.03}{(1.07)^2}\sum_{t=0}^{\infty}\left(\frac{.97}{(1.07)^2}\right)^t$$

$$= \frac{.03}{1.1449}\left(\frac{1}{1 - \frac{.97}{1.1449}}\right)$$

$$= .17153.$$

Then we obtain

$$Var(Z) = E[Z^2] - (E[Z])^2$$

$$= .17153 - (.30)^2$$

$$= .08153. \qquad \square$$

The concepts of mean and variance also apply to insurances payable at the moment of death; in fact, the formula $\overline{A}_x = \int_0^{\infty} v^t \, _tp_x\mu_{x+t}\,dt$, which was derived in Section 9.3, is just the expected value calculation for the random variable $Z = v^t$.

Example 10.2

Let Z denote the present value random variable, at policy issue, for a whole life policy with a death benefit of 1 payable at the moment of death, purchased by an individual for whom $\mu_x = .04$ for all x and $\delta = .07$. Find $E[Z]$ and $Var(Z)$.

Solution

$E[Z]$ is just $\bar{A}_x$, which is

$$\int_0^\infty v^t \, {}_tp_x\mu_{x+t} \, dt = \int_0^\infty e^{-.07t} e^{-.04t}(.04) \, dt$$

$$= .04 \int_0^\infty e^{-.11t} \, dt$$

$$= .04 \left(\frac{-1}{-.11} \right)$$

$$= .36364.$$

As in the previous example, to get $E[Z^2]$ we just square v^t, so

$$E[Z^2] = \int_0^\infty e^{-.14t} e^{-.04t}(.04) \, dt$$

$$= .04 \int_0^\infty e^{-.18t} \, dt$$

$$= .2\dot{2}.$$

Then

$$Var(Z) = .2\dot{2} - (.36364)^2 = .08999. \qquad \square$$

$E[Z^2]$ is called the *second moment* of the random variable Z. Note that in the last example, $E[Z^2]$ works out just like $E[Z]$, but with the force of interest doubled. Because of that, the notation ${}^2\bar{A}_x$ can be used to represent $E[Z^2]$ in cases like this.

Unlike the mean, the variance does not usually satisfy the linearity properties given by (10.1) and (10.2). However, it does satisfy the properties

$$Var(rZ) = r^2 \cdot Var(Z) \qquad (10.4)$$

and

$$Var(r+Z) = Var(Z), \qquad (10.5)$$

for any number r. Property (10.4) has an immediate and important application to all of our work.

| Example 10.3 |

Redo Example 10.1 if the death benefit is 1000 payable at the end of the year of death.

| Solution |

We know from Chapter 9 (or by using Property (10.2)) that the expected value is now $1000A_{20} = 1000(.30) = 300$. Property (10.4) tells us that the variance will now be equal to $(1000)^2(.08153) = 81,530$. (Keeping more decimals in Example 10.1 gives the more precise answer 81,526.587.)   □

When we turn our attention to life annuities, there is a problem that needs to be addressed at the outset. The expression $a_x = \sum_{t=0}^{\infty} v^t {}_tp_x$, while intuitively appealing, is of a conceptually different nature from $A_x = \sum_{t=0}^{\infty} v^{t+1} {}_tp_x q_{x+t}$. The latter consists of a sum of terms, each one of which is the product of a possible value of the present value random variable Z and the probability associated with that value. In the case of a_x, however, the possible values of the present value of all payments are sums of the v^i terms (depending on how long the individual survives). Nevertheless, the linearity properties given by (10.1) and (10.2) assure us that $a_x = \sum_{t=0}^{\infty} v^t {}_tp_x$ still correctly calculates the mean. However, the variance (which in general is not linear) is another matter entirely. The next example illustrates these problems and shows how to go about solving them.

| Example 10.4 |

In a very ill population of elderly people, we know that $p_{90} = .80$, ${}_2p_{90} = .50$, ${}_3p_{90} = .25$ and ${}_4p_{90} = 0$. A 90-year-old wishes to purchase a life annuity of 10,000 per year with the first payment in one year. If $i = .08$, find the mean and variance of the random variable for the present value of payments under this annuity.

Solution
The mean is just

$$10{,}000a_{90} = 10{,}000\left((.80)\left(\tfrac{1}{1.08}\right) + (.50)\left(\tfrac{1}{1.08}\right)^2 + .25\left(\tfrac{1}{1.08}\right)^3\right)$$

$$= 13{,}678.68.$$

The variance is more complicated; we will show two methods of finding it.

Method One
To start, we assume the annuity is 1 per year. There are three possibilities for the present value of future payments. If the person survives 1 year but not 2 (the probability of which is $.80 - .50 = .30$), the value will be $\tfrac{1}{1.08}$. If the person survives 2 years but not 3 (with probability $.50 - .25 = .25$), the value will be $\tfrac{1}{1.08} + \left(\tfrac{1}{1.08}\right)^2$. Finally, the person might survive 3 years (with probability $.25$) in which case the value will be $\tfrac{1}{1.08} + \left(\tfrac{1}{1.08}\right)^2 + \left(\tfrac{1}{1.08}\right)^3$. (Note that surviving 4 years is impossible.) Hence the second moment $E[Z^2]$ is

$$.30\left(\tfrac{1}{1.08}\right)^2 + .25\left(\tfrac{1}{1.08} + \left(\tfrac{1}{1.08}\right)^2\right)^2$$

$$+ .25\left(\tfrac{1}{1.08} + \left(\tfrac{1}{1.08}\right)^2 + \left(\tfrac{1}{1.08}\right)^3\right)^2 = 2.712567155.$$

Then the variance for an annuity of 1 per year is

$$2.712567155 - (1.367868211)^2 = .841503712.$$

Using Property (10.4), the answer to our question is

$$(10{,}000)^2(.841503712) = 84{,}150{,}371.20.$$

Method Two
Let Y be the present value random variable whose expected value is a_x, and let Z be the present value random variable whose expected value is A_x. We saw in Chapter 9 that $A_x = 1 - d\ddot{a}_x = v - da_x$, and consequently $a_x = \dfrac{v - A_x}{d}$. (This actually follows from the more general relation $Y = \dfrac{v - Z}{d}$, which is derived in the same way.) Properties (10.4) and (10.5) then tell us that

$$Var(Y) = Var\left(\frac{v}{d} - \frac{Z}{d}\right) = \frac{1}{d^2} \cdot Var(Z).$$

Then we can solve this by finding $Var(Z)$. First note that

$$E[Z] = A_{90} = .20\left(\frac{1}{1.08}\right) + .30\left(\frac{1}{1.08}\right)^2 + .25\left(\frac{1}{1.08}\right)^3 + .25\left(\frac{1}{1.08}\right)^4$$

$$= .8246023548$$

and

$$E[Z^2] = {}^2A_{90} = .20\left(\frac{1}{1.08}\right)^2 + .30\left(\frac{1}{1.08}\right)^4 + .25\left(\frac{1}{1.08}\right)^6 + .25\left(\frac{1}{1.08}\right)^8$$

$$= .6845863477.$$

Hence the variance of Z is ${}^2A_{90} - (A_{90})^2 = .0046173042$. Since $d = \frac{.08}{1.08}$, we get $Var(Y) = .8415037$, as before. In the usual situation where the number of future payments in a life annuity is potentially quite large, Method Two is the only reasonable way to proceed. $\square$

Example 10.5

Determine the variance of the present value random variable for a continuous life annuity of 1 per year assuming $\mu_x = .03$ for all x and $\delta = .05$.

Solution

In Chapter 9, we noted the identity $\overline{A}_x = 1 - \delta \overline{a}_x$. More generally we have $Z = 1 - \delta \cdot Y$, and consequently

$$Var(Y) = Var\left(\frac{1-Z}{\delta}\right) = \frac{1}{\delta^2} \cdot Var(Z).$$

In the insurance case, we know that

$$E[Z] = \int_0^\infty e^{-.05t} e^{-.03t}(.03)\,dt = \frac{3}{8}$$

and

$$E[Z^2] = \int_0^\infty e^{-.10t} e^{-.03t}(.03)\,dt = \frac{3}{13}.$$

Hence $Var(Z) = \frac{3}{13} - \left(\frac{3}{8}\right)^2 = \frac{75}{832}$, and the required variance is

$$Var(Y) = \frac{1}{.05^2}\left(\frac{75}{832}\right) = 36.06. \qquad \square$$

Another example of an expected value seen earlier was the notion of the *complete expectation of life* encountered in Section 7.5. Recall that the formula for this was

$$\overset{\circ}{e}_x = \int_0^\infty {}_t p_x \, dt.$$

This is the expected value of the future lifetime $T(x)$ of a person aged x.

Although $\overset{\circ}{e}_x$ is just the net single premium for a continuous life annuity in the case where $i = 0$, the approach just demonstrated for calculating the variance will not work here. The crucial observation is to recall Exercise 7-33 from Section 7.5, which gave the alternative formula

$$\overset{\circ}{e}_x = \int_0^\infty t \, {}_t p_x \mu_{x+t} \, dt.$$

We recognize that this integral is set up just like the integral for $\overline{A}_x$, since the term inside is the product of an amount t times the instantaneous probability ${}_t p_x \mu_{x+t}$. (The latter is called a *probability density function* in proper statistics terminology.) Hence we can calculate the variance in the same direct way as we did for $\overline{A}_x$.

| Example 10.6 |

Given $\ell_x = 1000\left(1 - \frac{x}{105}\right)$, $0 \leq x \leq 105$, find the mean and variance of $T(30)$, the future lifetime of a person currently aged 30.

| Solution |

The mean is just $\overset{\circ}{e}_{30} = \int_0^{75} {}_t p_{30} \, dt = \int_0^{75} \frac{75 - t}{75} \, dt = 37.5.$ Next we calculate the second moment as

$$E[T^2(30)] = \int_0^{75} t^2 \, {}_t p_{30} \mu_{30+t} \, dt$$

$$= \int_0^{75} t^2 \left(\frac{75 - t}{75}\right)\left(\frac{1}{75 - t}\right) dt$$

$$= \frac{1}{75}\left(\frac{(75)^3}{3}\right)$$

$$= 1875.$$

Then the variance is $1875 - (37.5)^2 = 468.75.$ □

To close this section, we would like to briefly mention the notion of median. The *median* of a set of measurements is a number m such that precisely half of the measurements are less than or equal to m. Questions involving the median are best answered from first principles. Here is an easy example.

|Example 10.7|

Find the median of $T(30)$ in Example 10.6.

|Solution|

To solve this, we simply need to find a time t such that precisely half of the time $T(30)$ will be less than t. But this just means that $_tp_{30} = \frac{1}{2}$, or $\frac{75-t}{75} = \frac{1}{2}$. Solving, we obtain $t = 37.5$. $\square$

We remark that although the mean and median were equal in the last example, this is not the usual situation.

10.2 NORMAL DISTRIBUTION

The primary purpose of the previous section was to introduce the notion of variance. In practical applications, however, we will be more interested in the square root of the variance. This is called the *standard deviation* and is denoted by σ, so we have

$$\sigma = \sqrt{Var(Z)}. \qquad (10.6)$$

Although $E[Z]$ is the expected value or mean of a random variable Z, it is unlikely that any specific value is exactly equal to $E[Z]$. We can be somewhat more confident, however, that a specific value might lie between $E[Z] - \sigma$ and $E[Z] + \sigma$. This confidence increases if we extend the interval to $(E[Z] - 2\sigma, E[Z] + 2\sigma)$, and continues to increase if we allow further and further deviation from the mean.

To be more precise about the ideas discussed in the last paragraph, we need to know the underlying distribution of Z. However, there is an observation due to Chebyshev which can be used in all cases.

Chebyshev's Rule

If $k > 0$, the probability that a specific value lies between $E[Z] - k\sigma$ and $E[Z] + k\sigma$ is greater than or equal to $1 - \frac{1}{k^2}$.

Chebyshev's Rule can be restated as saying that

$$Pr(|Z - E[Z]| < k\sigma) \geq 1 - \frac{1}{k^2}. \qquad (10.7)$$

For instance, setting $k = 2$ we see that $Pr(|Z - E[Z]| < 2\sigma) \geq .75$.

Example 10.8

In Example 10.1, use Chebyshev's Rule to find an interval for Z such that the probability that a specific value lies in the interval is at least (a) .75; (b) $\frac{8}{9}$.

Solution

We have $E[Z] = .30$ and $\sigma = \sqrt{.08153} = .28553$. For part (a) we know that $Pr(|Z - E[Z]| < 2\sigma) \geq .75$, so the interval is

$$(E[Z] - 2\sigma, E[Z] + 2\sigma) = (-.27106, .87106).$$

For part (b) we have $Pr(|Z - E[Z]| < 3\sigma) \geq \frac{8}{9}$, so the answer is

$$(E[Z] - 3\sigma, E[Z] + 3\sigma) = (-.55659, 1.15659). \qquad \square$$

A moment's thought, however, tells us that these intervals are not helpful. We already know from practical considerations that $Z > 0$, so a negative lower bound tells us nothing, and we also know that the largest value Z can take is $\frac{1}{1.07} = .93458$ (if death occurs in the first year). So in part (b) we actually know with probability 1 that Z is in the interval obtained. In part (a), we can easily calculate directly what the probability of Z being in the interval obtained is: since $\left(\frac{1}{1.07}\right)^3 = .816 < .87106$ and $\left(\frac{1}{1.07}\right)^2 = .873 > .87106$, Z will only be bigger than .87106 if death occurs in the first two years. The probability of this occurring is $.03 + (.97)(.03) = .0591$, so the probability is .9409 that we are in the interval (whereas Chebyshev only gives us .75).

Often what is of most interest in problems of this type is to find a constant c such that $Pr(Z < c)$ is relatively high, since this puts an upper bound on how large the payout is likely to be. If we assume the underlying distribution is symmetric, then Chebyshev's Rule can be applied to this sort of problem, but we saw in the last example that it is not likely to be very useful. A much stronger assumption would be to assume that the underlying distribution is *normal*. Normal distribution tables can be found in any statistics textbook, but the only values we will need are the following:

$$Pr(Z < E[Z] + .842\sigma) = .80 \qquad (10.8a)$$

$$Pr(Z < E[Z] + 1.282\sigma) = .90 \qquad (10.8b)$$

$$Pr(Z < E[Z] + 1.645\sigma) = .95 \qquad (10.8c)$$

$$Pr(Z < E[Z] + 1.960\sigma) = .975 \qquad (10.8d)$$

$$Pr(Z < E[Z] + 2.327\sigma) = .99 \qquad (10.8e)$$

| Example 10.9 |

Assuming a normal distribution in Example 10.1, find a constant c such that $Pr(Z < c)$ is equal to (a) .80; (b) .90; (c) .95; (d) .99.

| Solution |
(a) $c = E[Z] + .842\sigma = .30 + .842(.28553) = .54$
(b) $c = .30 + 1.282(.28553) = .666$
(c) $c = .30 + 1.645(.28553) = .769$
(d) $c = .30 + 2.327(.28553) = .964$ □

While the above answers seem more reasonable than those of Example 10.8, some of them are still inaccurate. For example, (c) indicates that we are 95% certain Z is less than .769, whereas an exact calculation reveals that Z is less than .769 only 91.3% of the time.

The moral is that we have to be very careful about drawing conclusions based on an assumption that the underlying distribution is normal. Students with a background in statistics are encouraged to think about why the normal distribution is not particularly appropriate in this last example.

10.3 CENTRAL LIMIT THEOREM

After examining the last section, the reader might feel that the normal distribution assumption will be of little use in our work. But this is not the case at all. In this section, we will see how it can be applied.

First we recall from Section 10.1 that, in general, $Var(Z_1 + Z_2)$ and $Var(Z_1) + Var(Z_2)$ are different. However, when Z_1 and Z_2 represent *independent* random events, these expressions are equal. Moreover, this observation extends to sums of more than two random variables. What do we mean by independent? Simply that the events have no effect on each other. The fundamental example for us will be the present value random variables for insurance (or annuities) sold to different individuals. Because the survival of one individual is assumed to have no effect on the survival of another, these random variables are independent. (Actually, we have tacitly assumed this in a number of places earlier in the text.)

| Example 10.10 |

In Example 10.1, assume 100 policies of the type described are sold to different individuals and let Z denote the present value of *aggregate* future death benefits for all those policies. Find $E[Z]$ and $Var(Z)$.

| Solution |

The expected value of aggregate death benefits is

$$E[Z] = 100(.30) = 30.$$

By assuming independence among the different individuals, the variance is

$$Var(Z) = 100(.08153) = 8.153. \qquad \square$$

Note that if instead of 100 unit policies sold to different people, we were talking about a single policy of face amount 100 sold to one individual, then we would still have $E[Z] = 30$ but $Var(Z)$ would now be equal to $(100)^2(.08153) = 815.3$. It makes sense that this answer should be larger than before. Any deviation of a single individual's present value of benefit from its expected value would be magnified if the face amount of the policy were increased, whereas deviations among a group of 100 individuals would tend to cancel each other out.

The important connection of all this with the normal distribution is given by the *Central Limit Theorem*, stated here in the way in which we will apply it.

Central Limit Theorem

If independent random variables $Z_1, Z_2, \ldots, Z_n$ have the same distribution, and if n is large, then the sum $Z = Z_1 + Z_2 + \cdots + Z_n$ is approximately normally distributed.

Although in general it is not that easy to decide how large n must be in order for the approximation to be very good, many authors use $n = 30$ as a rough yardstick. Here are some examples.

Example 10.11
In Example 10.10, find the value of c such that (a) $Pr(Z < c) = .95$ and (b) $Pr(Z < c) = .99$.
Solution
The Central Limit Theorem allows us to more confidently assume a normal distribution here, with $\sigma = \sqrt{8.153} = 2.855$. Then for part (a) we have $30 + (1.645)(2.855) = 34.7$, and for part (b) we have $30 + (2.327)(2.855) = 36.6$. ◻

Example 10.12
50 independent lives, each age 40, contribute equal amounts to establish a fund which will pay 1000 at the moment of death of each of the individuals. Given $\mu_x = .02$ for all x and $\delta = .07$, find the amount that each must contribute to have 90% confidence that all claims will be paid.
Solution
If Z_i is the random variable representing present value of the death benefit for the ith person, we have

$$E[Z_i] = 1000 \int_0^\infty (.02)e^{-.02t}e^{-.07t}\, dt$$

$$= \frac{2000}{9}$$

and

$$Var(Z_i) = (1000)^2 \int_0^\infty (.02)e^{-.02t}e^{-.14t}\, dt - (E[Z_i])^2$$

$$= (1000)^2 \left(\tfrac{1}{8}\right) - (1000)^2 \left(\tfrac{4}{81}\right)$$

$$= 75{,}617.28.$$

Since the lives are independent, if Z is the sum of the individual present values we then have

$$E[Z] = 50\left(\tfrac{2000}{9}\right) = 11{,}111.11$$

and

$$Var(Z) = 50(75{,}617.28) = 3{,}780{,}864.$$

Hence $\sigma = 1944.44$, and the total amount to be contributed for 90% confidence must be $11{,}111.11 + (1.282)(1944.44) = 13{,}603.88$. Each person must contribute $\tfrac{1}{50}(13{,}603.88) = 272.08$. $\square$

10.4 LOSS-AT-ISSUE

Consider a whole life insurance policy of 1, payable at the end of the year of death, purchased by a person age x who pays annual premiums of Q. If death were to occur at age $x+k$, the value at time of purchase of the death benefit would be v^{k+1}, whereas the value of the premiums paid would be $Q \cdot \ddot{a}_{\overline{k+1}|}$. The difference

$$L = v^{k+1} - Q \cdot \ddot{a}_{\overline{k+1}|} \tag{10.9}$$

is called the *loss-at-issue* for this policy.

This new random variable L is quite important because it measures whether the issuer of the policy has lost or profited from the given transaction. In this section, we will apply the ideas developed in previous sections to answer questions about L. It will be important to remember from before that $E[v^{k+1}] = A_x$.

Note that we are not assuming here that Q is necessarily equal to P_x. Instead, we are opening up the possibility that the premium Q may be different from that calculated earlier. In our first example, however, we will assume that $Q = P_x$.

Example 10.13

L is the loss-at-issue random variable for a whole life insurance of 1, payable at the end of the year of death, purchased by a life age 30 who pays annual premiums of P_{30}. Given $_tp_{30} = (.97)^t$ for all t and $i = .07$, find $E[L]$ and $Var(L)$.

Solution

First we calculate $P_{30} = \frac{A_{30}}{\ddot{a}_{30}} = \frac{1 - d\ddot{a}_{30}}{\ddot{a}_{30}}$. We find

$$\ddot{a}_{30} = \sum_{t=0}^{\infty} v^t \, _tp_{30} = \sum_{t=0}^{\infty} \left(\frac{.97}{1.07}\right)^t = \frac{1}{1 - \frac{.97}{1.07}} = 10.7,$$

so that

$$P_{30} = \frac{1 - \left(\frac{.07}{1.07}\right)(10.7)}{10.7} = \frac{3}{107}$$

and

$$A_{30} = 1 - \left(\frac{.07}{1.07}\right)(10.7) = \frac{3}{10}.$$

Next we find

$$L = v^{k+1} - \frac{3}{107}\ddot{a}_{\overline{k+1}|}$$

$$= v^{k+1} - \frac{3}{107}\left(\frac{1-v^{k+1}}{d}\right)$$

$$= v^{k+1} - \frac{3}{107}\left(\frac{1-v^{k+1}}{\frac{.07}{1.07}}\right)$$

$$= v^{k+1} - \frac{3}{7}(1-v^{k+1})$$

$$= \frac{10}{7}v^{k+1} - \frac{3}{7}.$$

Then

$$E[L] = \frac{10}{7}E[v^{k+1}] - \frac{3}{7}$$

$$= \frac{10}{7}A_{30} - \frac{3}{7}$$

$$= \frac{10}{7}\left(\frac{3}{10}\right) - \frac{3}{7} = 0.$$

Next we need to find

$$E[L^2] = E\left[\frac{100}{49}v^{2k+2} - \frac{60}{49}v^{k+1} + \frac{9}{49}\right]$$

$$= \frac{100}{49}E[v^{2k+2}] - \frac{60}{49}\left(\frac{3}{10}\right) + \frac{9}{49}.$$

We have

$$E[v^{2k+2}] = \sum_{k=0}^{\infty} {}_kp_{30}q_{30+k}v^{2k+2}$$

$$= \frac{.03}{(1.07)^2}\left(\frac{1}{1 - \frac{.97}{(1.07)^2}}\right)$$

$$= .17153,$$

so that

$$E[L^2] = \frac{100}{49}(.17153) - \frac{18}{49} + \frac{9}{49} = .16638,$$

and finally

$$Var(L) = .16638 - 0^2 = .16638. \qquad \square$$

In the above example, it was no surprise that $E[L]$ turned out to be zero. In fact, the reader will be asked to prove in the exercises that this occurs precisely when $Q = P_x$. Sometimes the phrase "the annual premium is determined by the equivalence principle" is used to describe this situation.

If a whole life policy has a benefit of 1 payable at the moment of death (rather than at the end of the year of death), and if the premiums are paid continuously, then the appropriate formula for L is

$$L = v^t - Q \cdot \bar{a}_{\overline{t}|}. \tag{10.10}$$

The next example illustrates this situation.

Example 10.14

Let L be the random variable for fully continuous (i.e., benefit payable at the time of death and premiums paid continuously) whole life insurance with face amount 1000 purchased by a 20-year-old. The total annual premium is 24. Assuming $\mu_x = .02$ for all x and $\delta = .08$, find $E[L]$ and $Var(L)$.

Solution
We have

$$L = 1000v^t - 24\bar{a}_{\bar{t}|}$$

$$= 1000v^t - 24\left(\frac{1-v^t}{\delta}\right)$$

$$= 1300v^t - 300.$$

Then

$$E[L] = 1300E[v^t] - 300$$

$$= 1300 \int_0^\infty {}_tp_{20}\mu_{20+t}v^t \, dt - 300$$

$$= 1300(.02) \int_0^\infty e^{-.10t} \, dt - 300$$

$$= -40.$$

We also find

$$E[L^2] = (1300)^2 E[v^{2t}] - (2600)(300)E[v^t] + 90{,}000$$

$$= (1300)^2 \int_0^\infty {}_tp_{20}\mu_{20+t}v^{2t} \, dt - 780{,}000(.20) + 90{,}000$$

$$= (1300)^2(.02)\left(\frac{1}{.18}\right) - 66{,}000$$

$$= 121{,}777.78.$$

Finally we have

$$Var(L) = 121{,}777.78 - (-40)^2 = 120{,}177.78. \qquad \square$$

The next example illustrates how the normal distribution can play a very important role in loss-at-issue calculations.

Example 10.15

In Example 10.14, find the minimum number of policies of the type described that an insurer must issue in order to be 95% certain that the total loss will be negative.

Solution
We must assume that the different policies are independent. Let the number of policies issued be n. From the last example, we know that the expected value of the total loss is $-40n$ and the variance is $120{,}177.78n$, so that the standard deviation is $346.7\sqrt{n}$. Using a normal approxi-

mation, we must have $-40n + (1.645)(346.7\sqrt{n}) \leq 0.$ Hence $\sqrt{n} \geq 14.258$ and $n \geq 204.$ $\square$

EXERCISES

10.1 Mean and Variance

10-1. Let Z denote the present value random variable, at policy issue, for a whole life policy with a death benefit of 1 payable at the end of the year of death purchased by a 30-year-old. Find $E[Z]$ and $Var(Z)$ if $i = .09$ and $_tp_{30} = (.97)^t$ for all t.

10-2. Do Question 1 if the death benefit is 1000 instead of 1.

10-3. Do Question 1 if the policy is for 30-year term insurance.

10-4. Do Question 1 if the policy is for 30-year endowment insurance.

10-5. Do Question 1 if the insurance is deferred for 30 years.

10-6. Do Question 1 if the death benefit is payable at the moment of death.

10-7. Let Z denote the present value random variable, at policy issue, for a whole life policy with a death benefit of 1 payable at the moment of death purchased by a 30-year-old, assuming $\mu_x = .03$ for all x and $\delta = .11$. Find $E[Z]$ and $Var(Z)$.

10-8. Do Question 7 if the policy is for 40-year term insurance.

10-9. Do Question 7 assuming $\delta = .11$ and $\ell_x = 100 - x$, $0 \leq x \leq 100$.

10-10. Let Z denote the present value random variable for a whole life policy of 1 payable at the moment of death. Find $E[Z]$ and $Var(Z)$ if $\mu = \mu_x$ and δ are both constant and if $\delta = 2\mu$.

10-11. Determine the mean and variance of the present value random variable for a life annuity of 1 per year, first payment in one year, given $i = .09$ and $_tp_x = (.975)^t$ for all t.

10-12. Do Question 11 if the annuity is continuous.

10-13. A three-year temporary life annuity will pay 2 at the end of the first year, 5 at the end of the second year, and 4 at the end of the third year.   Given that $p_{50} = .98$, $p_{51} = .978$, $p_{52} = .975$ and $i = .07$, find the mean and variance of the present value random variable for this annuity issued to a 50-year-old.

10-14. Given that μ_x is constant, $\delta = .09$, and $^2\overline{A}_x = .10$, calculate $\overline{a}_x$ and $^2\overline{a}_x$.   (Recall that the superscript to the left denotes a doubling of the force of interest.)

10-15. Given that μ_x and δ are both constant, find expressions for each of the following:
   (a)   The mean, variance and median of the present value random variable for a whole life insurance of 1 payable at the moment of death.
   (b)   The mean, variance and median of the present value random variable for a continuous life annuity of 1 per year.

10-16. Find the mean and variance of $T(40)$ in each of the following cases:
   (a) $\ell_x = 100 - x$, $0 \le x \le 100$
   (b) $_tp_x = (.97)^t$ for all t

10-17. Find the median of $T(40)$ in each of the cases in Question 16.

10-18. Given $\ell_x = 1000\left(1 - \frac{x}{110}\right)$ and $i = .07$, find the probability that $\overline{a}_{\overline{T}|} > 10$, where T represents the future lifetime of a life aged 50.

10-2   Normal Distribution

10-19. In Question 1, use Chebyshev's Rule to find an interval for Z such that the probability that a specified value lies in the interval is at least (a) .75; (b) $\frac{8}{9}$. Are these intervals useful?

10-20. What value of k is needed in Chebyshev's Rule in order to guarantee that $Pr(|Z - E[Z]| < k\sigma) \ge .95$?

10-21. Assuming a normal distribution in Question 1, find the constant c such that (a) $Pr(Z < c) = .90$; (b) $Pr(Z < c) = .95$; (c) $Pr(|Z - E[Z]| < c) = .90$; (d) $Pr(Z < c) = .975$.

10-22. Show that the standard deviation of rZ, where r is any positive number, is equal to r times the standard deviation of Z.

10-23. Using the result of Question 22, redo Questions 19 and 21 if the death benefit is 1000 instead of 1. (This could also be done using Question 2 but the suggested method is preferable.)

10-24. Redo Question 21 if the death benefit of Question 1 is payable at the moment of death.

10-3   Central Limit Theorem

10-25. In Question 1, assume 1000 policies of the type described are sold to different individuals and let Z denote the present value of aggregate future benefits for all these policies. Find $E[Z]$ and $Var(Z)$.

10-26. Redo Question 25 if a single policy with death benefit 1000 is sold.

10-27. Redo Question 25 if 10 policies with death benefit 100 each are sold.

10-28. 100 independent lives, each age 20, contribute equal amounts to establish a fund which will pay 10,000 at the end of the year of death of each individual. Given $_tp_{20} = (.98)^t$ and $i = .06$, find the amount that each must contribute to have 95% confidence that all claims will be paid.

10-29. Redo Question 28 if there are 1000 lives instead of 100. Explain the relative magnitude of your answers to the last two exercises.

10-30. Redo Question 28 if the insurance is payable at the moment of death.

10-4   Loss-at-Issue

10-31. Let L be the loss random variable for a fully discrete (i.e., annual premiums and benefit payable at the end of the year of death) whole life insurance of 1 purchased by a life age 25. Find $E[L]$ and $Var(L)$ in each of the following cases:

(a) $d = .08$, $A_{25} = .40$, $^2A_{25} = .23$, and the annual premium is 7% of the amount of insurance.

(b) $i = .08$, $\ell_x = 110 - x$ for $0 \leq x \leq 110$, and the annual premium is determined by the equivalence principle.

10-32. Let L be the loss random variable for a fully continuous whole life insurance of 1 purchased by a life age 40. Find $E[L]$ and $Var(L)$ in each of the following cases:

(a) $\delta = .06$, $\mu_x = .03$ for all x, and the annual premium is .04.

(b) $i = .06$, $_tp_{40} = (.96)^t$ for all t, and the annual premium is .05.

10-33. (a)   In a fully discrete setting, prove that $Q = P_x$ if and only if $E[L] = 0$.

(b)   In a fully continuous setting, prove that $Q = \overline{P}(\overline{A}_x)$ if and only if $E[L] = 0$.

10-34. Let L be the loss random variable for a fully continuous whole life insurance of 1 purchased by a life age x. Assume that the net annual premium is determined by the equivalence principle, but that 5% is added to each premium for expenses. Assume as well that $\mu = \mu_x$ and δ are both constant and that $\delta = 4\mu$. Find $E[L]$ and $Var(L)$.

10-35. In Questions 31(a) and 32(a), find the minimum number of policies of the type described that an insurer must sell in order to be 99% certain that the total loss will be negative.

CHAPTER ELEVEN
MULTI-LIFE THEORY

11.1 JOINT-LIFE ACTUARIAL FUNCTIONS

In the previous chapters we have discussed annuities and insurances relative to a single life: an annuity payable during the lifetime of a given individual or an insurance payable upon the death of that individual. In this chapter we will see how to extend this theory to handle problems involving the death or survival of more than one individual. Clearly there are many different types of questions which can arise, and rote memorization of formulae will not be very helpful. As in previous chapters, we will stress the solving of these problems from first principles.

There is some additional notation which must be introduced, and that will be done first. Then we will discuss life annuities which are dependent on the survival of a group of individuals, as well as life insurance payable upon the death of the first member of this group; these are called *joint-life functions*. In subsequent sections other types of multi-life problems will be discussed.

We saw briefly in earlier chapters how probabilities involving more than one person could be calculated. Here are two examples which will recall these ideas.

Example 11.1

Herman is 30 years old and Hermione is 25. Find expressions for each of the following:
(a) The probability that both Herman and Hermione live for 30 more years.
(b) The probability that at least one of them does not live for 30 more years.
(c) The probability that Herman and Hermione both reach age 60.
(d) The probability that one dies before age 45 and the other dies after age 55.
(e) The probability that at most one of them dies at age last birthday 45.

Solution

(a) $(_{30}p_{30})(_{30}p_{25})$
(b) $1 - (_{30}p_{30})(_{30}p_{25})$
(c) $(_{30}p_{30})(_{35}p_{25})$
(d)   There are two cases here since either person could be the first death. The answer is $(1 - _{15}p_{30})(_{30}p_{25}) + (_{25}p_{30})(1 - _{20}p_{25})$.
(e)   This is the complement of the case that both die at age last birthday 45, so we have $1 - (_{15}p_{30} - _{16}p_{30})(_{20}p_{25} - _{21}p_{25})$.   □

Example 11.2

Given $_{10}p_{20} = .9$, $_{15}p_{30} = .75$ and $_{10}p_{35} = .8$, find the probability that George (aged 20) and Ellen (aged 30) will both reach age 35, whereas Maurice (aged 20) and Bernadette (aged 30) will die between age 35 and age 45.

Solution

The answer is given by $(_{15}p_{20})(_{5}p_{30})(_{15}p_{20} - _{25}p_{20})(_{5}p_{30} - _{15}p_{30})$. Since not all of these probabilities are among the given values we must solve for them. We have $_{25}p_{20} = (_{10}p_{20})(_{15}p_{30}) = (.9)(.75) = .675$, and $_{15}p_{20} = \frac{_{25}p_{20}}{_{10}p_{35}} = \frac{.675}{.8} = .84375$. Also $_{5}p_{30} = \frac{_{15}p_{30}}{_{10}p_{35}} = \frac{.75}{.8} = .9375$.
Then we have $(.84375)(.9375)(.16875)(.1875) = .025028$.   □

In several of the above problems we calculated the probability of several lives all surviving for a number of years. In this case, a new notation is helpful: the probability that m independent lives of ages x_1, $x_2, \cdots, x_m$ will all survive for n years is denoted $_{n}p_{x_1 x_2 \cdots x_m}$. Our work on probability tells us that

$$_{n}p_{x_1 x_2 \cdots x_m} = (_{n}p_{x_1})(_{n}p_{x_2}) \cdots (_{n}p_{x_m}).$$ (11.1)

Other formulae follow naturally. For example, $_{n}q_{x_1 x_2 \cdots x_m}$, the probability that at least one of the lives dies during the next n years, is given by

$$_{n}q_{x_1 x_2 \cdots x_m} = 1 - _{n}p_{x_1 x_2 \cdots x_m}.$$ (11.2)

Note that it is *not* true that $_{n}q_{x_1 x_2 \cdots x_m} = (_{n}q_{x_1})(_{n}q_{x_2}) \cdots (_{n}q_{x_m})$.

Example 11.3

Show that $q_{x_1 x_2} = q_{x_1} + q_{x_2} - q_{x_1} q_{x_2}$.

Solution

$$q_{x_1} + q_{x_2} - q_{x_1}q_{x_2} = 1 - p_{x_1} + 1 - p_{x_2} - (1-p_{x_1})(1-p_{x_2})$$
$$= 1 - p_{x_1}p_{x_2} = 1 - p_{x_1x_2} = q_{x_1x_2}. \qquad \square$$

The relation given in Example 11.3 has a nice verbal interpretation. $q_{x_1x_2}$ is the probability that at least one of the two lives, aged x_1 and x_2, dies in the next year. q_{x_1} is the probability that the first life, aged x_1, dies, and q_{x_2} is the probability that the other life dies. In adding these together we are counting *twice* the case where both lives die, so we must subtract $q_{x_1}q_{x_2}$ to get a correct total.

We may now define life annuity and life insurance functions for a joint-life situation. A life annuity paying 1 at the end of each year as long as m lives, ages $x_1, x_2, \ldots, x_m$, all survive has a present value denoted by $a_{x_1x_2\cdots x_m}$. We have

$$a_{x_1x_2\cdots x_m} = \sum_{t=1}^{\infty} v^t \cdot {}_tp_{x_1x_2\cdots x_m}$$

$$= \sum_{t=1}^{\infty} v^t({}_tp_{x_1})({}_tp_{x_2})\cdots({}_tp_{x_m}). \qquad (11.3)$$

A life insurance policy paying 1 at the end of the year in which the first death occurs in a group of m lives, ages $x_1, x_2, \ldots, x_m$, has present value denoted $A_{x_1x_2\cdots x_m}$. We have

$$A_{x_1x_2\cdots x_m} = \sum_{t=0}^{\infty} v^{t+1}({}_tp_{x_1x_2\cdots x_m} - {}_{t+1}p_{x_1x_2\cdots x_m}). \qquad (11.4)$$

If one of the lives subscripted in an insurance present value symbol has a numeral over it, then the insurance pays at the end of the year of that death provided the deaths occur in the order named. For example, A_{xy}^1 is the present value of an insurance that pays on the death of (x) if (x) dies before (y), and A_{xy}^2 pays on the death of (x) if (x) dies after (y). Note that $A_x = A_{xy}^1 + A_{xy}^2$.

Other joint-life functions can be defined analogously to their single-life counterparts. For example

$$e_{x_1x_2\cdots x_m} = \sum_{t=1}^{\infty} {}_tp_{x_1x_2\cdots x_m}. \qquad (11.5)$$

A few problems involving joint-life annuities were actually given earlier in the text (see Exercises 13-15 of Chapter 8), since no theory was required beyond that developed at the time. Let us now give a solution to Exercise 8-13 using our new notation.

| Example 11.4 |

Julio's mortality for $1 \leq t \leq 4$ is governed by $_tp_x = .3(4 - t)$. Harold's mortality for $1 \leq t \leq 5$ is governed by $_tp_y = .25(5 - t)$. If $i = .07$, find the value at time 0 of a life annuity which pays 1000 at the end of each year as long as *both* Julio and Harold are alive.

| Solution |

We wish to calculate $1000a_{xy} = 1000\sum_{t=1}^{\infty} v^t(_tp_x)(_tp_y)$, in our new notation.

Substituting the above formulae for $_tp_x$ and $_tp_y$, we have

$$1000[(1.07)^{-1}(.9)(1) + (1.07)^{-2}(.6)(.75) + (1.07)^{-3}(.3)(.5)] = 1356.61.$$
□

For future problems we will require analogues of the commutation functions defined in Chapters 8 and 9. First, however, we need an analogue of ℓ_x. Since $_np_{x_1x_2\cdots x_m} = (_np_{x_1})(_np_{x_2})\cdots(_np_{x_m})$, we have

$$_np_{x_1x_2\cdots x_m} = \frac{\ell_{x_1+n}\,\ell_{x_2+n}\cdots\ell_{x_m+n}}{\ell_{x_1}\ell_{x_2}\cdots\ell_{x_m}}. \tag{11.6}$$

Thus it makes sense to define $\ell_{x_1x_2\cdots x_m} = \ell_{x_1}\ell_{x_2}\cdots\ell_{x_m}$. The only problem here is that the ℓ_x terms are often quite large, so this product might be unmanageable. This is dealt with by defining

$$\ell_{x_1x_2\cdots x_m} = k\,\ell_{x_1}\,\ell_{x_2}\cdots\ell_{x_m}, \tag{11.7}$$

where k is some fixed constant of proportionality, usually a power of 10^{-1}, so the size of the product is reasonable.

We then have

$$_np_{x_1x_2\cdots x_m} = \frac{\ell_{x_1+n:x_2+n\cdots x_m+n}}{\ell_{x_1x_2\cdots x_m}}. \tag{11.8}$$

We define

$$d_{x_1x_2\cdots x_m} = \ell_{x_1x_2\cdots x_m} - \ell_{x_1+1:x_2+1\cdots x_m+1}. \tag{11.9}$$

Hence

$$q_{x_1 x_2 \cdots x_m} = 1 - p_{x_1 x_2 \cdots x_m}$$

$$= 1 - \frac{\ell_{x_1+1:x_2+1\cdots x_m+1}}{\ell_{x_1 x_2 \cdots x_m}}$$

$$= \frac{d_{x_1 x_2 \cdots x_m}}{\ell_{x_1 x_2 \cdots x_m}}. \tag{11.10}$$

Recall that the force of mortality was previously defined by the formula $\mu_x = -D(\ln \ell_x)$. If we think of x as a "starting age" and use t as the variable, this can be rewritten as $\mu_{x+t} = -\frac{d}{dt}(\ln \ell_{x+t})$. This leads us to the joint-life analogue.

$$\mu_{x_1+t:x_2+t\cdots x_m+t} = -\frac{d}{dt}\left(\ln \ell_{x_1+t:x_2+t\cdots x_m+t}\right) \tag{11.11}$$

From Formula (11.11) we obtain the pleasing formula

$$\mu_{x_1+t:x_2+t\cdots x_m+t} = -\frac{d}{dt}\left(\ln (k\,\ell_{x_1+t}\,\ell_{x_2+t}\cdots \ell_{x_m+t})\right)$$

$$= -\frac{d}{dt}\left(\ln k + \ln \ell_{x_1+t} + \cdots + \ln \ell_{x_m+t}\right)$$

$$= -\frac{d}{dt}\left(\ln \ell_{x_1+t}\right) + \cdots + \left(-\frac{d}{dt}\left(\ln \ell_{x_m+t}\right)\right)$$

$$= \mu_{x_1+t} + \mu_{x_2+t} + \cdots + \mu_{x_m+t}. \tag{11.12}$$

What about commutation functions? Well, recall from (11.3) and (11.8) that

$$a_{x_1 x_2 \cdots x_m} = \sum_{t=1}^{\infty} v^t \,_t p_{x_1 x_2 \cdots x_m}$$

$$= \sum_{t=1}^{\infty} v^t \frac{\ell_{x_1+t:x_2+t\cdots x_m+t}}{\ell_{x_1 x_2 \cdots x_m}}. \tag{11.13}$$

It's a little tricky to see how to fit this into our Chapter 8 format, but observe that if we multiply both numerator and denominator of (11.13) by $v^{\frac{x_1 + x_2 + \cdots + x_m}{m}}$, we obtain

$$a_{x_1 x_2 \cdots x_m} = \sum_{t=1}^{\infty} \frac{v^{\frac{x_1 + x_2 + \cdots + x_m + mt}{m}} \ell_{x_1 + t : x_2 + t \cdots x_m + t}}{v^{\frac{x_1 + x_2 + \cdots + x_m}{m}} \ell_{x_1 x_2 \cdots x_m}}.$$

$$= \sum_{t=1}^{\infty} \frac{v^{\frac{(x_1 + t) + (x_2 + t) + \cdots + (x_m + t)}{m}} \ell_{x_1 + t : x_2 + t \cdots x_m + t}}{v^{\frac{(x_1 + x_2 + \cdots + x_m)}{m}} \ell_{x_1 x_2 \cdots x_m}}.$$

$$(11.14)$$

Hence we define

$$D_{x_1 x_2 \cdots x_m} = v^{\frac{x_1 + x_2 + \cdots + x_m}{m}} \ell_{x_1 x_2 \cdots x_m}. \qquad (11.15)$$

Similar reasoning leads us to the definition

$$C_{x_1 x_2 \cdots x_m} = v^{\left(\frac{x_1 + x_2 + \cdots + x_m}{m} + 1\right)} d_{x_1 x_2 \cdots x_m}. \qquad (11.16)$$

The joint-life functions N, M, S and R are then defined in the usual way as sums of D and C functions. The student should verify that the following formulae are consequences of the definitions just given:

$$a_{x_1 x_2 \cdots x_m} = \frac{N_{x_1 + 1 : x_2 + 1 \cdots x_m + 1}}{D_{x_1 x_2 \cdots x_m}} \qquad (11.17)$$

and

$$A_{x_1 x_2 \cdots x_m} = \frac{M_{x_1 x_2 \cdots x_m}}{D_{x_1 x_2 \cdots x_m}}. \qquad (11.18)$$

The case of 2 lives, aged x and y, is often encountered in practice. Here is an example illustrating that setting.

| Example 11.5 |
Show that $D_{xy} = k (1 + i)^{\frac{x+y}{2}} D_x D_y$.

Solution

$$k(1 + i)^{\frac{x+y}{2}} D_x D_y = k(1 + i)^{\frac{x+y}{2}} v^x \ell_x v^y \ell_y$$

$$= v^{x+y - \frac{x+y}{2}} k \ell_x \ell_y$$

$$= v^{\frac{x+y}{2}} \ell_{xy}$$

$$= D_{xy}. \qquad \square$$

We saw in Chapter 8 that the notation $N_x^{(m)} = N_x - \frac{m-1}{2m} \cdot D_x$ was useful because it led to the convenient formula $\ddot{a}_x^{(m)} = \frac{N_x^{(m)}}{D_x}$. This notation can also be extended to several lives, as we illustrate with the following example.

Example 11.6

John, aged 65, can collect 1000 a month for as long as he lives. Equivalently, John can elect a benefit paying X per month for the next 10 years guaranteed, and X per month thereafter as long as both John and his wife, currently aged 60, are alive. Each payment is made at the beginning of the month. Find X given $i = .07$, $D_{65} = 150$, $N_{65}^{(12)} = 1250$, $D_{60:65} = 650$ and $N_{70:75}^{(12)} = 1100$.

Solution

John's first benefit, the monthly life annuity, has present value equal to $12,000 \ddot{a}_{65}^{(12)} = 12,000 \left(\frac{1250}{150} \right) = 100,000$. We must compute the present value of the other benefit in two parts. Since the monthly interest rate is $j = (1.07)^{1/12} - 1$, the guaranteed portion has present value given by

$$X \left(\frac{1 - (1.07)^{-10}}{j} \right) (1 + j) = 87.4456830X.$$ The other portion has present

value equal to $12X \cdot \frac{N_{70:75}^{(12)}}{D_{60:65}} = 12X \left(\frac{1100}{650} \right) = 20.3076923X$. Thus the present value of the joint-life option is $107.7533753X$. Equating this to the present value of the single-life option, we obtain $X = 928.05$. $\qquad \square$

The next example illustrates one way in which continuous annuities can occur in joint-life situations.

Example 11.7

George, who has just retired, will receive a continuous annuity of 30,000 per year as long as both he and his wife are alive. The annual benefit reduces to 20,000 if exactly one of them is alive, with payments continuing until the second death. Find the net single premium for this annuity assuming $\mu_x = .07$ for George, $\mu_y = .06$ for his wife, and $\delta = .05$.

Solution

The required present value is

$$30{,}000\bar{a}_{xy} + 20{,}000(\bar{a}_x - \bar{a}_{xy}) + 20{,}000(\bar{a}_y - \bar{a}_{xy})$$

$$= 20{,}000\bar{a}_x + 20{,}000\bar{a}_y - 10{,}000\bar{a}_{xy}.$$

We have

$$\bar{a}_x = \int_0^\infty e^{-.05t} e^{-.07t}\, dt = \frac{1}{.12},$$

$$\bar{a}_y = \int_0^\infty e^{-.05t} e^{-.06t}\, dt = \frac{1}{.11},$$

and

$$\bar{a}_{xy} = \int_0^\infty e^{-.05t}\, {}_tp_{xy}\, dt = \int_0^\infty e^{-.05t} e^{-.07t} e^{-.06t}\, dt = \frac{1}{.18}.$$

Then the answer is

$$20{,}000\left(\frac{1}{.12} + \frac{1}{.11}\right) - 10{,}000\left(\frac{1}{.18}\right) = 292{,}929.29. \qquad \square$$

Note in the previous example that if the annuity were payable at the beginning or at the end of the year, we could obtain a good approximation to the present value by first doing the calculation as in the example and then using $\ddot{a}_x = \bar{a}_x + \frac{1}{2}$ or $a_x = \bar{a}_x - \frac{1}{2}$. We remark (without proof) that the same approximations apply to a_{xy} and $\ddot{a}_{xy}$.

We close this section by mentioning that if data is obtained from a life table which follows Makeham's law, then joint-life values can be reduced to those in which all lives are of the same age. It is beyond the scope of this book to discuss how this is done in general, but in the special case of two lives a Table of Uniform Seniority is often given indicating how this should be carried out. For example, if the table indicates that given an age difference of 4 then 2.4 should be added to the younger age, we could conclude that

$$a_{60:64} = a_{62.4:62.4} \approx a_{62:62} - .4(a_{62:62}-a_{63:63}).$$

If the life table follows Gompertz' law instead, an even greater simplification is possible in that all calculations can be reduced to the single-life case. Again, a Table of Uniform Seniority shows how this reduction can be carried out. For example, if the table indicates that given an age difference of 4 then 6.6 should be added to the older age, we obtain.

$$a_{60:64} = a_{70.6} \approx a_{70} - .6(a_{70}-a_{71}).$$

11.2 LAST-SURVIVOR PROBLEMS

The annuity and insurance problems considered in Section 11.1 were concerned either with a group of lives all surviving or with the first death in a given group of lives. Other situations are possible. For example an annuity may continue as long as at least one person is alive or, similarly, insurance may not be paid until all individuals have died. This is called a *last-survivor* situation, and will be discussed in more detail later in this section.

The reader will have no trouble dreaming up other possible scenarios. For example an annuity may be payable as long as at least half the individuals survive. All of these problems should be approached from first principles.

Here are two worked examples. The first (seen previously as Exercise 8-14) is actually a last-survivor situation and will be redone later in the section after appropriate theory has been developed, but we will do it here from first principles.

| Example 11.8 |

In Example 11.4 find the value at time 0 if the annuity pays 1000 as long as *either* Julio or Harold is alive.

Solution

We consider 3 cases separately and add the results. In Example 11.4 we saw that the value if *both* continue to be alive is 1356.61. Next we consider the cases of only one being alive. The value if Julio is alive but Harold is not is

$1{,}000[(1.07)^{-1}(.9)(0) + (1.07)^{-2}(.6)(.25) + (1.07)^{-3}(.3)(.5)] = 253.46.$

Similarly, the value if Julio is dead but Harold is alive is given by

$1000[(1.07)^{-1}(.1)(1) + (1.07)^{-2}(.4)(.75)$
$$+ (1.07)^{-3}(.7)(.5) + (1.07)^{-4}(1)(.25)] = 831.92.$$

Hence the total value is 2441.99. □

Example 11.9

Three lives are aged x, y and z. Find a nice expression for the net single premium for an annuity paying 1 at the end of each year as long as *at least two* of the lives survive.

Solution

a_{xy} is the premium to pay for the annuity while x and y survive, and a_{xz} and a_{yz} are similarly defined. Thus $a_{xy} + a_{xz} + a_{yz}$ is the premium for the annuity while two lives survive, but the case where all three survive is counted 3 times here. We do want it counted once, so to get the correct answer we must subtract off $2a_{xyz}$, obtaining $a_{xy} + a_{xz} + a_{yz} - 2a_{xyz}$. □

The last-survivor situation is important enough to warrant some new notation. We let $_np_{\overline{x_1x_2\cdots x_m}}$ denote the probability that *at least one* of a group of m lives, aged $x_1, x_2, \cdots, x_m$, will survive for n years. We have

$$_np_{\overline{x_1x_2\cdots x_m}} = 1 - (1 - {_np_{x_1}})(1 - {_np_{x_2}})\cdots(1 - {_np_{x_m}}). \qquad (11.19)$$

To compare this with $_np_{x_1x_2\cdots x_m}$, we multiply out and obtain

$$_np_{\overline{x_1x_2\cdots x_m}} = ({_np_{x_1}} + {_np_{x_2}} + \cdots + {_np_{x_m}})$$
$$- ({_np_{x_1x_2}} + {_np_{x_1x_3}} + \cdots + {_np_{x_{m-1}x_m}})$$
$$+ \cdots + (-1)^{m+1}\, {_np_{x_1x_2\cdots x_m}}$$
$$= \sum_i {_np_{x_i}} - \sum_{i<j} {_np_{x_ix_j}} + \cdots (-1)^{m+1}\, {_np_{x_1x_2\cdots x_m}}.$$

$$(11.20)$$

We also have $_nq_{\overline{x_1x_2\cdots x_m}} = 1 - _np_{\overline{x_1x_2\cdots x_m}}$, where $_nq_{\overline{x_1x_2\cdots x_m}}$ denotes the probability that all individuals die within n years. Hence

$$_nq_{\overline{x_1x_2\cdots x_m}} = (_nq_{x_1})(_nq_{x_2})\cdots(_nq_{x_m}). \tag{11.21}$$

In practice, the case of two lives, aged x and y, occurs quite often. In this special case, the above formulae become

$$_np_{\overline{xy}} = _np_x + _np_y - _np_{xy} \tag{11.22}$$

and

$$_nq_{\overline{xy}} = (_nq_x)(_nq_y). \tag{11.23}$$

Other last survivor functions follow easily. For example,

$$a_{\overline{x_1x_2\cdots x_m}} = \sum_{t=1}^{\infty} v^t \, _tp_{\overline{x_1x_2\cdots x_m}}. \tag{11.24}$$

Using Formula (11.20) for $_tp_{\overline{x_1x_2\cdots x_m}}$, we obtain

$$a_{\overline{x_1x_2\cdots x_m}} = \sum_i a_{x_i} - \sum_{i<j} a_{x_ix_j} + \cdots + (-1)^{m+1} a_{x_1x_2\cdots x_m}. \tag{11.25}$$

The special case of two lives gives

$$a_{\overline{xy}} = a_x + a_y - a_{xy}. \tag{11.26}$$

The reader is encouraged to give a verbal explanation for this identity.
    In the case of insurance, we have

$$A_{\overline{x_1x_2\cdots x_m}} = \sum_{t=0}^{\infty} v^{t+1} \left(_tp_{\overline{x_1x_2\cdots x_m}} - _{t+1}p_{\overline{x_1x_2\cdots x_m}} \right). \tag{11.27}$$

| Example 11.10 |

Repeat Example 11.8 using our new notation.

Solution

This time we use the formula $1000a_{\overline{xy}} = 1000a_x + 1000a_y - 1000a_{xy}$. In Example 11.4, we had $1000a_{xy} = 1356.61$. If x refers to Julio we have $1000a_x = [(1.07)^{-1}(.9) + (1.07)^{-2}(.6) + (1.07)^{-3}(.3)] = 1,610.07$.
Similarly with y referring to Harold, we have

$$1000a_y = 1000[(1.07)^{-1}(1) + (1.07)^{-2}(.75)$$

$$+ (1.07)^{-3}(.5) + (1.07)^{-4}(.25)] = 2,188.53.$$

Hence $1000a_{\overline{xy}} = 1610.07 + 2188.53 - 1356.61 = 2441.99$. □

11.3 REVERSIONARY ANNUITIES

A reversionary annuity is an annuity which begins at the end of the year of death of a given individual, now aged y. The payments are made to a second individual, now aged x, as long as he is alive. Note that x must be alive when y dies for payments to begin. The notation for this annuity is $a_{y|x}$, and a formula for its present value is easily derived. Clearly a payment occurs at time t if, and only if, y is dead but x is still alive. Hence

$$a_{y|x} = \sum_{t=1}^{\infty} v^t(_tp_x)(1 - _tp_y)$$

$$= \sum_{t=1}^{\infty} v^t \, _tp_x - \sum_{t=1}^{\infty} v^t \, _tp_{xy}$$

$$= a_x - a_{xy}. \tag{11.28}$$

Formula (11.28) makes sense. Our reversionary annuity is an annuity to x, which has present value a_x, but will not pay during the joint lifetime of x and y, so we must subtract a_{xy}.

Example 11.11

In Example 11.4, find the value at time 0 of a reversionary annuity to Julio payable upon the death of Harold.

Solution

We can carry out a direct calculation, obtaining a present value of $1000[(1.07)^{-1}(.9)(0) + (1.07)^{-2}(.6)(.25) + (1.07)^{-3}(.3)(.5)] = 253.46$.

Note that this is just one of the terms calculated in the solution to Example 11.8. Alternatively, we could use $a_{y|x} = a_x - a_{xy}$. As before, $a_x = (1.07)^{-1}(.9) + (1.07)^{-2}(.6) + (1.07)^{-2}(.3) = 1.61007$, which gives us $1000a_x = 1610.07$. From Example 11.4 we have $1000a_{xy} = 1356.61$. Thus we have $1610.07 - 1356.61 = 253.46$. $\qquad\square$

More complicated reversionary annuities can also be worked out, as we see in the following examples.

| Example 11.12 |

State verbally the meaning of $a_{\overline{xy}|z}$, and then express it in terms of joint-life functions.

| Solution |

$a_{\overline{xy}|z}$ is an annuity payable to z upon the death of *both* x and y. Then

$$a_{\overline{xy}|z} = \sum_{t=1}^{\infty} v^t (1 - {}_t p_{\overline{xy}})\,{}_t p_z$$

$$= \sum_{t=1}^{\infty} v^t \left({}_t p_z - {}_t p_z({}_t p_x + {}_t p_y - {}_t p_{xy}) \right)$$

$$= a_z - a_{zx} - a_{zy} + a_{zxy}. \qquad\square$$

The symbol $a_{y|x}^{(m)}$ is used to denote a reversionary annuity payable m times a year. Analogous to (11.28) we have

$$a_{y|x}^{(m)} = a_x^{(m)} - a_{xy}^{(m)}. \tag{11.29}$$

If approximate formulae are used for $a_x^{(m)}$ and $a_{xy}^{(m)}$, the correction terms $\dfrac{m-1}{2m}$ will cancel out, and we obtain the approximation

$$a_{y|x}^{(m)} \approx a_x - a_{xy}. \tag{11.30}$$

A more careful approximation, whose derivation is beyond the scope of this text, is given by

$$a_{y|x}^{(m)} \approx a_x - a_{xy} + \frac{m^2-1}{12m^2} \cdot \mu_y. \tag{11.31}$$

Many interesting problems involving reversionary annuities are included in the exercises. We will close with an example showing that problems are often not as difficult as they might first appear.

| Example 11.13 |

Siegfried has the option of choosing any of the following three annuities, first payment in one year:
(a)   A life annuity of 1000 per year.
(b)   A life annuity of 750 per year, together with a reversionary annuity of 600 per year to his wife after his death.
(c)   A life annuity of T per year payable as long as *either* Siegfried or his wife survives.

If all three annuities are equivalent, find T.

| Solution |

Let x be Siegfried's age and y be his wife's age. Equating the present values of options (a) and (b) we have $1000a_x = 750a_x + 600(a_y - a_{xy})$, from which we find $a_x = \frac{600}{250}(a_y - a_{xy}) = 2.4(a_y - a_{xy})$. The present value of option (c) is $Ta_{\overline{xy}} = Ta_x + T(a_y - a_{xy})$. Equating this to the value of option (a) we have $Ta_x + T(a_y - a_{xy}) = 1000a_x$, so that

$$T = \frac{1000[(2.4)(a_y - a_{xy})]}{(2.4)(a_y - a_{xy}) + (a_y - a_{xy})} = \frac{2400}{3.4} = 705.88. \qquad \square$$

EXERCISES

11.1 Joint-Life Actuarial Functions

11-1.   Mary is 15 years old and Helen and Harry are 25-year-old twins. Find expressions for each of the following:
   (a)   The probability that all three live 40 years.
   (b)   The probability that at least one does not live for 40 years.
   (c)   The probability that at most one does not live for 40 years.
   (d)   The probability that Mary reaches age 50 and exactly one of the twins lives for 20 years.

11-2.   Show that $\frac{{}_np_{x:y-1}}{p_{y-1}} = (p_x)({}_{n-1}p_{x+1:y})$.

11-3. Show that the probability that two lives, one aged 30 and the other aged 40, will die at the same age last birthday is equal to $_{10}p_{30}(1+e_{40:40}) - 2 \cdot {}_{11}p_{30}(1+e_{40:41}) + (p_{40})({}_{11}p_{30})(1+e_{41:41})$.

11-4. If two lives are both governed by the formula $\ell_x = 120 - x$, for $0 \le x \le 120$, find $\mu_{45+t:50+t}$.

11-5. Prove each of the following identities:
   (a) $C_{xy} = vD_{xy} - D_{x+1:y+1}$
   (b) $D_{xy} = \sqrt{(D_{xx})(D_{yy})}$

11-6. If 6 students all graduate at age 22, find expressions for each of the following:
   (a) The probability that not more than 3 of the students will be alive at age 50.
   (b) The probability that not less than 3 of the students will be alive at age 50.
   (c) The probability that not more than one of the students will die at age 50 last birthday.

11-7. Francis, aged 65, purchases a life annuity paying 1000 at the end of each year provided she and her husband, aged 60, are both alive. Find the net single premium for this annuity if $N_{60:65} = 1500$ and $D_{60:65} = 85$.

11-8. Repeat Question 7 if the first payment occurs immediately.

11-9. Repeat Question 8 if the first 3 annuity payments are guaranteed. Assume $N_{63:68} = 1280$ and $i = .09$.

11-10 The curtate-future-lifetime of a given situation is said to be n if the situation survives for n years but does not survive for $n+1$ years. If $q_x = .05$, $q_{x+1} = .07$, $q_y = .08$ and $q_{y+1} = .11$, determine the probability that the curtate-future-lifetime of the joint life status (xy) is equal to 1.

11-11. Given two independent lives, each subject to a force of mortality $\mu_x = \frac{1}{x}$, determine the probability that the joint life status (40, 50) fails during the next 5 years.

11-12. Repeat Question 11 if the 40-year-old is subject to $\mu_x = .0005x$ and the 50-year-old is subject to $\mu_y = .001y$.

11-13. George and Sarah purchase a continuous annuity of 20,000 per year, payable as long as both of them survive. Assuming $\mu_x = .05$ for George, $\mu_y = .04$ for Sarah, and $\delta = .08$, find the present value of this annuity.

11.2   Last-Survivor Problems

11-14. Do Example 11.8 if the annuity pays 1000 as long as *exactly one* of Julio or Harold is alive.

11-15. A life insurance policy is payable at the end of the year in which occurs the second death of two lives, aged 50 and 60. Show that the probability that the death benefit will be paid exactly 11 years later is

$$_{10}p_{50}(1-p_{60}) + {}_{10}p_{60}(1-p_{70}) - {}_{10}p_{50:60}(1-p_{60:70}).$$

11-16. Express the answer to Question 15 in terms of single-life probabilities.

11-17. An annuity of 1 is payable yearly to a person aged x as long as both she and another life aged y survive, and for n more years after the death of y (provided x is alive), except that no payments will be made after m years from the present time $(m > n)$. Show that the present value of this annuity is

$$a_{x:\overline{n}|} + \frac{D_{x+n}}{D_x} \cdot a_{x+n:y:\overline{m-n}|}.$$

11-18. An n-year temporary annuity pays 1 while both lives survive, $\frac{1}{3}$ if the first life only survives, and $\frac{1}{4}$ if the second life only survives. If the ages are x and y, find the present value in terms of annuity functions.

11-19. Rank the following in increasing order of magnitude: a_x, a_{xy}, a_{yx}, $a_{\overline{xy}}$.

11-20. If two independent lives (x) and (y) are both subject to the force of mortality $\mu_{x+t} = \mu_{y+t} = .03$, $0 < t \leq 10$, find the probability that the last survivor status $(\overline{xy})$ will survive for 6 years.

11-21. George and Sarah purchase a continuous annuity of 20,000 per year payable as long as at least one of them survives. Assuming $\mu_x = .05$ for George, $\mu_y = .04$ for Sarah, and $\delta = .08$, find the net single premium for this annuity.

11-22. George and Sarah purchase 100,000 of whole life insurance. Assuming $\mu_x = .05$ for George, $\mu_y = .04$ for Sarah, and $\delta = .08$, find the net single premium for this insurance in each of the following cases.
   (a)   The insurance is payable at the time of the first death.
   (b)   The insurance is payable at the time of the second death.

11-23. Smith is age 50 and Brown is age 51. A life annuity of 100 per year is payable to Smith. The net single premium for this annuity is equal to the net single premium for an annuity of K per year payable as long as either Smith or Brown is alive. Annuity payments are made at the end of each year. A life table following Gompertz' law tells us that $a_{50} = 16.08$, $a_{51} = 15.72$, $a_{59} = 12.76$, and $a_{60} = 12.39$. A table of uniform seniority is as follows:

Difference in Ages	Addition to Older Age
0	9.12
1	8.63
2	8.16
3	7.71
4	7.27
5	6.86

Find K.

11.3   Reversionary Annuities

11-24. Paul, aged 65, purchases a reversionary annuity of 1000 per year for his wife, aged 60. Find the net single premium for this annuity given the values $N_{61} = 1350$, $D_{60} = 300$, $N_{61:66} = 620$ and $D_{60:65} = 370$.

11-25. Can you calculate the present value of a reversionary annuity payable to Paul upon his wife's death, from the data given in Question 24? If not, what additional information is required?

11-26. Show that $a_{x|y} - a_{y|x} = a_y - a_x$.

11-27. Bertha, aged 40, wishes to purchase an annuity. She is offered two equivalent plans:
   (a)   500 per month for life, with 300 continuing to her husband after her death.
   (b)   600 per month for life, with 150 continuing to her husband after her death.
Given $\ddot{a}_{40}^{(12)} = 31$, and that the first payment under either plan will be made immediately, find the present value of the benefits payable to Bertha and her husband.

11-28. In Question 27, what is the present value of the benefits payable to Bertha's husband after her death in each of the two cases?

11-29. On January 1, 1998, Martha, aged 40, purchases a reversionary annuity to benefit her child, aged 15. Any payment made on or before December 31, 2008, will be 10,000, and subsequent payments will be 5000. Find the net single premium for this annuity, given $a_{15} = 31.5$, $a_{40:15} = 19.6$, $a_{15:\overline{11|}} = 19.3$ and $a_{40:15:\overline{11|}} = 10.1$.

11-30. Marcella, aged 35, and Maria, aged 40, purchase a life insurance policy which will pay annual benefits to the survivor upon the death of one of the women, first payment at the end of the year of death. If Marcella dies first, Maria receives 2000 per year for life. If Maria dies first, Marcella receives X per year for life. The policy is purchased by net annual premiums of 400, payable at the beginning of each year as long as both women are alive. Given $a_{35} = 15$, $a_{40} = 13.6$ and $a_{35:40} = 12.1$, find X.

11-31. Given $\ell_x = 120 - x$, find the probability that a reversionary annuity bought by Alphonse, aged 60, for his girlfriend Brigitte, aged 19, will be in payment status after 10 years.

11-32. Given $a_{x|y} + a_{y|x} = 4$, $2a_{xy} + 2a_{x|y} + a_{y|x} = 24$, and $2a_{xy} + a_{x|y} + 2a_{y|x} = 22$, find the present value of a 10,000 last-survivor annuity to two individuals aged x and y.

11-33. Tim is aged 40 and Yvette is aged 30. Tim purchases a deferred annuity, paying 100 per month commencing at his age 65, with payments of 50 per month continuing to Yvette for her life, beginning at Tim's death after age 65. If Tim dies before age 65, no benefits are payable. Find the net single premium for this annuity given $D_{30} = 191$, $D_{40} = 157$, $D_{55} = 52$, $D_{65} = 39$, $\ddot{a}_{55}^{(12)} = 16.1$, $\ddot{a}_{65}^{(12)} = 12$, $\ddot{a}_{55:65}^{(12)} = 10.7$ and $i = .05$.

11-34. Assume in Question 33 that if Tim dies before age 65, Yvette will receive 50 per month for life beginning at her age 55. Can you answer the question now? If not, what further data is required?

11-35. Barney is aged 55 and Hilda is aged 65. An annuity of X per month at the beginning of each month is payable to Barney for life. If Barney dies before Hilda, a reversionary annuity of $X - 100$ per month will continue to Hilda for life. The net single premium for this annuity is 50,000. Find X given $\ddot{a}_{55}^{(12)} = 12$, $\ddot{a}_{65}^{(12)} = 8.5$ and $\ddot{a}_{55:65}^{(12)} = 7.2$.

11-36. Ethel, aged 60, purchases an annuity paying 80 per month for life, first payment occurring immediately, with 50 per month continuing to her husband, aged 65, if she dies. If her husband dies before Ethel, the annuity to Ethel increases to 100 per month. Find the net single premium for this annuity given $\ddot{a}_{60}^{(12)} = 10$, $\ddot{a}_{65}^{(12)} = 8.5$ and $\ddot{a}_{60:65}^{(12)} = 6.5$.

11-37. Wally, aged 65, purchases an annuity paying 400 per month as long as both he and his wife, aged 60, survive, with the first payment occurring immediately. If either dies, the benefit is reduced to 300 per month for the life of the survivor. Find the net single premium for this annuity given $\ddot{a}_{60}^{(12)} = 10$, $\ddot{a}_{65}^{(12)} = 8.5$ and $\ddot{a}_{60:65}^{(12)} = 11.7$.

11-38. (a)   Prove algebraically that $a_{y|x} = \sum\limits_{t=1}^{\infty} v^t \, {}_tp_x \, ({}_{t-1}|q_y) \, \ddot{a}_{x+t}.$

(b)   Give a verbal explanation for the identity in part (a).

11-39. Darryl and David are both 30 years old. Annuity A pays 1 per year as long as exactly one of the men is alive. Annuity B pays 3 per year while Darryl is alive, and 2 per year to David after Darryl dies. Annuity A has present value 8.50 and Annuity B has present value 32.25. Find the present value of an annuity paying 1 per year while both Darryl and David are alive.

11-40. George has just retired at age 65, and his retirement benefit entitles him to 1000 per month for life (starting immediately), with 500 per month continuing to his surviving spouse if he should die. George is four years older than his wife. A unisex life table gives us the values $\ddot{a}_{66}^{(12)} = 9.15$, $\ddot{a}_{57}^{(12)} = 11.43$ and $\ddot{a}_{57:66}^{(12)} = 8.17$. We are told that the table should be set forward one year for males and set back four years for females. Find the present value of George's retirement benefit.

11-41. A reversionary annuity provides payments of 100 at the beginning of each month during the lifetime of Brown, aged 60, after the death of Smith, aged 65. You are given the following values from a life table which follows Makeham's law:

x	$\ddot{a}_x^{(12)}$	$\ddot{a}_{xx}^{(12)}$
60	10.5	8.8
61	10.2	8.5
62	10.0	8.2
63	9.8	8.0
64	9.6	7.8
65	9.3	7.5

You are also given the following values from a table of uniform seniority.

Difference in Ages	Addition to Younger Age
1	0.5
2	1.0
3	1.6
4	2.2
5	2.8

Find the net single premium for this annuity.

CHAPTER TWELVE
PENSION APPLICATIONS

One of the major areas of application for life contingencies, and annuities in particular, is in the calculation of the values of benefits and contributions for participants in a pension plan, and we have devoted the final chapter of this text to pension applications.

The reader will be pleased to learn that no new mathematics is required here. The terminology differs somewhat from that used in earlier chapters, and this may initially cause some confusion, but it should be quite temporary. We will spend the entire chapter presenting a large number of worked examples, which, hopefully, will prepare the reader for most problems which can arise. This can be put to the test in the exercises at the end of the chapter.

Example 12.1
Francisco, aged 45, works for a large oil company. At age 65 he will retire and begin collecting a pension of 20,000 per year for life, with the first payment coming one year after retirement. Find the present value of Francisco's future benefits given $N_{66} = 950$ and $D_{45} = 180$.

Solution

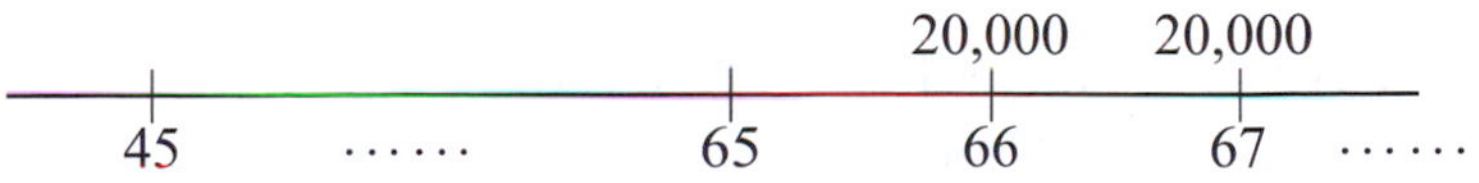

```
                            20,000   20,000
├─────────────┼──────────────┼────────┼────────────
45    ......        65           66       67  ......
```

FIGURE 12.1

The present value is $20{,}000\left(\dfrac{N_{66}}{D_{45}}\right) = 20{,}000\left(\dfrac{950}{180}\right) = 105{,}555.56.$ □

Example 12.2
Repeat Example 12.1 if the payments are 5000 per quarter instead of 20,000 per year, with the first payment coming 3 months after retirement. Assume $D_{65} = 80$.

Solution

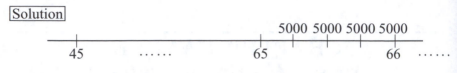

5000 5000 5000 5000

45 ...... 65 66 ......

FIGURE 12.2

The answer is

$$20{,}000\left(\frac{D_{65}}{D_{45}}\right)a_{65}^{(4)} = 20{,}000\left(\frac{D_{65}}{D_{45}}\right)\left(a_{65} + \frac{3}{8}\right)$$

$$= 20{,}000\left(\frac{N_{66} + \frac{3}{8} \cdot D_{65}}{D_{45}}\right)$$

$$= \frac{20{,}000(950 + 30)}{180} = 108{,}888.89. \quad \square$$

Some pension applications may require just the theory of interest and not life contingencies. The next two examples illustrate this point.

Example 12.3

At the end of each year, Wanda's employer will contribute 10% of Wanda's salary to a pension fund. Wanda's salary increases by 5% each year, and the contributions earn interest at a rate of 9% per year. If Wanda's current salary is 20,000 per year, how much will the fund contain after 15 contributions assuming Wanda remains alive and employed throughout the period?

Solution

The answer is

$$2000[(1.09)^{14} + (1.05)(1.09)^{13} + (1.05)^2(1.09)^{12} + \cdots + (1.05)^{14}]$$

$$= 2000(1.09)^{14}\left[1 + \frac{1.05}{1.09} + \cdots + \left(\frac{1.05}{1.09}\right)^{14}\right]$$

$$= 2000(1.09)^{14}\left[\frac{1 - \left(\frac{1.05}{1.09}\right)^{15}}{1 - \left(\frac{1.05}{1.09}\right)}\right] = 78{,}177.71. \quad \square$$

In general, any time a pension calculation assumes, for convenience, that the probabilities of mortality are negligible, the calculation is then done at interest only.

In Section 2.3 we saw how to calculate the time-weighted rate of investment return, as opposed to the dollar-weighted rate, which is just our usual yield rate when compound interest is assumed. Each of these measures of investment return are encountered in pension situations, as we see in the following example.

Example 12.4

On January 1, 2000, a pension fund has a market value of 3,000,000. On March 31, 2000, a contribution of 160,000 is made. Immediately after this contribution is made, the market value of the assets is 3,300,000. On August 31, 2000, a lump sum distribution of 12,000 is made. Immediately after this distribution is made, the market value of the assets is 3,250,000. On December 31, 2000, the assets have a market value of 3,500,000.

(a) Find the dollar-weighted rate of return of the fund during 2000. Assume simple interest for periods less than a year.

(b) Find the time-weighted rate of return of the fund during 2000.

Solution

(a) In calculating dollar-weighted rates, the market values at intermediate times are of no significance; we are only concerned with the amount of each deposit or withdrawal. The equation of value, using simple interest for periods less than a year, is

$3,000,000(1+i) + 160,000(1+\frac{3}{4}i) - 12,000(1+\frac{1}{3}i) = 3,500,000,$

leading to $3,116,000i = 352,000$, so $i = .11297$.

(b) In this case the market values at intermediate times are very important. Without such information we simply could not calculate a time-weighted return. The fund value just *before* the March 31 deposit is $3,300,000 - 160,000 = 3,140,000$, and the accumulation rate from January 1 to March 31 is given by $1 + i_1 = \frac{3,140,000}{3,000,000}$. The fund value just *before* the August 31 withdrawal is $3,250,000 + 12,000 = 3,262,000$. We see that the fund actually lost money during the summer, and the accumulation rate between March 31 and August 31 is $1 + i_2 = \frac{3,262,000}{3,300,000}$. The accumulation rate in the final four months of 2000 is $1 + i_3 = \frac{3,500,000}{3,250,000}$. The dollar-weighted return for the year is then obtained by subtracting 1 from the product of these fractions, and is equal to .1142. □

Example 12.5

Vivienne's retirement benefit is 50% of her final year's salary, paid in equal monthly installments for life with the first payment made at age 65. She is currently age 20 and earns 20,000 per year. Assuming Vivienne's salary increases at 5% per year, find the present value of all future retirement benefits. You are given $i = .09$ and $\ddot{a}_{65}^{(12)} = 11$, and you are to assume that Vivienne does not die or leave the company before age 65.

Solution

Vivienne's salary on retirement will be $20{,}000(1.05)^{44}$, and her annual pension is $10{,}000(1.05)^{44} = 85{,}571.50$, payable monthly. The present value of these payments at retirement is $(85{,}571.50)\ddot{a}_{65}^{(12)} = 941{,}286.50$. Its value at the present time is $(941{,}286.50)(1.09)^{-45} = 19{,}477.33$, which is calculated at interest only since survival to age 65 is assumed. □

Example 12.6

Upon retirement at age 65, Bruce, now aged 55, will receive a pension of 500 per month, increasing by 20 per month for each completed year of retirement for life. Find the present value of these benefits, given that $D_{55} = 1400$, $D_{65} = 550$, $N_{65} = 4800$, $S_{65} = 34000$.

Solution

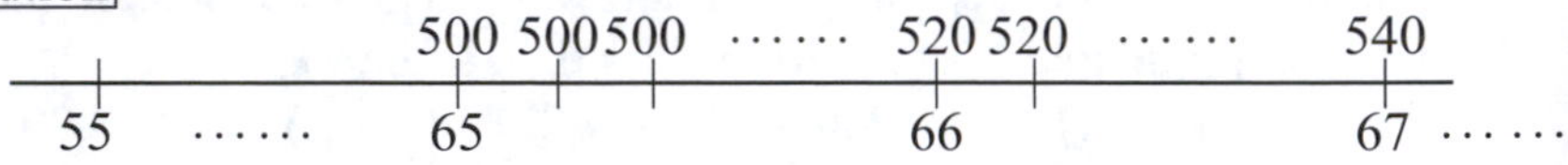

```
            500 500 500    ······  520 520   ······     540
    +----+------+---+---+-----------+----+---------------+------
    55  ······   65             66              67  ······
```

FIGURE 12.3

The benefit is 500 per month in the first year, 520 per month in the second and so on. The present value at age 55 (see Exercise 8-48) is

$$\frac{D_{65}}{D_{55}}\left[(12)(480)\ddot{a}_{65}^{(12)} + (12)(20)(I\ddot{a})_{65}^{(12)}\right]$$

$$= \frac{(12)(480)\left[N_{65} - \frac{11}{24}\cdot D_{65}\right] + (12)(20)\left[S_{65} - \frac{11}{24}\cdot N_{65}\right]}{D_{55}}$$

$$= 24{,}162.86. \qquad\qquad □$$

Example 12.7

Corinne, aged 60, will retire at age 65. If she should die before reaching retirement age, her estate is entitled to a benefit of 1000 for each completed year of service, payable at the end of the year of death. Find the present value of this future death benefit if Corinne was hired at age 45, and if $M_{60} = 790$, $M_{61} = 765$, $M_{62} = 729$, $M_{63} = 693$, $M_{64} = 656$, $M_{65} = 614$ and $D_{60} = 2500$.

Solution

The death benefit is 15,000 at age 60, 16,000 at age 61, ..., 19,000 at age 64. Its present value is equal to

$$15,000\left(\frac{C_{60}}{D_{60}}\right) + 16,000\left(\frac{C_{61}}{D_{60}}\right) + \cdots + 19,000\left(\frac{C_{64}}{D_{60}}\right)$$

$$= \frac{1000[15M_{60} + M_{61} + M_{62} + M_{63} + M_{64} - 19M_{65}]}{D_{60}}$$

$$= 1210.80.$$

□

It is quite possible that an employee's benefit package would involve both a preretirement death benefit, as in Example 12.7, and a pension plan upon retirement, as in the earlier examples. In such a case the present value of all future benefits can be calculated by working out the two benefits separately and adding the results.

Example 12.8

Rosalind's defined benefit pension is 50% of her final salary, payable in monthly installments for life beginning when she turns 65, offset by the annuity provided by the participant's defined contribution plan account balance. 10% of salary is contributed to the defined contribution plan at the end of each year. Salary increases are 6% per year, and the defined contribution plan earns 8% per year. At age 45, Rosalind is earning 30,000 per year and has accumulated 11,000 in the defined contribution plan account, just after the last contribution is made. Find Rosalind's projected defined monthly benefit, assuming she will still be alive and employed at the time of retirement. Assume $\ddot{a}_{65}^{(12)} = 9$.

Solution

The defined contribution plan balance in 20 years will be of amount

$$11,000(1.08)^{20} + \sum_{t=0}^{19}(.1)(30,000)(1.06)^t(1.08)^{19-t}$$

$$= 11,000(1.08)^{20} + (3,000)(1.08)^{19}\left[\frac{1 - \left(\frac{1.06}{1.08}\right)^{20}}{1 - \frac{1.06}{1.08}}\right] = 269,343.78.$$

Dividing the above by $\ddot{a}_{65}^{(12)}$, we see that the defined contribution plan will provide an annual pension of 29,927.09, payable in monthly installments. The final salary is $30,000(1.06)^{19} = 90,767.99$, so her defined benefit pension is 45,384 annually minus the defined contribution value, giving 15,456.91. Hence her projected monthly benefit is 1,288.08. ☐

Example 12.9

A pension plan offers three equivalent options. Option I pays the participant 1000 per month for life. Option II pays the participant 800 per month for life, and pays the participant's spouse a reversionary annuity of 600 per month for life. Option III pays the participant K per month for life, and pays the participant's spouse a reversionary annuity of K per month for life. Find K.

Solution

If x is the age of the participant and y is the age of the spouse, then we have $1000a_x^{(12)} = 800a_x^{(12)} + 600a_{x|y}^{(12)}$, so that $a_x^{(12)} = 3a_{x|y}^{(12)}$. Likewise $1000a_x^{(12)} = K\left(a_x^{(12)} + a_{x|y}^{(12)}\right)$, so $(1000 - K)a_x^{(12)} = Ka_{x|y}^{(12)}$. This gives us $3(1000 - K) = K$, so $4K = 3000$ and $K = 750$. ☐

Example 12.10

Agatha's retirement plan pays 200 per month during the joint lifetime of Agatha and her husband, plus 300 per month during the lifetime of the survivor following the first death. The first payment comes at the time of retirement. If Agatha retires at age 65 and is 4 years older than her husband, find the present value of these benefits on the date of retirement. You are given $12\ddot{a}_{61}^{(12)} = 115$, $12\ddot{a}_{65}^{(12)} = 105$ and $12\ddot{a}_{\overline{61:65}}^{(12)} = 130$.

[Solution]
The present value is

$$2400\ddot{a}^{(12)}_{61:\overline{65}} + 3600\ddot{a}^{(12)}_{\overline{61:65}} = 2400\left(\ddot{a}^{(12)}_{61} + \ddot{a}^{(12)}_{65} - \ddot{a}^{(12)}_{\overline{61:65}}\right) + 3600\ddot{a}^{(12)}_{\overline{61:65}}$$

$$= 200(115+105) + 100(130)$$

$$= 57{,}000. \qquad \square$$

EXERCISES

12-1.   Pauline, aged 20, will retire at age 60 on a pension of 4000 per month.   Given $D_{20} = 2800$, $N_{60} = 7500$ and $N_{61} = 7000$, find the present value of all future benefits.   Assume the first payment occurs at retirement.

12-2.   Repeat Question 1 if the pension payments are 48,000 per year, the first payment at the time of retirement.

12-3.   Repeat Question 2 if the first payment occurs one year after the time of retirement.

12-4.   Repeat Question 1 if the first monthly payment occurs one month after the date of retirement.

12-5.   Is it possible to answer Question 1 if the pension payments will only continue for a maximum of 10 years?   If not, what additional information is required?

12-6.   Is it possible to answer Question 1 if the pension payments are guaranteed into perpetuity?   If not, what additional information is required?

12-7.   Miguel's retirement benefit is 1000 per month, payable for 15 years certain, beginning on January 31, 1999.   Half of this benefit is financed by his company, and half is financed by a defined contribution plan consisting of quarterly payments for 10 years beginning March 31, 1989.   Assuming Miguel survives to retirement and $i = .06$, find the quarterly payment to the defined contribution plan.

12-8.   Repeat Question 7 if we no longer assume that Miguel survives to retirement at age 65. Which commutation functions are needed to answer the question?

12-9.   A pension fund has a value of 1,000,000 on January 1, 1999. On June 30, 1999, a withdrawal of 10,000 is made. On September 30, 1999, a further withdrawal of 20,000 is made. On December 31, 1999, the fund has a value of 1,115,000.
        (a)   Find (if possible) the dollar-weighted rate of investment return for 1999. Assume simple interest for periods less than a year.
        (b)   Find (if possible) the time-weighted rate of investment return for 1999.

12-10. Repeat Question 9 given that the fund has values of 1,070,000 just *before* the June 30 withdrawal, and 1,100,000 just *after* the September 30 withdrawal.

12-11. A pension fund has a value of 1,000,000 on January 1, 1999. Withdrawals of 10,000 are made from the fund on March 31, 1999, October 31, 1999, and April 30, 2000. Immediately *after* these withdrawals the fund has balances of 1,035,000, 1,085,000 and 1,120,000. On December 31, 2000, the value of the fund is 1,200,000.
        (a)   Find (if possible) the dollar-weighted rate of investment return for the two-year period from January 1, 1999 to December 31, 2000.
        (b)   Find (if possible) the time-weighted rate of return for the same period.
        (c)   Find (if possible) the effective annual rate corresponding to the rate calculated in part (a).
        (d)   Repeat (if possible) parts (a) and (b) for the year 1999 only.

12-12. Redo Question 11 if, in addition to the given information, we know that the fund has a value of 1,100,000 on December 31, 1999. There is no deposit or withdrawal on that date.

12-13. Roger, aged 25, earns 20,000 per year. His annual retirement benefit, beginning at age 65, is 60% of his final year's salary. This benefit is paid monthly, with the first payment on the date of retirement. It is assumed that Roger survives and stays with this firm until retirement. If Roger's salary increases at 4% per year and $i = .07$, find the present value of future retirement benefits given $\ddot{a}_{65}^{(12)} = 8$.

12-14. Repeat Question 13 if the retirement benefit is 60% of the average of the final 5 years' salaries.

12-15. Repeat Example 12.6 assuming that the monthly payments reach a maximum of 700 per month, and then remain at that level for life. Use some of the values $N_{75} = 1080$, $N_{76} = 980$, $N_{77} = 900$ and $S_{75} = 6180$.

12-16. Karen, aged 55, must choose between two actuarially equivalent retirement options. Option I offers annual payments commencing at age 65; the initial payment will be 10,000 and each subsequent payment will be 4% greater than the previous one. Alternatively, she can choose early retirement by picking Option II, which offers annual payments commencing immediately; the initial payment will be K and each subsequent payment will be 4% greater than the previous one. At 4%, we are given the values $D_{55} = 150$, $D_{65} = 80$, $N_{55} = 2000$, $N_{65} = 900$, $\overset{\circ}{e}_{55} = 20$, $\overset{\circ}{e}_{65} = 13$. Find K.

12-17. Tom's company offers a preretirement death benefit of 2000 for each completed year of service, payable at the end of the year of death. Tom is currently age 63, was hired at age 30, and will retire at age 65 if he survives to that age. Find the present value of this benefit given $M_{63} = 1000$, $M_{64} = 960$, $M_{65} = 915$, $N_{63} = 30,000$ and $N_{64} = 28,000$.

12-18. Edward's normal retirement benefit at age 65 is 1100 per month, with 600 continuing as a reversionary annuity to his spouse. If Edward's spouse dies before him, then Edward's benefit increases to 1500 per month. Edward is exactly 3 years older than his spouse. Find the value of the benefits to Edward and his spouse on the date of his retirement, given $\ddot{a}_{62}^{(12)} = 9.25$, $\ddot{a}_{65}^{(12)} = 8.62$ and $\ddot{a}_{62:65}^{(12)} = 7.5$.

12-19. Brian's normal retirement benefit is 300 per month. An actuarially equivalent joint and 50% to surviving spouse benefit pays 250 per month. Find the actuarially equivalent joint and 100% to surviving spouse benefit.

12-20. Greta, aged 55, is entitled to a pension paying 2000 per month beginning in 10 years. She is offered the option of using part of this fund to pay her recently divorced husband, aged 60, a life annuity of 500 per month commencing immediately. The rest of the fund would be used to pay her a reduced monthly pension benefit, again beginning in 10 years. Find the new payment given $\ddot{a}_{60}^{(12)} = 9.5$, $\ddot{a}_{65}^{(12)} = 8.5$, $D_{55} = 200$ and $D_{65} = 85$.

12-21. Leslie selects an optional pension benefit which entitles her to monthly payments of X, beginning at age 60, for 10 years certain and thereafter as long as Leslie and her spouse are both alive. Leslie is 5 years older than her spouse. The normal pension benefit at the time of retirement is a single-life annuity of 1,000 per month. Find X under the optional form, given $i = .09$, $D_{60} = 280$, $D_{55:60} = 900$, $N_{60}^{(12)} = 2500$ and $N_{65:70}^{(12)} = 2800$.

12-22. Allan retires at age 65 and is entitled to a monthly pension of X for life, with the first payment occurring immediately. In lieu of this, he may elect a pension paying 250 per month for life, with 200 per month continuing to his spouse for life after his death. Alternatively, he may elect a pension paying 260 per month, with 180 per month continuing to his spouse for life after his death. Find X.

12-23. Can you solve Question 22 if X is a yearly pension for life? If not, state what additional information is required.

12-24. The normal form of a pension benefit pays a life annuity to those retiring in years up to and including 1996, and a life annuity with 50% continuing to a surviving spouse for those retiring after 1996. We are given that $i = .09$ and that 75% of employees are married, and we will assume that the spouse is always the same age as the participant. Retirement occurs at age 65. The present value of all future benefits on January 1, 1997, is 10,000,000 for active participants and 2,000,000 for retired participants. Given $\ddot{a}_{65}^{(12)} = 8$ and $\ddot{a}_{65:65}^{(12)} = 6.5$, find the increase in the present value as of January 1, 1997, of future benefits due to the change in the normal form.

12-25. Roland's normal retirement benefit is a life annuity of 1000 per month, beginning at age 65. Alternatively, he decides to select an equivalent benefit paying X per month beginning at age 70, with the first 5 years guaranteed. Find X given that $i = .06$, $\ddot{a}_{\overline{5|}.06}^{(12)} = 4.348$, $D_{65} = 500$, $N_{65} = 4950$, $D_{70} = 365$, $D_{75} = 200$ and $N_{75} = 1580$.

ANSWERS
TO THE EXERCISES

CHAPTER 1

1. a) 20,720.00 b) 22,216.24   c) 14,202.52   d) 16,497.82

2. a) 23,590.81 b) 22,110.67   c) 24,273.33

5. b) No

6. a) Amount of interest earned in the nth year of the investment.
    c) The total interest earned, $A(n) - A(0)$, is the sum of amounts earned each year.
    d) No. The i_r are rates, not amounts.

7. a) $3\frac{1}{3}$ b) .08333   c) 2.96899   d) .06991

8. 700.00

9. 14,710.39

10. .12988

12. (a)

13. a) 681.47   b) .136364   c) 681.47

14. a) 7092.84   b) 6501.66

15. b) The present value t years in the past is $\frac{1}{(1+it)}$; $1 - it$ will turn negative in $\frac{1}{i}$ years.

18. Expression (c) is id^2; all the others are i^2d.

19. 2700.00

20. C is most advantageous to the investor (effective annual rate of .12603); A is most advantageous to Acme Trust (effective annual rate of .12551).

21. 3947.80

22. a) .12360   b) .11486   c) .11711   d) .00976

23.   a) .07   b) .14   c) .14490   d) .13232

24.   24

25. $7\left[1 - \left(1 + \frac{i^{(5)}}{5}\right)^{-5/7}\right]$

29.   a) .12222   b) .13926   c) .12793   d) .13171

33. $(1 + t)^{.04}$

34. $\ln a + 3t^2 \ln b + d^t \ln d \ln c$

36. $1 - \delta + \frac{\delta^2}{2!} - \frac{\delta^3}{3!} + \frac{\delta^4}{4!} - \cdots,$

37. $i - i^2 + i^3 - i^4 + \cdots$

42. $i - \delta = \frac{\delta^2}{2!} + \frac{\delta^3}{3!} + \frac{\delta^4}{4!} + \cdots,$ and $\delta - d = \frac{\delta^2}{2!} - \frac{\delta^3}{3!} + \frac{\delta^4}{4!} - \cdots,$ so
      $i - \delta$ is larger.

CHAPTER 2

1.   6053.01

2.   5852.81

3.   1377.92

4.   3.86582 years

5. $i = \frac{1}{9}$ and $i = 0$

6.   a) 4.26   b) 2.68938

7.   342.84

8.   19.05945 years

9.   20,279.91

10.   a) 11,168.05 b) 4112.94   c) 2113.17

11. $\frac{14}{21} < i < \frac{19}{21}$

12.   .12928

13.   .097

14.   a) 316.02   b) .17923

15.   a) .07   b) .08313   c) .08049

16. .20

17. a) .27105   b) .27027   c) .26316

18. a) .21053   b) .20513

   c) No, we need the fund balance on July 1, 1997.

19. b) $\dfrac{C-A-W}{A+\frac{1}{2}\cdot W}$; $\left(\dfrac{B}{A}\right)\left(\dfrac{C}{B+W}\right)-1$

   c) $\dfrac{C-A-W}{A+\frac{1}{2}\cdot W}$; $\left(\dfrac{B-W}{A}\right)\left(\dfrac{C}{B}\right)-1$

CHAPTER 3

1. a) 82; 297   b) 23; 616   c) 103; 286   d) 215,233,605; 442,865

   e) $\dfrac{3}{4^{16}}$; $\dfrac{2,516,583}{1,048,576}$ f) $\dfrac{59,049}{8,388,608}$; $\dfrac{4,017,157}{1,492,992}$

3. 1098.41

4. 86.49

5. 22,240.31

6. a) 5746.64   b) 11,487.56   c) 8443.70   d) 32.7312 years
   e) This is not possible; the present value of an annuity of 1000 per
   year at $i = .08$ cannot exceed 12,500.00, which is less than 3 times
   our current value.

12. $a_{\overline{n}|} < n < s_{\overline{n}|}$; they are equal if $i = 0$.

13. 865.57

18. 3896.13

19. a) 619.14   b) 648.58   c) 850.82

20. a) 791.44   b) 811.94   c) 986.14

21. 19,856.34

25. a) 14,245,831.44
   b) 13,889,685.65 $\Big\}$ at 4%
   c) 14,599,612.40

   a) 13,479,564.11
   b) 13,395,316.83 $\Big\}$ at 6%
   c) 13,248,156.69

26.   (c) is greatest for $i < .05155$

     (a) is greatest for $.05155 < i < .06667$

     (b) is greatest for $i > .06667$

32. $a_{\overline{25}|} + \dfrac{a_{\overline{26}|}(1+i)}{s_{\overline{2}|}}$

33. $\dfrac{2x - y}{x^2 + 2x - y}$

34.   1810.03

35.   32.8125

36.   .10248

37.   49,999.50

39.   a) 666.67   b) 766.67   c) 381.17

40.   .20

41.   10,760.60

42.   546.84

43.   .04881

44.   2,147,717.73

45.   .07177

46.   a) 24   c) 6

47.   17; 569.88

48.   159; 56.01

49.   24; 573.46

50.   12; 369.94

51.   .005637

54.   .08795

55.   .09952

58.   5973.56

59.   (d) < (c) < (a) = (b) < (e)

60.   719.85

61. a) $\dfrac{1}{i} + \dfrac{1}{i \cdot s_{\overline{2}|i}}$ b) $\dfrac{(Ia)_{\overline{n}|}}{i \cdot a_{\overline{n}|}}$ c) $(Ia)_{\overline{\infty}|} = \dfrac{1}{i} + \dfrac{1}{i^2}$

63. 12,652.20

64. 18,377.37

65. $v^5\left[n \cdot a_{\overline{2n-1}|} - (a_{\overline{n-1}|})^2\right]$

66. 887.16

67. b) $-\dfrac{n(n+1)}{2}$

68. a) $\dfrac{q}{p-q}$ b) $\dfrac{2q}{p-q}$

CHAPTER 4

1. a) 27,629.66 b) 1795.93; 2741.89

2. a) 2665.34   b) 373.15; 26.85

3. 7595.17

4. 797.34

5. a) True   b) False   c) True

6. 750.43

7. a) 54.82; 842.53   b) 84,077.57   c) 110.26; 787.09

    d) 179,205.00   e) 1101.04

9. 27th

10. 538.58

11. .04535

12. a) $v_i^3(1 - i \cdot a_{\overline{10}|j})$ b) $\dfrac{j}{1+j}$

13. $B(1 + i \cdot s_{\overline{r}|j}) + (A - B)(1+j)^r - X \cdot s_{\overline{r}|j}$

14. 3544.22

15. $\dfrac{X(a_{\overline{10}|.16} - a_{\overline{4}|.14})}{a_{\overline{7}|.14} - a_{\overline{4}|.14}}$

16. 36.83

17.

Year	Payment	Interest	Principal	Outstanding Balance
0				5000.00
1	1285.79	700.00	585.79	4414.21
2	1285.79	617.99	667.80	3746.41
3	1285.79	524.50	761.29	2985.12
4	1285.79	417.92	867.87	2117.25
5	1285.79	296.42	989.37	1127.88
6	1285.79	157.90	1127.88	0

18.

Year	Payment	Interest	Principal	Outstanding Balance
0				50,000.00
1	4537.82	3250.00	1287.82	48,712.18
2	4537.82	3166.29	1371.53	47,340.65
3	4537.82	3077.14	1460.68	45,879.97
4	4537.82	2982.20	1555.62	44,324.35
5	4537.82	2881.08	1656.74	42,667.61
6	4537.82	2773.39	1764.43	40,903.18
7	4537.82	2658.71	1879.11	39,024.07
8	4537.82	2536.56	2001.26	37,022.81
9	4537.82	2406.48	2131.34	34,891.47
10	4537.82	2267.95	2269.87	32,621.60
11	4537.82	2120.40	2417.42	30,204.18
12	4537.82	1963.27	2574.55	27,629.63
13	4537.82	1795.93	2741.89	24,887.74
14	4537.82	1617.70	2920.12	21,967.62
15	4537.82	1427.90	3109.92	18,857.70
16	4537.82	1225.75	3312.07	15,545.63
17	4537.82	1010.47	3527.35	12,018.28
18	4537.82	781.19	3756.63	8,261.65
19	4537.82	537.01	4000.81	4,260.85
20	4537.82	276.97	4260.85	0

19.

Year	Payment	Interest	Principal	Outstanding Balance
0	2462.10			
1	300	344.69	− 44.69	2506.79
2	300	350.95	− 50.95	2557.74
3	300	358.08	− 58.08	2615.82
4	300	366.21	− 66.21	2682.03
5	300	375.48	− 75.48	2757.51
6	400	386.05	13.95	2743.56
7	400	384.10	15.90	2727.66
8	400	381.87	18.13	2709.53
9	400	379.33	20.67	2688.86
10	400	376.44	23.56	2665.30
11	400	373.14	26.86	2638.44
12	400	369.38	30.62	2607.82
13	400	365.09	34.91	2572.91
14	600	360.21	239.79	2333.12
15	600	326.64	273.36	2059.76
16	600	288.37	311.63	1748.13
17	600	244.74	355.26	1392.87
18	600	195.00	405.00	987.87
19	600	138.30	461.70	526.17
20	600	73.66	526.34	0

20.

Year	Payment	Interest	Principal	Outstanding Balance
0				1000.00
1	200.00	160.00	40.00	960.00
2	200.00	153.60	46.40	913.60
3	200.00	146.18	53.82	859.78
4	200.00	137.56	62.44	797.34
5	200.00	127.57	72.43	724.91
6	200.00	115.99	84.01	640.90
7	200.00	102.54	97.46	543.44
8	200.00	86.95	113.05	430.39
9	200.00	68.86	131.14	299.25
10	200.00	47.88	152.12	147.13
11	170.67	23.54	147.13	0

21. | Year | Payment | Interest | Principal | Outstanding Balance |
|------|---------|----------|-----------|---------------------|
| 0 | | | | $a_{\overline{n}|}$ |
| 1 | 1 | $1 - v^n$ | v^n | $a_{\overline{n-1}|}$ |
| 2 | 1 | $1 - v^{n-1}$ | v^{n-1} | $a_{\overline{n-2}|}$ |
| 3 | 1 | $1 - v^{n-2}$ | v^{n-2} | $a_{\overline{n-3}|}$ |
| 4 | 1 | $1 - v^{n-3}$ | v^{n-3} | $a_{\overline{n-4}|}$ |
| 5 | 1 | $1 - v^{n-4}$ | v^{n-4} | $a_{\overline{n-5}|}$ |
| . | . | . | . | . |
| . | . | . | . | . |
| . | . | . | . | . |
| 20 | 1 | $1 - v^{n-19}$ | v^{n-19} | $a_{\overline{n-20}|}$ |
| . | . | . | . | . |
| . | . | . | . | . |
| . | . | . | . | . |
| $n-2$ | 1 | $1 - v^3$ | v^3 | $a_{\overline{2}|}$ |
| $n-1$ | 1 | $1 - v^2$ | v^2 | $a_{\overline{1}|}$ |
| n | 1 | $1 - v$ | v | 0 |

26. a) 1086.91   b) 1886.91

   c) .07483

27. Sinking Fund Deposit is 1912.22;   New Total Payment is 6349.48

   Old Total Payment was 6278.78

28. a) .042775   b) .125

29. a) 115.00   b) 34.06   c) 375.63   d) 15th

30. a) 380.08   b) .09590   c) 565.12   d) 87.30

31. a) 556.50   b) .13164   c) 554.34

32. a) 749.85   b) .17488   c) .19

33. a) 374.67   b) .18805   c) .17687   d) .13148; .12083

34. 9839.98

35. 2760.22

36. 423.63

37. a) 4545.92   b) 4911.00   c) 7140.71

CHAPTER 5

1. 1067.95

2. 978.94

4. a) .035   b) $27\frac{1}{2}$ years

5. 1120.42

7. $1 - \frac{1}{2}p$

8. .03293

9. .07267

10. 12 years, assuming an exact number of years

11. 76.82

13. a) 1049.93   b) 1077.93   c) 1091.93

14. a) 1037.68; 982.68   b) 990.83; 990.83

    c) 1015.19; 996.85   d) 1052.36; 999.79

16.

Time	Coupon	Interest	Principal	Book Value
0				1055.08
1	35.00	26.38	8.62	1046.46
2	35.00	26.16	8.84	1037.62
3	35.00	25.94	9.06	1028.56
4	35.00	25.71	9.29	1019.27
5	35.00	25.48	9.52	1009.75
6	35.00	25.25	9.75	1000.00

17.

Time	Coupon	Interest	Principal	Book Value
0				973.79
1	35.00	38.95	− 3.95	977.74
2	35.00	39.11	− 4.11	981.85
3	35.00	39.27	− 4.27	986.12
4	35.00	39.44	− 4.44	990.56
5	35.00	39.62	− 4.62	995.18
6	35.00	39.81	− 4.81	1000.00

18.

Time	Coupon	Interest	Principal	Book Value
0				1067.95
.	.	.	.	.
.	.	.	.	.
.	.	.	.	.
8	45.00	42.00	3.00	1046.93
.	.	.	.	.
.	.	.	.	.
.	.	.	.	.
17	45.00	40.73	4.27	1013.88

20. 5048.19

21. 172.05

22. 865.04

23. 68.34

24. a) 903.47   b) 869.48

25. a) 12.7; 12.0 b) 15.25

26. a) 929.76   b) 953.74

27. a) 1046.94   b) .12963

28. a) 875.91   b) 1128.21   c) 1000.00

29. .06064

30. a) 89.53   b) 111.41

31. 9272.10

32. a) 50.00   b) $\frac{X}{i}$ c) $\dfrac{X}{(1+i)^{1/4}-1}$

33. a) 100.00   b) Infinite

CHAPTER 6

1. a) $\frac{1}{52}$ b) $\frac{1}{4}$ c) $\frac{16}{52}$ d) $\frac{2}{52}$ e) $\frac{103}{2704}$

2. a) $\frac{1}{6}$ b) $\frac{4}{6}$ c) $\frac{5}{36}$ d) $\frac{1}{9}$ e) 0

3. a) $\frac{1}{4}$ b) $\frac{1}{8}$ c) $\frac{3}{8}$ d) $\frac{1}{2}$

4. $\frac{13}{20}$

5. 1; $\frac{5}{2}$

6. $\frac{20}{26}$

7. $\frac{21}{37}$

8. 43.75

9. 11

10. .221

11. 6141.30

12. 2192.98; .1696

13. .0574

14. .6875

15. 10,258.31

16. 108,888,888.89

17. 2749.31

18. 2343.75

19. 116.18

20. .1987

21. .012

22. a) 858.02   b) 1120.88   c) .08237 per half year

CHAPTER 7

1.

Age	ℓ_x	d_x	q_x
0	1000	700	.7
1	300	90	.3
2	210	84	.4
3	126	126	1

2. a) $\dfrac{\ell_{45}}{\ell_{20}}$ b) $\dfrac{\ell_{25}}{\ell_{20}}$ c) $\dfrac{\ell_{25}-\ell_{26}}{\ell_{20}}$ d) $\dfrac{\ell_{60}}{\ell_{20}}$ e) $1-\left(\dfrac{\ell_{60}}{\ell_{20}}\right)^2$

3. .13043

4. a) $4\left(\dfrac{\ell_{60}}{\ell_{30}}\right)^3\left(\dfrac{\ell_{50}-\ell_{55}}{\ell_{30}}\right)$ b) $1-\left(\dfrac{\ell_{60}}{\ell_{30}}\right)^4-4\left(\dfrac{\ell_{60}}{\ell_{30}}\right)^3\left(\dfrac{\ell_{30}-\ell_{60}}{\ell_{30}}\right)$

6.

x	ℓ_x	d_x	p_x	q_x
0	1000	100	.90	.10
1	900	150	.8\.3	.1\.6
2	750	150	.80	.20
3	600	300	.50	.50
4	300	180	.40	.60
5	120	120	.00	1.00
6	0			

7. a) .95   b) .0975   c) .01073   d) .0486

8. $\dfrac{\frac{1}{2}d_{35}}{\ell_{30}}$

11. .16

12. .32

13. a) 1000   b) 0   c) 8   d) .7\.7   e) .3   f) .05263   g) .07465

14. $p_x=\dfrac{119-x}{120-x};\ q_x=\dfrac{1}{120-x};\ \mu_x=\dfrac{1}{120-x}$

16. $\mu_x=-\ln s-2x\ln w-c^x(\ln c)(\ln g)$

21. a) 90   b) 90   c) .2857   d) .1385

22. a) .5   b) $\dfrac{1}{30}$ c) 80

23. a) .99830   b) .99154   c) .00170   d) .00846

   e) .00169   f) .00505

25. .12857

28. a) $\dfrac{1000\ell_{35}}{T_{35} - .4T_{50} - .6T_{65}}$ 　　　　 b) $\dfrac{400\ell_{50}}{T_{35} - .4T_{50} - .6T_{65}}$

   c) $\dfrac{1000(\ell_{35} - .4\ell_{50} - .6\ell_{65})}{T_{35} - .4T_{50} - .6T_{65}}$

29. .0194

32. 540,000

33. $e_{90} = 4.5$; $\overset{\circ}{e}_{90} = 5$ (both exactly and approximately)

35. 63.63

36. a) 70 　　　 b) 80 　　　 c) 54.375 　　　 d) 42.2

37. a) 60 　　　 b) 20

38. a) 80 　　　 b) 10

39. $40 + \dfrac{T_{40} - T_{50} + T_{75} - 10\ell_{50} + 35\ell_{75}}{\ell_{40} - \ell_{50} + \ell_{75}}$

40. a) $\dfrac{100(T_{20} - T_{65})}{T_{65}}$ 　　　 b) 45

41. i) $\left(_{7}p_{40}^{(\tau)}\right) q_{47}^{(b)}$

   ii) $\left(_{4}p_{40}^{(\tau)}\right)\left(q_{44}^{(b)} + q_{44}^{(c)}\right) + \left(_{5}p_{40}^{(\tau)}\right)\left(q_{45}^{(b)} + q_{45}^{(c)}\right)$
   $\qquad + \left(_{6}p_{40}^{(\tau)}\right)\left(q_{46}^{(b)} + q_{46}^{(c)}\right) + \left(_{7}p_{40}^{(\tau)}\right)\left(q_{47}^{(b)} + q_{47}^{(c)}\right)$

   iii) $q_{30}^{(a)} = \dfrac{d_{30}^{(a)}}{\ell_{30}^{(\tau)}}$; 　 $m_{30}^{(a)} = \dfrac{d_{30}^{(a)}}{\ell_{30}^{(\tau)} - \frac{1}{2}d_{30}^{(\tau)}}$

   iv) decrement (c) only acts on ages $x < 50$

43. $\dfrac{1 - \frac{1}{2}(a + b)}{1 + \frac{1}{2}(a + b)}$

44. 103

45. a) .737 　　　 b) .194 　　　 c) .0163

CHAPTER 8

1. a) 618.16   b) 267.01   c) 225.53   d) 520.54   e) 628.04
2. 287,223.64
3. 1110.50
4. a) 36,923.08   b) 34,528.49
5. a) 11,773.36   b) 10,138.45
6. a) 36,693.42   b) 34,404.64
7. $500 \sum\limits_{t=1}^{\infty} (1.13)^{-2t} \, {}_{2t}p_{45}$
8. 1296.93
9. 1567.84
10. 4099.37
13. 1356.61
14. 2441.99
15. a) 1799.00   b) 13,256.14
16. a) 55,647.06   b) 53,882.35   c) 57,647.06 d) .06
17. a) $\dfrac{20,000N_{48}}{D_{38}}$ b) $\dfrac{20,000(N_{48} - N_{62} + N_{72})}{D_{38}}$
    c) $\dfrac{20,000(D_{38} \cdot v^{10}\ddot{a}_{\overline{5}|} + N_{53})}{D_{38}}$
19. .112
20. (a), (b), (d) are equal to each other, but (c) is different
21. 5027.59
22. 2.8167
23. a) .3863   b) .568
24. a) 81,400   b) 81,000   c) 81,800   d) No
28. $\dfrac{N_x - N_{x+n} - (\frac{m-1}{2m})(D_x - D_{x+n})}{D_x}$ or $\dfrac{N_x^{(m)} - N_{x+n}^{(m)}}{D_x}$
29. 270.02
30. 267.10

31. 263,780.49

32. 279,822.15

33. 78,214.11

34. 82,970.66

35. 65,699.85; 69,695.35

36. 461.82

38. $\bar{a}_{x:\overline{n}|} = \dfrac{N_x - \frac{1}{2}D_x - (N_{x+n} - \frac{1}{2}D_{x+n})}{D_x};\quad {}_{n|}\bar{a}_x = \dfrac{N_{x+n} - \frac{1}{2}D_{x+n}}{D_x}$

39. a) 10,000.00 b) 9502.13   c) 9295.00

40. 18,804.27

41. 105,600

42. 27,466.67

43. 62,933.33

44. 3733.33

46. $\dfrac{10N_x + S_{x+1} - 2S_{x+6} + S_{x+21}}{D_x}$

47. ${}_{n|}(I\ddot{a})_x = \dfrac{S_{x+n}}{D_x};\quad (D\ddot{a})_{x:\overline{n}|} = \dfrac{(n+1)N_x - S_x + S_{x+n+1}}{D_x}$

52. 2165.03

53. 197.46

54. 216.84

55. 334.86

56. 1.4286

CHAPTER 9

1. a) 30,769.23 b) 10,255.34

2. a) 25,527.41 b) 7912.74

3. a) 30,087.74 b) 9994.20

4. a) 32,302.58 b) 11,528.11

5. a) 31,842.58 b) 11,146.28

6. a) 23,977.21   b) 10,511.82

9. 77,482.30

10. 84,582.90

11. 87,343.87

15. $(1-{}_{10}p_x)\,v^{10} + ({}_{10}p_x)\,v^{10}A_{x+10}$

17. 7466.67

18. a) 48,076.92   b) 40,828.40

19. 41,346.15

20. $\dfrac{50,000(M_{30} - M_{80} + D_{80} + M_{50} - M_{70})}{D_{30}}$

22. a) .0476   b) 19,800.00

23. 6148.89

24. 22,461.17

25. 79,348.05

26. a) 17,164.35   b) 15,965.94   c) 19,456.91

27. a) 44,444.44   b) 41,457.53   c) 48,178.08

28. a) 27,708.65   b) 22,196.28   c) 34,946.58

29. 9648.56

30. 45,600.74

31. 118,181.82

32. 53,289.68

33. a) Decrease   b) Increase

36. $\dfrac{ln(2\mu + \delta) - ln\mu}{\mu + \delta}$

37. 42,606.65

38. a) 28,571.43   b) 57,243.34

40. 29,600.00

41. 11,800.00

42. 26,200.00

43. 31,920.00

45. $\dfrac{1000(R_0-R_{10}) + 40,000M_{51}}{D_0}$

46. 651.36

47. 9270.83

49. a) 681.82   b) 824.18   c) 59.55

50. a) 74.07   b) 61.39

52. 1318.18

53. 1966.67

54. 206.55

55. 215.84

56. 1179.25

57. 1182.76

58. 20,176.47

59. 3431.88

60. $\dfrac{11,000\, A_{50}}{\ddot{a}_{50:\overline{30|}} + 1.1(DA)^{1}_{50:\overline{29|}}}$

61. $\dfrac{(1+r)M_x + kD_x + h(N_x-N_{x+n})}{(1 - \frac{j}{100})(N_x - N_{x+n})}$

62. a) 1118.64   b) 9274.78   c) 15,040.63   d) .63586

63. a) $\dfrac{5000R_{20}}{N_{20} + 2N_{30}}$

    b) $\dfrac{5000R_{20}}{N_{20} + 2N_{30}}$

    c) $\dfrac{25,000M_{25} + 5000R_{25} - \left(\frac{5000R_{20}}{N_{20}+2N_{30}}\right)\left(N_{25} + 2N_{30}\right)}{D_{25}}$

    d) $\dfrac{150,000M_{50} + 5000R_{50} - 3\left(\frac{5000R_{20}}{N_{20}+2N_{30}}\right)N_{50}}{D_{50}}$

65. a) 285.32   b) 1995.23   c) 2103.56   d) 0

66. a) 437.22   b) 3057.45   c) 3223.45   d) 0

67. .64

69. .143865

72. a) .03788   b) .03861   c) .04   d) .04

73. a) .1739   b) .1875

CHAPTER 10

1. .25; .07505
2. 250; 75,051.58
3. .24244; .07846
4. .27267; .09398
5. .00756; .000256
6. .26115; .08198
7. .21429; .07410
8. .21350; .07441
9. .12987; .04807
10. $\frac{1}{3}$; $\frac{4}{45}$
11. 8.47826; 10.276
12. 8.96897; 10.303
13. 9.07; 3.14
14. $\frac{100}{11}$; 5
15. a) $\dfrac{\mu}{\mu+\delta}$; $\dfrac{\mu\delta^2}{(\mu+2\delta)(\mu+\delta)^2}$; $\left(\dfrac{1}{2}\right)^{\delta/\mu}$

    b) $\dfrac{1}{\mu+\delta}$; $\dfrac{\mu}{(\mu+2\delta)(\mu+\delta)^2}$; $\dfrac{1-\left(\frac{1}{2}\right)^{\delta/\mu}}{\delta}$
16. a) 30; 300   b) 32.83; 1077.9
17. a) 30   b) 22.76
18. .72193
19. a) $(-.2979, .7979)$ b) $(-.5719, 1.0719)$
    The upper end of the interval in (a) is of some use, but a direct calculation gives a higher probability; (b) is not useful.
20. 4.47
21. a) .601   b) .701   c) .451   d) .787
23. Question 19: a) $(-297.9, 797.9)$ b) $(-571.9, 1071.9)$

    Question 21: a) 601   b) 701   c) 451   d) 787

24. a) .628 b) .732 c) .471 d) .822

25. 250; 75.05

26. 250; 75,050

27. 250; 7505

28. 2955.80

29. 2644.14

30. 3044.04

31. a) $-.125$; .2461 b) 0; .0675

32. a) $-.1111$; .2469 b) $-.0926$; .3097

34. $-.01$; .1133

35. 86; 109

CHAPTER 11

1. a) $(_{40}p_{15})(_{40}p_{25})^2$ b) $1 - (_{40}p_{15})(_{40}p_{25})^2$
    c) $(_{40}p_{25})^2 + 2(_{40}p_{15})(_{40}p_{25})(1 - _{40}p_{25})$
    d) $2(_{35}p_{15})(_{20}p_{25})(1 - _{20}p_{25})$

4. $\dfrac{145 - 2t}{(75 - t)(70 - t)}$

6. a) $(1-_{28}p_{22})^6 + 6(1-_{28}p_{22})^5(_{28}p_{22}) + 15(1-_{28}p_{22})^4(_{28}p_{22})^2$
    $$+ 20(1 - _{28}p_{22})^3(_{28}p_{22})^3$$
    b) $20(1 - _{28}p_{22})^3 (_{28}p_{22})^3 + 15(1 - _{28}p_{22})^2 (_{28}p_{22})^4$
    $$+ 6(1 - _{28}p_{22})(_{28}p_{22})^5 + (_{28}p_{22})^6$$
    c) $[1 - (_{28}p_{22}-_{29}p_{22})]^6 + 6[1 - (_{28}p_{22}-_{29}p_{22})]^5(_{28}p_{22} - _{29}p_{22})$

7. 16,647.06

8. 17,647.06

9. 17,817.94

10. .1506

11. .1919

12.   .3084

13.   117,647.06

14.   1085.38

16. $_{10}p_{50}(1 - p_{60}) + {}_{10}p_{60}(1 - p_{70}) - ({}_{10}p_{50})({}_{10}p_{60})(1 - p_{60}\,p_{70})$

18. $\frac{5}{12}a_{xy:\overline{n}|} + \frac{1}{3}a_{x:\overline{n}|} + \frac{1}{4}a_{y:\overline{n}|}$

19. $a_{yx} = a_{xy} < a_x < a_{\overline{xy}}$

20.   .97286

21.   202,865.76

22.   a) 52,941.18   b) 18,853.70

23.   83.43

24.   2824.32

25.   No; N_{66} and D_{65} are needed

27.   260,400.00

28.   74,400.00; 37,200.00

29.   105,500.00

30.   772.41

31.   .15017

32.   125,000.00

33.   4319.08

34.   Yes; 4736.73

35.   323.06

36.   11,640.00

37.   50,280.00

39.   3.67

40.   129,360.00

41.   2952.00

CHAPTER 12

1.   124,642.86
2.   128,571.43
3.   120,000.00
4.   123,928.57
5.   No; N_{70} and D_{70}
6.   No; i
7.   1110.66
8. D_{55}, N_{56}, D_{65} and N_{65}
9.   a) .14646   b) Impossible
10.   a) .14646   b) .14598
11.   a) .23418   b) .23368   c) .11094   d) Not possible
12.   a) .23418   b) .23368   c) .11094   d) .12111; .12086
13.   29,595.14
14.   27,404.47
15.   23,365.57
16.   3512.20
17.   2850.00
18.   131,760.00
19.   214.29 per month
20.   685.12
21.   907.69
22.   350.00
23.   No, we need to know $\ddot{a}_{65}$ or $\ddot{a}_{65}^{(12)}$
24.   703,125.00
25.   1535.05

INDEX